achers and others with a role in nurturing the faith of the
ll discover a fresh and incisive approach in this
ısive and challenging book. God, humanity, creation and
ıporary Church are examined and Christian Spirituality,
lways about experiencing Jesus in the events of life and
ther, is celebrated. This is a wise, sympathetic and
readable book.

O'Gara (Marino Institute of Education)

ı*ng Christian Faith: Free to Be"* is a timely publication
·oclaims Jesus and His message in a fresh and challenging
)rawing on a lifetime of reflection and pastoral
ıce, Gleeson communicates the Gospel in a study that is at
ıtimate and provocative. It affords comfort by addressing
while at the same time taking us beyond our comfort zone.
the teacher, Gleeson anticipates the questions of the reader
'fers a framework and apparatus that will allow group study
ructured reflection. This volume offers the Gospel message
ınd" from the limitations of human parameters - it presents
ıanity as a relationship which profoundly alters all others.

ı*ire Keogh (author of "Edmund Ignatius Rice")*

ı*ding Christian Faith: Free to Be"* is a truly remarkable,
ζeous and challenging work that covers a huge range of
onal theological issues - including the dialogue between
ιe and religion, God and the imagination, interpreting
ure and what the Kingdom of God really is about - as well as
ırn contemporary issues such as the family, poverty and
ın rights, the environment and the Church for the future.
;on draws on a wide range of sources from many disciplines to
the reader to consider what Christianity is about, how it
ιcts upon the world and what direction a truly missionary
știan Church might consider for the future. This is not a book
ıose who espouse a 'comfortable' form of Christianity and is
hat most certainly will 'disturb the peace' of the reader. It is a
that all those who seek to become genuine disciples of the

young rabbi from Nazareth should see as essential reading. *Dr. Aidan Donaldson (author of "Come Follow Me: Recalling the Dangerous Memory of Jesus and the Church Today")*

The contemporary Church is in crisis and Gleeson offers not only a thoughtful diagnosis of what fetters our minds and hearts as Church today but proposes a concrete pathway towards liberating ourselves into a transformed people of God. I have been excited and heartened by the scope and depth of this book.

Under fourteen clear chapter headings Gleeson explains why we are where we are! He brings scholarship and personal vulnerability to his analysis and as the expert spiritual guide that he is, schools us in the most satisfying elements of our faith, engaging with mystery, exercising our imaginations in relation to our images of God, eschewing oppositional thinking and encountering the person of Jesus in all its healing and re-vitalizing essence. This is a book for slow, reflective reading, chapter by chapter.

It would be an exciting prospect if small reading groups were to form in parishes and communities and adopt this book, chapter by chapter, over 13 or 14 weeks. Such a project could offer fresh enterprise and facilitate a transformed consciousness, a more alert and vocal laity, and an opportunity for further renewal for our church today. Can I dare to believe that by becoming a fully free disciple of Jesus I can allow him, even yet, do something new in me?

Dr. Una Agnew (author of "The Mystical Imagination of Patrick Kavanagh")

Unbinding Christian Faith
Free to Be

Denis Gleeson

Cluain Mhuire Press

2015

First Printing : 2015

ISBN : 978-1-326-47676-2

Cluain Mhuire Press

Email : cluainmhuirepress@icloud.com

In memory of my parents
who introduced me to Christian faith and
Br. John C. Moore who
introduced me to Christian spirituality and
in gratitude to my family, my friends and
my Brothers in religion, all of whom
sustain me in both.

Contents

Acknowledgements

The inspiration for this book and the theme of the unbinding of Lazarus that is central to the book resulted from a conversation with my good friend, Don Bisson. I am grateful to him. Particular thanks also to Donal Dorr, Daire Keogh, Una Agnew, Anne O'Gara and Aidan Donaldson. All were most generous with their time and offered invaluable comments and observations on the draft. Their gracious and positive feedback ensured that the book would actually see the light of day.

The book would not have been possible without much support and encouragement from friends and colleagues. In that regard I am indebted to Geraldine McLaverty, Gerry Scannell, Liam Perry and Ann Lyons who share countless years of varied and distinguished experience within Catholic education. Dorothy Donnelly and Fiona Rooney offered sympathetic perspective from outside the world of education at an early stage in the project.

My thanks to my community, the Congregation of Christian Brothers who have supported, with much patience and generosity over the last several years, the ministry out of which this book has grown. A special word of gratitude to Martin O'Flaherty and David Gibson whose daily, fraternal concern and good humour made sure that I did not give up nor drive myself or anyone else to distraction.

Finally, I add a word of thanks to Paul Shevlin for kindness and wise counsel.

Biblical quotations from the NRSV Bible, Catholic Edition.
Cover illustration by the author.

Preface

What a tremendous goal to "unbind" the negativities, lack of maturity, distorted thinking, skewed interpretation of traditions as well as freeing up the true message of Christianity in a new light! As a spiritual director and formator of supervisors and directors, I know firsthand how women and men genuinely on the search have difficulties re-engaging their Christian traditions and have, at times, thrown out the baby with the bathwater. No book can in itself solve the enormous challenges of transforming Christianity and releasing its archetypal powers for a new era, but this book does engage us in a dialogue and set us in the right direction.

Denis Gleeson is first and foremost an educator, one who spent years in a high stress environment trying to communicate the basics of Christianity under the most difficult of circumstances. A good teacher takes the most complicated of issues and presents the material with clarity and vision. He successfully accomplishes this challenge. This book can be used by anyone who wants an overview of issues that need attention and transformation in our present reality within the structures of church life, now and in the future. He holds the tension between new insights from contemporary theological scholarship and the realities of practical everyday life.

When Denis speaks of a "flawed familiarity", he challenges the church to turn from the safety of regression into saying the old things in the old way. Yet, he is obviously deeply committed to renewal of the tradition beyond the mediocrity of liturgical and theological reflection available to most Christians. Any unbinding needs the prophetic energy of lovingly questioning authority, by probing into the natural sciences, psychology, inter faith dialogue and western mystics. He generously shares the fruit of his research and deep reflection and encourages us to go further.

I would recommend this book to my spiritual directees, or those on my training programmes for spiritual directors, for them to have a "Lazarus" experience, a metaphorical coming into new light around their own tradition. This is not about a few new insights, but an invitation to transformational space. I can also envision groups reading **Unbinding Christian Faith: Free to Be** in book clubs, parish renewal teams, religious communities, teacher training programmes, religious education departments, staff faculties in Christian Schools, etc. Enjoy and share with your friends, family members, and anyone who seeks to hold the tension between new breakthroughs and the best of an ancient tradition - a tradition that feels asleep at the moment.

Don Bisson fms

Introduction

Picture the scene. There is quite a crowd following Jesus. It is hot and dusty and very uncomfortable out on the open road in the blazzing sunshine. The crowd is making its way towards the tombs and Martha, in obvious distress, is struggling to keep pace with Jesus' determined stride. In between breathless sobs she explains how things could have been so different had Jesus arrived some four days earlier. He could have saved poor Lazarus their beloved, and now deceased, brother. Jesus who is clearly upset himself tries to calm them as they walk along. He is aware that consternation is growing in the faces of the crowd as they near the tombs. They are puzzled by his sense of purpose. What is he going to do? They have already exhausted all the possibilities in their minds but the one thing they do know about Jesus is that you can expect the unexpected. Finally, they reach the tomb of Lazarus. Jesus immediately calls for the tombstone to be rolled aside and the wave of initial consternation at this request quickly gives way to dismay, disbelief and shock. This cannot be! It is not proper! They will be unclean! There is no need for this! Jesus, however, insists.

Eventually, when the tombstone has been pushed and dragged clear, Jesus, his face already stained by tears, bows his head and prays. Then, in a strong and clear voice, he thanks the Father for hearing his prayer and calls upon Lazarus to come out of the tomb. The crowd is stunned into silence and then there is a collective intake of breath as a ghostly shape looms from the darkness and slowly comes into focus. There are some muffled screams as the figure, bound in white bandages from head to toe, emerges fully into the light. It is Lazarus! Jesus calls for him to be unbound and to be set free.

Some two thousand years or so after the raising of Lazarus, Christianity perhaps, in many respects, finds itself bound and entombed. If this is so, it will only escape its entombment and its bonds by turning to Jesus and listening once again with an open heart to the Good News of the Kingdom of God. The remedy seems simple enough, so, at a personal level and at the level of Christian community, what holds us back? Do we understand the nature of our entombment and of our bonds? Why do we resist Jesus' call to us, to come out of the tomb and to break free? These are the questions that will be explored in the pages that follow. I hope many will find them relevant and helpful. As one who has been involved in education all of my adult life, I will be particularly delighted if they are found to be so by parents and teachers and anyone who has a role in nurturing the faith of the young.

1. Freeing Up our View of the World

How do we see each other? What prevents us from seeing each other as God sees us? What is my worldview and is it truly my own? How do I see the relationship between science and religion? Is my universe a mechanical one or a totally unpredictable one?

In the early 1960's, Thomas Merton, a Trappist monk, found himself away from his Monastery of Gethsemane situated in the green, rolling hills of Kentucky. He was on a visit to the neighbouring city of Louisville. The city was just an hour or so away from the monastery but in truth he was in a different world. There was no ordered silence here, as he stood on the corner of 4th and Walnut in the busy centre of the shopping district. Here he was jolted into a different world and he realised that different though it was, it was not a separate world.

Merton thought to himself that the monks back in the monastery and the people of Louisville who were hurrying about their business shared a world that was trying to live with the terrible reality and possible consequence of nuclear proliferation. They also shared a world of racial tension, mass media, big business and technological and political revolution. True, the monks were conscious of the spiritual dimension of the world they inhabited, but that did not make them any better than others outside of the monastery who were also aware of the spiritual dimension or, indeed, others outside of the monastery who were not aware of it. He almost laughed aloud at the very thought that in the monastery they could foster the illusion of difference and separateness. The mystery of the incarnation itself gave the lie to any such thought.

Then an amazing thing happened. As he looked at the people around him, Merton not only knew he was one with them and loved them, he experienced that oneness and that love. His own words describe it best:

"Then it was as if I suddenly saw the secret beauty of their hearts, the depths of their hearts where neither sin nor desire nor self-knowledge can reach, the core of their reality, the person that each one is in God's eyes. If only they could all see themselves as they really *are.* If only we could see each other that way all the time. There would be no more war, no more hatred, no more greed...I suppose the big problem would be that we would fall down and worship each other. But this cannot be *seen* only believed and 'understood' by a peculiar gift."

What a thought! If only we could see each other as God sees us and as we really are it would be an end to war, hatred, greed and all kinds of violence and abuse! The world would be utterly transformed. I wonder if this touches something of what Jesus meant by the kingdom of God? However, Merton goes on:

"At the centre of our being is a point of nothingness which is untouched by sin and by illusion, a point of pure truth, a point or spark which belongs entirely to God, which is never at our disposal, from which God disposes our lives, which is inaccessible to the fantasies of our own mind or the brutalities of our own will. This little point of nothingness and of *absolute poverty* is the pure glory of God within us. It is so to speak His name written in us, as our poverty, as our indigence, as our dependence, as our sonship. It is like a pure diamond, blazing with the invisible light of heaven. It is in everybody, and if we could see it we would see these billions of points of light coming together in the face and the blaze of a sun that would make all the darkness and cruelty of life vanish completely... I have no program for this seeing, It is only given. But the gate of heaven is everywhere." [1]

This glimpse of the true nature of humanity was not merely a powerful insight that Merton had. It was not merely an idea, for, in truth, we have all had such ideas now and again. We all consider, idly as it were, the oneness of humanity, the equality of all human kind irrespective of race, colour or creed. Our intellect is exercised but we soon enough go about our daily business unaffected. No, this experience of Merton's was precisely that – an actual experience. It was an experience born out of his contemplative lifestyle and affecting him deeply and forever. It was as if the gates of heaven had, for a fraction of a second, been left ajar. He knew that it was an experience that was "given" and that was not available to all. If only it were! But I wonder what is it that prevents us from having this same experience? Maybe we are being offered it every day. What holds us back from accepting it? What veils our vision? What clouds our mind?

Well, in the course of these pages, we may surface some anwers to these questions, but, for the moment, I want to suggest that in the Western world, at least, one of the answers lies in the attitude we have to science and, specifically, how many of us tend to see the relationship between science and religion.

Science and Religion

Now, I was never very good at mathematics. The reason, probably, is that I just did not have any great aptitude for it. However, I suspect that another contributory factor is that at some stage I gave acceptance to the idea that mathematics is simply difficult and that there was no great gain to be had by struggling with it. This seems to be a common enough response and not just to mathematics but to science as well. Science is difficult, we reason, and therefore it is best left to the scientists and they will tell us, or even better, show us and demonstrate to us, what we need to know. Keep it simple we

Unbinding Christian Faith: Free to Be   Denis Gleeson

ask, keep it brief and if it can be made entertaining, then, all the better. Now, undoubtedly, this approach does have the advantage of saving us effort but it also has its limitations because it means, of course, that we are left to accept on faith what the scientists choose to tell us. In addition, our understanding of what we are told will be limited and the vast majority of us may never get beyond the media sound bites. Clearly, this does not pay any great respect to our intelligence and it does not give us any really sound basis upon which to form opinion, make judgments and consider ethical issues.

Interestingly, many of us have taken the very same approach with religious matters and are prepared to accept the word of others when it comes to what we believe about God, humanity and creation. Again, the approach does not do us justice and ensures only that our spiritual growth and development is likely to be very limited and, sadly, may even owe more to our years at school than to any steps we may have taken in our adult life.

Furthermore, the situation with respect to any attempts we may make to understand ourselves and our world is further complicated for us because I think that it is fair to say that there has been and there is some tension between the world of religion and the world of science. In fact, over the past few centuries, some have asserted, and many more have assumed, that there is an irreconcilable rift between religion and science and certainly in the popular imagination today I would guess that the two are seen almost as opposites. If you are on the side of science, any religious worldview is viewed as dubious, if not downright superstitious and if you are on the side of religion, the worldview of science is viewed as presumptive if not incredibly arrogant. Well, for me, the division seems to be unnecessary and constitutes one of the great and most harmful prejudices and misunderstandings of our times.

With respect to the reality of our universe and of human existence itself, there can be only the one truth of the matter and it is neither a scientific truth only nor a religious truth only. It has to be both and very much more. We now know that the universe, of which earth is just a miniscule part, is vaster and more complex than we ever imagined. Whatever lens we choose to view it through, be it an actual lens or a conceptual, philosophical, or theological lens, it will most certainly be inadequate and will give us only a tiny glimpse of the reality that we are trying to focus upon.

In general terms, science concerns itself with the establishment of facts and religion with the exploration of meaning and it is only when they trespass without invitation or welcome on each other's territory that serious problems arise, or so the theory goes. There are areas of overlap such as ethics and psychology but the tragedy is that such has been the level of recrimination between science and religion that meaningful dialogue even in these areas is minimal.

The ironies abound, of course. Science proclaims itself to be open to the whole of reality, even those realities it cannot explain and which will never be fully explained. Religion aspires, for its part, to be pastoral and compassionate towards all and to reverence all of creation in all of its wonder. However, none of us, including all who would invest in this debate, is ever beyond the need to improve communication and to hone our listening skills. Science and religion, quite simply, need to begin to listen to each other and to take each other seriously before any respectful and meaningful dialogue can begin.

Two Scientific Views of the World

My father died unexpectedly. When I awoke on the morning of his funeral, I lay in my bed and stared at the familiar ceiling above me. One thing I knew, at that moment, with searing clarity was that my life and my world were now, devastatingly, changed forever. Sometimes change is like this. It is brutal, immediate, undeniable and irreversible. When change comes about in this manner, our response to it, as we know, is more vexed than when changes occurs over a period of time. It also takes us a lot longer to process the change and adapt to it. We may never even manage this satisfactorily at all and we may opt instead to struggle on, allowing immersion in the daily preoccupations of life, dull the shock that change visits on our system.

However, much of the time, for better or for worse, change is not so sudden and creeps up on us. A vague awareness gives way to a strengthening conviction that things are not as they once were. Social and cultural change can sometimes be like this. It may be hard, for example, to pinpoint the exact moment when a society finally decides to preoccupy itself more with the material rather than with any consideration of the spiritual. It may take us time to notice that our sense of community has faded and is being replaced by an overarching and irrepressible accommodation of the individual. We may miss the exact moment when a critical mass is reached in public opinion and the loudest voice and moral relativism seem to have replaced a sense of shared and lasting values. We may not be able to identify just when the previously unthinkable and unacceptable actually became acceptable and even commonplace. Changes of this kind, as I said, can creep up on us and can leave us in shock and bewilderment.

This has been the case, as over the past one hundred years or so, we have struggled to change our scientific perspective on the world. In fact, I think that we are still struggling to do this and that many of us now operate with a scientific perspective on the world that is long out of date. It also impacts negatively on our state of mind and on our general happiness with life. The fact that we may not be aware of this and that our view of the world operates at a level below consciousness does not lessen its importance and its influence upon us day to day.

The Mechanical Universe

Isaac Newton gave us a view of the world about us that we could refer to as classical physics. [2] This world view maintained that we lived in a material world, the world that we could see, hear, smell, taste and touch and that this material world was nothing less than what we termed, "reality". Furthermore, this material world had one great distinguishing and comforting feature – it was predictable. It had a very reassuring cause-and-effect tidiness. [3] This meant that we could exercise a certain degree of control over our world. We could explain things. We knew why the world worked the way it did and why things around us were the way they were. Primitive religious belief and superstition were a thing of the past. We declared ourselves to know why the planets kept to their elliptical paths, why lightning flashed across the sky and why the tides ebbed and flowed. Our world was seen as a giant, mechanical, clockwork creation and our static universe was defined in terms of tiny, solid particles floating in a sea of space and extending infinitely in all directions. [4] John Polkinghorne writes:

> "So complete did this new science seem to be that, by the end of the 18th century, the greatest of Newton's successors, Pierre Simon Laplace, could make his celebrated assertion that a being equipped with unlimited calculating power and given complete knowledge of the dispositions of all particles at some instant of time, could use Newton's equations to predict the future, and to retrodict with equal certainty the past, of the whole universe." [5]

What a sweeping and amazing claim! But we went further. We also convinced ourselves that we knew not just certain details about the likely development of humankind but that we had more or less resolved the question of how humanity had come to be. Having achieved this, we then confidently placed ourselves at the apex of all creation. Human beings were superior to all else that existed. We worked a kind of Copernican revolution in reverse. Having established that our planet, the earth, was not, in fact, the centre around which all of creation revolved, we put ourselves at the centre of creation.

In time, however, even humanity itself came to be seen, at least by some, as machine-like and predictable. A very extreme example of this came in the theories of psychologist John Watson who sought to explain all that we needed to know about human behaviour. Thoughts and emotions were explained away as conditioned responses. There was no such thing as fear. There was simply a human being's conditioned fear response. There was no such thing as love. There was simply a human being's conditioned love response. Chemical interaction and electrical impulses in the brain were seen to account for music, poetry, art and mystical experience alike. There was, in reality, no autonomous, independent, totally unique, personal inner life.[6] We were flesh and blood robots.

Now, whilst the brilliance of Newtonian physics was considered irrefutable and remains a towering intellectual achievement, not everyone, of course, would have condoned its application to humanity, in the way described, without hesitation or question. The mechanical model, however, proved to be highly resilient and it persisted and it did gradually eat its way into our psyche where it remains a powerful influence to this day. I believe that, consciously or unconsciously, it is still the basis of the world-view of many people, even people who hold firm to religious belief. It continues, as a result, to contrive to impoverish human existence and to provide a foundation upon which unease between religion and science stubbornly rests.

Despite this and the fact that those who held religious belief attempted to resist, if not the brilliance of Newtonian physics itself, then at least its use to shape a view of human existence that effectively stripped humanity of its soul, it could be argued, that religion and theology fell under its cause-and-effect spell to some extent. The mechanical mindset extended even to the relationship with God. If you dutifully attended Church on a Sunday and kept the commandments then your individual soul was automatically saved. If, as a Catholic, the rites of a sacrament were properly observed, then the sacrament was automatically effective.

The great irony of all of this is that science itself has moved on and left classical Newtonian physics far behind. A new world-view based on quantum physics is now firmly in its place. The story of quantum physics[7] and of this new world-view goes at least as far back as the year 1900. That was the year that a German physicist called Max Planck proposed that light existed not as a continuous unbroken stream of particles but as packets of energy that he would later call, "quanta". Innocuous as it may at first appear, this was an assertion that would, in time, revolutionize science.

The Quantum Story

The quantum story is inextricably interwoven with the story of light. As we know, life on earth depends on the light and heat received from our nearest star, the sun. Anything we can learn, therefore, about the nature and behaviour of light is hugely important because it will help us better understand life on our own planet and the make-up of the stars that we can gaze upon every clear night. Learning about light can also inform us about the microscopic world of the atom and we know how our very survival has been threatened by the little knowledge we possess of that small world.

Finally, we now know that the speed of light, which is 300,000 kilometres per second, provides us with no less than a cosmic reference point for all other physical reality. So, the quantum story offers us, in fact, an entirely different way of looking at the world, our place in the world and the universe itself.

It offers us a different mindset, a new perspective, an outlook that is dynamic and vibrant rather than static and mechanical.

The story really begins, as I have said, with Max Planck. However, an important preface was written nearly a hundred years before in 1801 when Thomas Young carried out a famous experiment by shining a light beam through a metal plate that had two parallel rectangular slots cut into it. Instead of finding an even spread in the light pattern on the far side of the metal plate, Young found a pattern of light and dark stripes. This pattern could only have been produced by the light beam behaving like a parted wave as it passed through the slots. On the far side of the slots, the crests of the waves coming through combined, at times, to give a light stripe and, alternatively, the crest of one wave combined with the trough of the other wave to give a dark stripe. [8] Because of the way the waves interfered with each other, the pattern of stripes became known as an interference pattern.

By 1873 what proved to be another giant step had been taken when James Clerk Maxwell established that light, in fact, consisted of electromagnetic waves. [9] However, coming back to Max Planck, it was he who took not so much a giant step but, as we have come to say today, a quantum leap that shook the scientific world. Planck proposed that light came not in one continuous, unbroken stream but in parcles, or packets of energy, or "quanta", but which would finally become known as photons. [10]

To you and I this may seem unremarkable but what disquieted the scientists was the realisation that if light was a spread out wave, as it were, it was very difficult to understand or visualise it being absorbed or being produced by atoms of matter that could not even be seen under the most powerful microscope. [11] For light to penetrate an atom it would have to come as a bullet-like particle. So, was light a wave, or was it a particle?

The only conclusion that could be arrived at was that light actually behaved like a wave in some instances and in others it behaved like a particle. Michael Chown puts it this way:

"Light really is both a particle and a wave. Or more correctly, light is 'something else' for which there is no word in our everyday language and nothing to compare it with in the everyday world."[12]

This was a disaster because it meant that the world of atoms did not behave with any predictability at all. Traditionally, science was based upon detailed observation followed by rigorous analysis. In turn, then, and given a controlled set of circumstances, clear, confident predictions could be made about an outcome. Nature, however, in the miniscule form of the atom was telling us that this, simply, was not necessarily so. We were now far from a clockwork world and were facing a world not of predictability but, of all things, uncertainty. So much so, that uncertainty itself would become a new principle of physics, the Heisenberg Principle, named after the famous scientist, Werner Heisenberg.

What happened was that things went from bad to worse after Max Planck's discovery because it was found that not only could light behave either as a particle or as a wave but that its option in doing so seemed to depend upon the fact that it was being observed. The act of observation seemed to influence its behaviour and replace the probability of it being one or the other with a definite state as either particle or wave. This seemed outrageous. The scientist was no longer a detached and objective observer. He, or she, was a participant.

Scientists were driven to distraction and so much so that they conceived of some bizarre experiments. By far the most famous thought experiment was that of Schrodinger's cat.[13] Briefly, Schrodinger imagined a box that had a perfectly even chance of either releasing, or not releasing, a lethally poisonous gas, over a period of thirty minutes. He visualised a cat being put into it and the lid being closed, so that it could not be seen what was going on. The question now was, after the thirty minutes, was the cat dead or alive or did that depend upon the box being opened and someone making an observation? Well, the arguments went back and forth

Unbinding Christian Faith: Free to Be   Denis Gleeson

but eventually, Heisenberg won the day with the view that nature makes the choice and that nature is unpredictable in the making of the choice. So, the poor cat would be either dead or alive before the box was opened and the opening of the box would play no part in its fate. Unpredictability, randomness was here to stay. By 1958, Neils Bohr could say that:

> "It is wrong to think that the task of physics is to find out how nature is. Physics concerns what we can say about nature." [14]

Eleven years later, Eugene Wigner could assert that the classical laws of physics and chemistry were a, "matter of the past." [15]

A truly profound shift had taken place. With the advent of quantum theory, we now no longer believed that we could master the mysteries of nature and, in time, explain them away. Nature's inherent unpredictability had convinced us that all we would ever really be able to do would be to observe nature and talk and theorise about our observations.

Einstein, notably, was unsettled by this development and he resisted it passionately.[16] However, he also resisted other things the mathematics was telling him such as the existence of black holes and the origin of the universe in a big bang. Even his extraordinary mind found the unpredictability, randomness and mystery of nature hard to accept, so, we should hardly be surprised when we find nature and the world that we inhabit impossible to fathom. Yet, quantum physics has opened up for us explanations for the burning of stars, the structure of elementary particles, the order of elements in the periodic table and the birth of the universe itself.[17] Its understanding have also given us technologies that include, "transistors, lasers, semiconductors, light-emitting diodes, scans, PET scans, and MRI machines." [18]

Psychologically and, of course, religiously and spiritually, it is taking most of us a long time to catch up on the science. Some of us still approach the world with the old Newtonian mindset and that means our approach to the world is dated and out of touch, and even incompatible, with a lot of new thinking that is going on around us. In particular, as has been noted, this can make it difficult for us to get our heads around the idea of God and to fit God in, as it were, to our daily life.

Though the quantum world is a much more God friendly world, all our thinking about God, in fact, relies not so much upon who God is, as upon who we think He, or She, is. The image we have of God is so important and is directly related to our world view because it is directly related not just to the scope of our imagination and the breadth of our vision but to our ability to accept the existence of the incomprehensible, the ineffable, the totally other, the unpredictable and the random. With quantum physics, mystery has been rehabilitated, as has human responsibility and conscience. We can no longer claim to be mere cogs in the great cosmic machine.[19] Interconnectedness, interdependence, relationship and consciousness are established as terms in the new scientific vocabulary and these are the terms that are already shaping the world view and the mindset of the twenty-first century.

Summary

At the corner of 4th and Walnut in Louisville Thomas Merton not only glimpsed the oneness of humanity, he actually experienced it. We wonder what holds the rest of us back from such an experience. Perhaps the way we view the world we live in and, in particular the way we view science and religion are a part of our difficulty. In general, science explores fact and religion explores meaning, but, there is only one truth about our reality and that of the universe and it is not exclusive to either religion or science. A respectful dialogue between the two is needed.

That religion struggles with change is well known. That science too struggles with change is not so readily recognised. Isaac Newton gave us what we can now call the classical view of our "reality". Our world was seen as a giant clockwork mechanism comprised of solid particles floating in an infinite sea of space. As for human beings, they came to be viewed by some as chemically conditioned, flesh and blood machines. Music, art and mystical experience were merely electrical activity in the brain. Now, whereas science itself has moved on from this view, surprisingly, it actually remains embedded in the popular psyche manifesting sometimes as a rejection of religious belief.

Today, quantum physics offers a much more dynamic and vibrant perspective of our world. Newtonian certainties have been replaced by unpredictability and randomness. Mystery has been rehabilitated. Yet, many of us struggle with concepts of interconnectedness, interdependence and a developing human consciousness. Strangely enough, this includes more than a few holding religious belief, or, maybe more correctly, static religious certainties.

Quotation for Discussion

"With the advent of quantum theory, we now no longer believed that we could master the mysteries of nature and, in time, explain them away. Nature's inherent unpredictability had convinced us that all we would ever really be able to do would be to observe nature and talk and theorise about our observations. Einstein, notably, was unsettled by this development and he resisted it passionately.[16] *However, he also resisted other things the mathematics was telling him such as the existence of black holes and the origin of the universe in a big bang. Even his extraordinary mind found the unpredictability, randomness and mystery of nature hard to accept, so, we should hardly be surprised when we find nature and the world that we inhabit impossible to fathom."*

Unbinding Christian Faith: Free to Be   Denis Gleeson

Questions for Discussion:

- What are the certainties in our world and in life that I subscribe to, if there are any, and how do I feel about the reality of randomness?
- How important for me are interconnectedness, interdependence, the development of consciousness and a creative dialogue between religion and science?

1. "Conjectures of a Guilty Bystander" Thomas Merton. Image Books (1989) cf p156-158.
2. "The Mind and the Brain" Jeffrey Schwartz M.D., and Sharon Begley. Regan Books (2002) cf p255-289
3. ibid cf p262
4. "Quantum Theory Cannot Hurt You." Marcus Chown. Faber and Faber (2007) cf p143.
5. "Quantum Theory: A Very Short Introduction" John Polkinghorne. Oxford (2002) p1.
6. Schwartz and Begley. Op. Cit. Cf p258-259.
7. Ibid cf p261ff.
8. Op. Cit. Polkinghorne. Cf p2
9. Ibid cf p4.
10. Op. Cit. Schwartz and Begley. Cf p261.
11. Op. Cit. Chown cf p18.
12. Ibid p19.
13. Op. Cit. Schwartz and Begley. Cf p275
14. Ibid p274.
15. Ibid p261
16. Ibid Cf p274
17. Ibid Cf p262
18. Ibid p262
19. Ibid Cf p276

2. Adopting a Different Mindset

What mindset do I usually bring to daily life? Is it a mindset open to change, difference and possibility? Is it a mindset that is cautious and defensive and thinks in terms of "us" and "them"? Do I have very definite opinions or do I welcome views different to my own? What kind of mindset did Jesus have?

"Do not be conformed to this world, but be transformed by the renewing of your minds, so that you may discern what is the will of God – what is good and acceptable and perfect." (Rom: 12.2)

The classical world view brought with it a mindset that is often referred to as dualistic. By way of contrast, the quantum world view offers us a mindset that is unitive. I actually prefer the term oppositional to dualistic and the term relational to unitive, but, the choice of term is wide. Richard Rohr,[1] for example, speaks of dualistic thinking in contrast to nondualistic thinking, or, polarity thinking in contrast to nonpolarity thinking. Then, instead of dualistic thinking, he sometimes refers to binary thinking or even, all-or-nothing thinking. Whatever terms are used, the idea, however, is the same and the important thing is to be aware of the mindset out of which we operate. Clearly, there are consequences to living out of any mindset and that is why it is crucial to bring it to consciousness.

Oppositional thinking is an inevitable corollary of the classical Newtonian world view because a mechanical and unchanging world, allied with the empirical method, demands division, distinction and the breaking down of things into parts. At times this is not just useful, it is even a necessity [2] but when fragmentation and exclusion become an habitual mindset and are adopted as a general approach to life, then, a problem arises. Things are seen in black and white. Opinions are either right or wrong. Choices are reduced to either this choice or that choice.

Unbinding Christian Faith: Free to Be   Denis Gleeson

People are either included or excluded. Passing judgement on everything and everyone becomes an instinctive, abiding and compulsive preoccupation. I know that I have demonstrated an oppositional mindset when, I have insisted, for example, on my point of view being the only correct one, my plan of procedure being the only viable one, my experience being the only valid experience. In doing so, I have been dismissive of other viewpoints. I have impoverished planning and invalidated the experience of others. The oppositional mindset operates with an "us" and "them" stance and favours hierarchy, privilege, independence and individualism. It perpetuates a competitive, success and failure perspective towards life. It is, As Richard Rohr puts it, an "all-or-nothing" approach.

Relational thinking follows from taking a quantum world view. Perpetual and dynamic change are, as we have seen, its major characteristics. Acceptance of ongoing process, integration and collaboration are distinctive of its mindset. Opinion is nuanced and accommodating. Decision making follows the creation of options and the exploration of possibility. The whole is seen as more than just the sum of the parts. Consensus and inclusion allow participants to exercise ownership of an enterprise. Preoccupation, such as it is, is with listening, acceptance, intuition, imagination and creativity. I know that I have demonstrated a relational mindset when I have shown a willingness to broaden my horizons, to compromise and to take on board, as valid alternatives, approaches which I recognise as simply different to my own. Outcomes are thereby strengthened and enriched. The relational, unitive, nondualistic mindset is more comfortable with "we" than with "I" and favours equality, interdependence and community. Barbara Fiand sums up the situation for us when she writes:

"The dualistic perspective, which has ruled our self-understanding for so many centuries, valued distinction and, with it, 'specialness'. We identified ourselves by our differences and treasured them. From them we derived our notions of superiority and inferiority, a sense of better and worse, of inclusion and exclusion, of togetherness and segregation. From them, also, hierarchy was born. Today, however, we are invited toward identity through 'at-onement' and interconnectivity. We have no choice, really, for we know now what we did not know before: Nothing happens anywhere in the universe that does not affect everything, everywhere, instantly." [3]

In our homes, at the workplace, at the mall, in our Churches and in our schools and universities, it matters what mindset we adopt. It matters if we place value on what we do and on what we aspire to. It matters if we place value on people. If we want to release the energy, creativity, goodwill and potential of those around us, it will always be more difficult to do that with oppositional thinking and easier to do it with relational thinking. Unfortunately, however, we have engaged with oppositional thinking as if we had no alternative. I do not know how many times I have listened to a political, social or economic debate on the radio, or watched one on television and ended up more confused over the issues than I was at the beginning. This is because the approach of the participants, invariably, is from an oppositional mindset. Rather than take a relational stance by pooling information and collaborating in the search for the next step forward, the idea seems to be for each person involved to try to better everyone else by sheer force of argument and have their opinion and definitive solution dominate. The media, of course, sometimes collude as, they are often more interested in spectacle, controversy and spectacular headlines than in providing a service that informs us on the issues and is genuinely educational for the general public.

However, it is not only some of our politicians, business people and journalists who indulge in oppositional and dualistic thinking, I think that most of us in the Western world tend to do so and we do it on a daily basis. When we convince ourselves, for example, that we have not enough time to pray, or that prayer is not relevant to the task in hand, that is oppositional thinking. We are seeing the elements of our day as isolated events unrelated to each other and as having no connection to God, who is the source of all being. If we believe in God at all, then, logically, this does not make any sense. Our oppositional mindset, however, in its search for definition, compartmentalisation and predictability, locks us into a life defined by fragmentation and limited by a lack of awareness and a stifled consciousness. This is why Jesus declines to reprimand Mary when Martha complains that she has been left by her sister with a lot to do (cf Lk 10:38-42). Martha has missed the point, her thinking is narrowly focussed on the immediate and she takes, therefore, an oppositional stance. Mary knows the one thing that is necessary. She knows who Jesus is and understands the relational kingdom of which he speaks. She is aware with a consciousness that has expanded. Martha has still some way to go.

Relational thinking can offer us a breadth of vision, a feel for the "more" in life and limitless possiblities, options and potential. It will also bring surprise, unpredictabilty and lots of loose ends, but, can we really say that life itself is not just like that? Margaret Wheatley, an organisational consultant, outlines how the quantum world view has changed her mindset and approach. She writes:

"My growing sensiblity of a quantum universe has affected my organisational life in several ways. First, I try hard to discipline myself to remain aware of the whole and to resist my well trained desire to analyse the parts to death. I look now for patterns of movement over time and focus on qualities like rhythm, flow, direction and shape. Second, I know I am wasting time whenever I draw straight lines between two variables in a cause-and-effect diagram, or position things as polarities, or create elaborate plans or time lines. Third, I no longer argue with anyone about what is real.

Fourth, the time I formerly spent on detailed planning and analysis I now use to look at the structure that might facilitate relationships. I have come to expect that something useful occurs if I link up people, units, or tasks, even though I cannot determine the outcomes. Lastly, I realise more and more that the universe will not cooperate with my desires for determinism." [4]

What Wheatley is describing is a change from an oppositional mindset to a relational mindset. Her preoccupation now is with an awareness of the whole and she sees her task in terms of the facilitation of relationships. If this is the case in a business context, how much more can it be the case in religious, spiritual and environmental contexts?

Why, for example, are the Beatitudes such a puzzle to us? Even when they are the subject of reflection by quite brilliant minds, we can be impressed by theological insightfulness but still be left with a feeling that we have not quite grasped the essence. Otherwise, I would suggest, the Beatitudes would occupy a much more prominent place in the Western Christian psyche than they appear to. We do not seem to get the point, just as we are somewhat uneasy about the vineyard owner who pays all of his workers the same wage irrespective of their hours of work. Likewise, we have a sneaking sympathy for the older brother who complains when he comes home to find a feast in full swing in honour of his younger sibling who had squandered half of the inheritance. The reason is that Jesus speaks out of a relational mindset, whereas we are much more at home with the apportioning of what we consider to be justice and fairness.

A parent or teacher confronted with an irrational, foul-mouthed, out-of-control teenager may wish that there were formulaic, clear-cut, strategies and procedures for dealing with the situation, but, there are not. There is only the slow, messy, uncertain, almost arbitrary process of trying to build, or continue to build, a relationship in the face of rank unreasonableness. This calls for a cultivated ability not to take what is said personally and a heroic effort to put the young person and their needs first. Such a relational approach offers some hope of success, whereas any other approach will only compound and complicate matters.

Going from the domestic to the global, we can ponder why, anyone should be without adequate food and shelter, with all the wealth, technology, economic muscle and logistical expertise that there is in the world. We are smart enough to be able to tackle world poverty, but, we seem to lack the collective will. Stuck in the oppositional paradigm, we still think on personal, local and national scales rather than on a global scale. We buy arms and aircraft carriers and invest billions in security rather than reach out to others. Despite evidence to the contrary, we convince ourselves that our Western lifestyle does not have to change, that our ecological and environmental issues can be contained and are neither urgent nor a priority.

Thomas Keating says that our mindset does not allow us to ask the right questions and our world view is simply out of date. [5] Richard Rohr puts it another way. He says that we do not see the "big picture", we lack a "contemplative gaze". [6] Because we do so, we can avoid what is in front of our eyes and fail to understand the message of compassion and unity our religious traditions have been offering us for centuries. Embracing a quantum mindset and cultivating relational thinking would be positive steps to take in positioning ourselves for the future. A further positive step would be to review our idea, or image, of God.

Summary:

The classical world view brought with it a dualistic, oppositional mindset. It was important to be able to make distinctions and categorise. Robust debate tended to precede the passing of judgement between accurate and inaccurate, right and wrong.

Competition and hierarchy dictated success in many aspects of science, politics, religion and life.

The quantum worldview offers us a different dynamic and is nondualistic, relational or unitive. Here the emphasis is on acceptance, integration and collaboration. Change and possibility are happily explored. Teamwork, equality, interdependence and community are the hallmarks of the preferred methods of operation. Barbara Fiand suggests that this relational mindset is really our only option because we have now come to know that all activity in the universe is interconnected.

In general, Western society, however, remains competitive, confrontational and oppositional both in the way society is organised and in the way we prefer to think and to go about life. Analysis, planning and compartmentalisation are still our daily, default positions. We tend to see ourselves as in control, so, God is not relevant and, consequently, there is little space for prayer. By way of contrast, in the Gospel, Mary, Martha's sister, knew that there was only one thing necessary and this is why Jesus refuses to accept criticism of her. The mindset of Jesus is a unitive, relational mindset with a focus on those attitudes of being which will open us up to each other and to life in the Divine.

The great religious traditions have pleaded for compassion for centuries. Yet, rather than address such issues as economic injustice, world poverty and hunger, our collective mindset remains one of defending the indefensible and securing entitlement, wealth and privilege.

Quotation for Discussion:

"We are smart enough to be able to tackle world poverty, but, we seem to lack the collective will. Stuck in the oppositional paradigm, we still think on personal, local and national scales rather than on a global scale. We buy arms and aircraft carriers and invest billions in security rather than reach out to others. Despite

evidence to the contrary, we convince ourselves that our Western lifestyle does not have to change, that our ecological and environmental issues can be contained and are neither urgent nor a priority."

Questions for Discussion

- Can you recall a recent incident, confrontation or conversation that illustrates either oppositional thinking, or relational thinking either on your part, or locally, nationally, or internationally?
- Being completely honest, what is the one thing necessary in my life and what evidence is there to support that?

1. "The Naked Now" Richard Rohr. Crossroad Publishing (2009) cf p32ff.
2. Ibid cf p32.
3. "Awe-Filled Wonder" Barbara Fiand. Paulist (2008) p53-54.
4. Margaret Wheatley. Source as yet not known.
5. "Foundations for Centering Prayer and the Christian Contemplative Life" (Invitation to Love) Thomas Keating. Continuum (2002) cf p232.
6. Richard Rohr. Op cit. Cf p29.

3. God, Nurture, Metaphor and Imagination.

What, for you, are the most powerful Christian compositions, images or symbols? Has any Christian art influenced your image of God? How do you think of God? Is God with us or not? Do you experience the presence of God in your life? What is the mark of a proper relationship with God? What is the true nature of freedom and of love? Is God's presence veiled for me?

In Islam, images of God are prohibited and given our experience in Christianity, I can see a certain wisdom in that, although it must surely be acknowledged that the artistic Christian heritage numbers among the great achievements of human kind. That having been said, if we consider some of the most famous Christian works of art, we cannot but wonder at the role they have played in shaping our concept of God and of things spiritual. One of the most magnificent illustrated pages in the ninth century Book of Kells, for example, features Christ enthroned. The artwork and intricate filigree are stunning and the most common reaction to it is probably one of sheer amazement. However, I am always somewhat disconcerted by the hollow eyed Christ that stares back at me from that wondrous page. What does that face evoke in my spiritual psyche? It is certainly not the joy of Christ in his glory. It has more to do, I think, with an interpretation of Christ's suffering and his fearful passion and yet, undeniably, the illustration is still of Christ enthroned in heaven.

Then, in the fourteenth century in Italy, Dante Alighieri produced his epic poem the Divine Comedy with its description of hell, the Inferno. So powerful has its influence been that some wonder if we do not owe our ideas of the afterlife much more to this work of art than to anything in scripture or in Christian dogma. And if this is so, how has this undoubted masterpiece of world literature impacted upon our ideas about God with its powerful images of everlasting punishment?

Taking just one further example, how have we been influenced by Michaelangelo's painting of God's creation of Adam on the ceiling of the Sistine chapel? This has been such an iconic image since it was painted in the sixteenth century that it is no great surprise that the image of God as an old man with a flowing white beard appears to have worked its way into our subconscious. However it may have filtered through to them from cultural exposure, some small children certainly seem to identify God in these classic terms. We as adults, of course, while openly marvelling at the artistic execution, may consider ourselves too spiritually sophisticated for such an image to weigh significantly with us.

So, leaving my supposed sophistication aside, what actually is my own image of God? This is a question that I found myself struggling with many times during retreats and spiritual programmes and a question that I think we can all usefully spend time with. I was never quite sure how to approach the question for myself and never happy that I had answered it fully or accurately. A breakthrough of sorts came when I finally understood what had been suggested to me often and that was that my image of God surely depended in some measure, at least, on the relationship that I had with my own parents. It was a matter of nurture and so I came to conclude that my image of God was of a God who was caring, kindly, somewhat undemonstrative and who had expectations that certain standards be maintained. This meant that my image of God, therefore, was simply that - an image that I myself had unconsciously crafted! It had much more to do with my own personal experience of life and my interpretation of that experience than it had to do with God. Of course, I knew that God was a God of love, but, could I honestly say that that had been my direct experience of God? Here was another question to struggle with as, presumably, a person's image of God owes something also to their actual inner experience of God, however they name that experience!

For me, a further breakthrough came when I actually ventured to say to a friend that I experienced God as a God of kindness. He did not respond immediately but later queried whether I would consider using the word "tenderness" rather than the word "kindness". Somehow, I knew that the nuance he was suggesting was right and that if I felt discomfort around the word "tenderness" then that was entirely my own problem. Perhaps, the issue was not so much my image of God as the assumptions and preconceptions that I had around God?

Seeds are sown as soon as an adult attempts to answer a child's first question about who, or what, God is. Better by far that the answer is one that the child has to grow into, than one that the child will have to grow out of. Otherwise, God may well suffer the same inevitable fate as Santa Claus. Often, for example, a child is introduced to God as a God who takes care of them and keeps them safe.[1] Later, God may become a God who rewards and punishes. With adutlhood, a person is challenged to move beyond images such as these. Whereas, if God is introduced to the child simply as the creator of all that exists, that view of God may become more sophisticated in adulthood with learnings from cosmology. It will never be invalid and can eventually grow into the notion of God as Being itself.

Thinking of God as pure Being is nothing new. In medieval times both John Duns Scotus and Thomas Aquinas[2] preoccupied themselves with the idea and in the twentieth century it was this concept that led Thomas Merton to Christianity.[3] Though it may sound modern, therefore, it is scarcely that and it also fits in with the God we meet in the pages of the sacred scriptures. We do well to remember, however, that the notion of God as pure Being, along with all the other descriptions of God we find in the scriptures and other spiritual writings are just notions. They are images, descriptions and attempts to express the inexpressible. Barbara Fiand writes that, "everything that *can* in fact be spoken about God, even by the most inspired mystic – is *metaphor*."[4] She adds:

vibrate with the energy of the one God. The exclusive and elitist social and political systems we create among ourselves, the insurmountable distinctions we insist upon are really nonsense. The rigid, intractable religious barriers we have sometimes established in the very name of God are at best, a tragic misunderstanding of tradition and at worst, a betrayal of the richness of our spiritual inheritance. They actually verge on blasphemy. Blasphemous also is the disdain we have often shown as humanity for the rest of creation, for it too beats to the rhythm of God's breath. What change we could bring about if we allowed the concept and image of the breath of God inform our social, economic and moral thinking!

The Presence of God in Relationship

In the Old Testament the question of God's presence is never far away. The people ask, is God present or not? How is God present? Does God's presence make a difference? Should we be fearful of God's presence? When God is present, what does he ask of us?

The story really begins with Abram who will later be called Abraham. God suddenly appears in Abram's life and tells him to leave his country in return for a blessing - the assured survival of his descendants and a land that Abram, his wife Sarai and their descendants can call their own (cf Gn:12.1-3 and 17.1-27). So, Abram does so and after God has renamed Abram and Sarai, Abraham and Sarah, they have a son, Isaac, even though both of them are quite old. Everything, therefore seems to be going as God has promised and then God does the most extraordinary thing, He asks Abraham to make a sacrifice of his son, Isaac (cf Gn:22). If Isaac is sacrificed, of course, where will that leave God's promise of many descendants? Nevertheless, Abraham does not hesitate. He makes his preparations, takes Isaac with him and sets out, as he had been told to do, for the land of Moriah.

Now, as we know, an angel intervenes and at the last moment, Isaac is saved. But, what are we to make of this game of life and death that God was playing? The angel declares that Isaac has been saved because his father, Abraham, has shown his "fear" of God. Yet, Abraham does not show any signs of fear, as we understand it. What he does show is trust in God, a steadfast belief that God will be true somehow to His promises. More importantly, Abraham shows love for God because he chooses his relationship with God above those promises. The God of Abraham is not just a God of power, who can ordain a favourable future. He is a God who is present as a God who seeks out personal relationship.

In turn, Isaac is blessed by God (cf Gn: 25.11 and 26.13) and enters into relationship with Him (cf Gn:26.24-25), as does Isaac's younger son, Jacob. Jacob, in fact, ends up wrestling with God and in so doing, he models for us all, the struggle that we have with God as we seek to define the real and make sense of life and of our own humanity. John A. Sanford says that:

> "Everyone who wrestles with his spiritual and psychological experience, and no matter how dark or frightening it is, refuses to let it go until he discovers its meaning, is having something of the Jacob experience." [7]

So, Jacob's name is changed to Israel, meaning the one who has struggled with God.[8] Then, Israel asks God His name (cf Gn: 32.23-32). However, God's name, as we have seen, is revealed not to Jacob, or to his son, Joseph, but some generations later, to Moses as God begins to enter into relationship with His people, the people of Israel. God's people must now forge their relationship with Him as he leads them to nationhood. As with Abraham, the nation's relationship with God begins with a promise. This time the promise is a promise of freedom (cf Ex: 3.16-17). The exodus is God's delivery on that promise and is the central event in the Old Testament. But the Israelites still doubt God's presence and His good intentions towards them (cf Ex: 15.22- 16.35). This, despite that fact that God has overseen their escape through the Sea of Reeds from the pursuing Egyptian army (cf Ex:14). So, at Massah and Meribah they ask, "Is the LORD among us or not?" (Ex: 17.7) This is the question that has reverberated down through the centuries since. It finds articulation in every age, expression in every language and an echo in every human heart. It is also a question that keeps repeating itself with each new circumstance in our individual lives. Is God with me or not? How can God be present in this crisis I now have to face?

Therefore, even though God's presence is a powerful presence bestowing freedom on the Israelites and giving them a land of their own, it does not prove to be enough to guarantee their fidelity to Him. They are remembered in the Psalms as:

"...a stubborn and rebellious generation,
a generation whose heart was not steadfast,
whose spirit was not faithful to God." (Ps: 78.8)

The people constantly stray from the covenant God has made with them and as well as neglecting their duty to Him, they show scant respect for each other. As we know, only the first three commandments deal directly with the relationship between God and His people and their demands are simple: worship no other God; respect God's name and observe the Sabbath. All the other commandments deal with how the Israelites are to behave towards each other (cf Ex: 20.1-17; 22.20-7) if they are to live beside each other as neighbours and as one people.

After the great Exodus event, the bible story, in some respects, constitutes a series of appeals by God to His people to be faithful to Him and to treat each other properly. By the time of the prophets, God has tired of sacrifices that are really meaningless and are an empty ritual.

"What to me is the multitude of your sacrifices?
says the LORD;

I have had enough of burnt offerings of rams
and the fat of fed beasts;
I do not delight in the blood of bulls,
or of lambs or of goats.
When you come to appear before me,
who asked this from your hand?
Trample my courts no more;
bringing offerings is futile;
incense is an abomination to me....
even though you make many prayers;
I will not listen;
your hands are full of blood."
(Is: 1.11-13a, 15b)

God makes it clear that if His people are to be present in relationship to Him, they must be in respectful and just relationship with each other. Again, this is underscored in the famous opening chapter from Isaiah.

"Wash yourselves; make yourselves clean;
remove the evil of your doings
from before my eyes;
cease to do evil,
learn to do good;
seek justice,
rescue the oppressed,
defend the orphan,
plead for the widow.
(Is: 1.16-17)

Pleading with His people, however, is not enough and God goes a step further. He promises to bestow on Israel the ability to do what Israel cannot bring itself to do, which is, to be faithful and to be just. He vows to plant his law and his covenant deep in the human heart so that the least and the greatest will know Him (cf Jer: 31.33-34).

Now, the God of the Old Testament can be seen as problematical in some respects and images used of Him are often in need of explanation and context. But, it is clear that He is consistently a God who calls us to relationship with Him and with each other. His presence in relationship is a powerful presence that changes us and changes our lives. Our interaction with God leads us to an experience of freedom and brings us home to the truth regarding our own existence and that is that we exist only in God. Certainly, we can and do rebel against the idea and assert our independence but this independence too is God given and whatever our use of it, God always allows us our choice. Freedom is a prerequisite of love and we are made to love and to live in God who is love. Thomas Merton puts it as follows:

"To say that I am made in the image of God is to say that love is the reason for my existence, for God is love. Love is my true identity. Selflessness is my true self. Love is my true character. Love is my name." [9]

God's most dramatic Word on the Divine presence to humanity in relationship and on the nature of freedom, love and life, comes in the person of Jesus. Jesus is Immanuel, "which means 'God is with us.' " (Mt: 1.23). His mission is to heal, to help the blind to see, the deaf to hear and to raise the dead to life. He comes to bring the Good News to the impoverished (cf Lk: 7.22). In other words, God offers us new life in Jesus. Which of us is not in need of healing and is not blind and deaf? Which of us does not need to be reinvigorated? Which of us does not need our lives to be enriched? Which of us does not need to be set free? (cf Lk: 4.18).

As Jesus breathes his own Spirit into us (cf Jn: 20.22), he also gives us the task of reinvigorating, enriching and caring for each other (cf Mt: 25: 31-46). We are to be his presence upon the earth. God, in and through the person of Jesus, is again being consistent. In the New Testament, He not only offers us new life, He empowers us with the Spirit and expects us to be just with each other.

In fact, the beatitudes that Jesus puts before us go well beyond what was required by the commandments. The commandments were basic requirements for civilized living and form the bedrock of any society. If we are to live alongside each other at all, the very least that can be expected is that we do not kill each other, or abandon the elderly, or lie about each other, or steal, or have irresponsible sexual relations. The beatitudes assume all of that and look to the mindset that drives all of our activity (cf Mt: 5.1-12). We are to be free of attachment and self-promotion; we are to be gentle and hunger and thirst only for what God wants; we are to reflect God's mercy and compassion; we are to be peacemakers and are to put up with persecution and abuse when they come our way because we are prepared to stand up for what we see is right and be loyal to the person and values of Jesus. A society founded on adherence to this mindset would indeed be a new society, a new kingdom in which God would be powerfully present to His people.

But, we shrink from the beatitudes and we shrink also from love because both make us vulnerable. Maybe, we understand the love of God and the beatitudes well enough. In fact, maybe we understand them all too well and just cannot bring ourselves to let go in their embrace. God as revealed in Jesus is a vulnerable God. He is a God whose love brings him to the cross. I think we are uncomfortable with a vulnerable God. In that illustration, in the Book of Kells, of Christ enthroned, perhaps after all, it is his vulnerability that disconcerts me.

In ancient times and in the Jewish Temple in Jerusalem, incense was burnt to give homage to God but also to protect the priest from God's presence. The belief was that to look on the face of God would result in death, so a cloud of incense was raised as a protective veil between the worshipper and the worshipped in case God should appear. Today, in worship, in prayer and in life in general, our sense of God's presence has become blunted and veiled by our upbringing, culture and imagination. But, of course, God's presence in life does not depend, at all, on our sensitivity to it, but our sensitivity to it does need to be sharpened. Thomas Keating writes:

> "The present moment, every object we see, our inmost nature are all rooted in God. But we hesitate to believe this until personal experience gives us the confidence to believe in it. This involves the gradual development of intimacy with God. God constantly speaks to us through each other as well as from within. The experience of God's presence activates our capacity to perceive God in everything else – in people, in events, in nature." [10]

Where can we gain such personal experience? Well, Keating gives us the answer. It is to be gained through, "gradual development of intimacy with God." And that gradual development, as we shall see later on, comes through the development of our relationship with God by our practice of prayer. Specifically, the prayer in question here is non-vocal, non-conceptual prayer. It is a prayer of quiet, a prayer of centering, an entering into contemplative silence.

Receptive silence allows God to be God. Unhindered by our thoughts and images, and no longer bound by the limitations of our small minds, God can work in our inner depths and heal the assumptions and misconceptions we have. God can breathe the breath of life into us afresh, and invite us to come into His, or Her, presence. Then, with ever growing consciousness, we can grow, more and more, into relationship. When Jesus called Lazarus out of the tomb, he called him to a completely new experience of life and a new awareness of God.

Summary:

Down through the centuries, Christian art has influenced our image of God and the way we think about God. It seems our image of God is shaped by our experience of our parents, by our upbringing and by our own personal inner experience of the Divine. Based on these we make assumptions about God and form conceptions that we may well have to grow out of.

It is important to remember that images of God are just images and however lyrically we may speak about our God our words are merely necessary metaphor. One such metaphor is found in the first chapters of Genesis when we read that creation pulses to the spirit and the breath of God. Even the name God gives to Moses. "I AM, WHO I AM" resonates with this idea.

The God of the Old Testament is a God who is present and a God who seeks out personal relationship with Abraham, Isaac and Jacob. Our struggle with the presence and idea of God is a struggle with our own reality. This was also the struggle of the Hebrew people in the desert during the Exodus. Their question "Is the LORD among us or not?" reverberates down through the ages.

As for our relationship with God and our presence to God, that is measured, the prophets consistently tell us, by the justice evident in our relationships with each other. God's covenant is planted deep in the human heart.

True human freedom is found only in God. We are made to love and to live in God who is love. Jesus is God's most dramatic word on the Divine presence to humanity, on freedom and on love. In the beatitudes, Jesus invites us to just relationships. In Jesus, a vulnerable God invites us to intimacy.

Quotation for Discussion:

"In ancient times and in the Jewish Temple in Jerusalem, incense was burnt to give homage to God but also to protect the priest from

God's presence. The belief was that to look on the face of God would result in death so a cloud of incense was raised as a protective veil between the worshipper and the worshipped in case God should appear. Today, in worship, in prayer and in life in general, our sense of God's presence has become blunted and veiled by our upbringing, culture and imagination. But, of course, God's presence in life does not depend, at all, on our sensitivity to it, but our sensitivity to it does need to be sharpened."

Questions for Discussion

- When you look back over your life, what were the moments that were significant in the evolution of your relationship with God?
- What interconnectedness do you experience between your awareness of the presence of God, your consciousness of yourself and your attitude towards other people?

1. "Divine Therapy and Addiction" by Thomas Keating. Lantern Books (2009) cf p18.
2. "The Naked Now" Richard Rohr. Crossroad Publishing (2009) cf p130.
3. "The Seven Storey Mountain" by Thomas Merton. SPCK (1990) cf 172ff.
4. "Awe-Filled Wonder" Barbara Fiand. Paulist (2008) p18.
5. Ibid p18.
6. Richard Rohr. Op. Cit. cf p25-26.
7. "The Man Who Wrestled With God' John A. Sandford. Paulist (1981) p40.
8. Ibid cf p40.
9. "New Seeds of Contemplation" by Thomas Merton. Shambhala (2003) p63.
10. "Open Mind, Open Heart" by Thomas Keating. Continuum (2006) p33-34

4. Trusting that God can Heal the Brokenhearted

If God is good and all-powerful, why is there so much suffering? Also, why does God tolerate human evil? Do suffering and evil make me angry with God? Is God punishing us when we suffer? What are we to make of Jesus' suffering on the cross? How much of my suffering is self-inflicted?

Conversations on the topic of religion generally do not go very far before someone brings up the related questions of suffering and evil. If God is both good and all-powerful, the reasoning goes, how can He allow a world in which there is so much suffering and in which people perpetrate such awful deeds? Any nature programme will illustrate the extent of the suffering that occurs so casually in nature and we will find ourselves fascinated and appalled in equal measure. Any news broadcast will remind us of the terrible cruelties that we, as human beings, sometimes endure and daily visit upon each other. Why does God allow it all?

Of course, a little reflection may bring us to concede suffering and evil are not quite the same thing. There is a qualitative difference, for example, between suffering that occurs due to natural causes and suffering that is caused by evil acts. So, in our reflection, we may further allow that such things as crime, war, ignorance, selfishness, mindlessness, poverty, deprivation and disadvantage are, for the most part, human products and God, who gifts us with free-will, can hardly be held to account for them. However, among these human acts, some at the very least, have their origins in sheer malice and evil. Why did God bestow upon us such a propensity for that? And, in the case of suffering due to natural causes, why, in any event, does God "send" natural disasters. How can God stand over the suffering of innocent children in such catastrophes, or even the suffering of one sick child, for that matter?

This chapter attempts to address some of these questions and move us from an oppositional mindset to a unitive mindset. The anger that many of us hold towards God is a huge burden on us and is one of the tightest bonds that bind and restrict us in our relationship with the Divine and in our development as truly human beings. How can we have a positive image of God if we believe God is passive and uncaring in the face of evil and suffering? How can we love a God if we cannot trust that God genuinely wants to heal our hearts when they are broken? Let us begin by looking at some common answers to these questions. What we will see is their inadequacy.

Responses to Suffering and Evil

Our attempts to explain suffering and evil have really been endless. They include the notion that suffering is a punishment from God. Now, on the surface of it, this may seem a rather primitive idea for us to entertain in the twenty-first century. However, even though we may consciously reject this idea at an intellectual level, we often have a very poor image of ourselves and, by way of projection, we can imagine that God shares this poor image of us. So, despite ourselves, we cannot escape a vague, unspoken and unsophisticated suspicion that the suffering, misfortune or evil that befalls us is, in some way, a punishment and a reckoning for something that we have done or have failed to do. In fact, our suspicion can appear to be confirmed by a quite literal interpretation of some passages in the scriptures. We read in Isaiah, for example:

"Tell the innocent how fortunate they are,
for they shall eat the fruit of their labours.
Woe to the guilty! How unfortunate they are,
for what their hands have done shall be done to them. "
(Isaiah: 3.10-11)

This is the idea that the book of Job explores and is what Marie A. Conn terms, "retribution theology" [1] It maintains that God ordains that good people will prosper in life as a result of their good deeds and bad people will suffer. Now, our human experience tells us that this is simply untrue. Most of us need hardly look beyond our own families for proof that it is untrue and all of us know that some, who are suspected of very bad deeds, appear to be beyond the reach of the law of the land and to enjoy the good life. Yet, as I have said, we hold onto the idea on both a personal and a social level and it continues to have purchase for us. Crude as it is, it is also a potent political idea articulated in the belief that the rich deserve what they have because they have worked hard for it and that the poor are poor by virtue of their laziness and lack of initiative.

If we look to the gospel, however, we see that Jesus will have none of this. He rejects entirely the idea that suffering is in any way a punishment from the Father. When he is told that Pilate has killed some Galilean worshippers, he asks his audience if those killed were greater sinners than any other Galileans. Answering the question himself, he says that they were not. He then repeats the question citing the example of eighteen people killed when the tower of Siloam collapsed. Again, he answers his own question saying that those unfortunates were no more guilty than anyone else who happened to be in Jerusalem at the time. After both of these answers, he urges his listeners to repent and warns them, that if they do not, they too will perish. Here, however, he is talking of a spiritual fate, a spiritual death (cf Lk: 13.4). Human evil and natural disaster, he is saying, are not punishment from God. But, ever the skilled teacher using an opportunity to deliver a message, he adds that our own failure to turn our lives towards God can lead to even greater disasters than Pilate's bloody atrocity or the collapse of an ancient tower.

A further opportunity to convey this message comes when Jesus and his disciples meet a man blind from birth and the disciples' query whether the poor man is blind because of his own sin or because of that of his parents (cf Jn: 9.1ff). Jesus tells them that neither the man nor his parents sinned. He then cures the man, declaring that the man "…was born blind so that the works of God might be displayed in him." Now after rejecting the idea of suffering as punishment from God, Jesus is hardly proposing that suffering was instead designedly inflicted on this man so that it could be used by God as a means of His own glorification. No, Jesus is simply saying that the curing of the man, who was born blind by no fault either of his own or of his parents, will be a glorification of God. God is glorified when suffering is overcome. This is entirely in keeping with Jesus' own mission, received from God, which is to combat illness, suffering and evil of all kinds, including that imposed by religious institution. To this end, Jesus is the great healer wherever he goes in Galilee and Judah. His healings are not just statements of power they are statements of hope that suffering and evil can and will be overcome.

Now, even if the man who was born blind was not born so by a design of God, could it be that on the grand scale, the cosmic scale, suffering and evil are part of some grand design that is just outside of and beyond our limited human understanding? Harold S. Kushner dismisses this idea in his classic text, *"When Bad Things Happen to Good People"*. He writes:

"If a human artist or employer made children suffer so that something immensely impressive or invaluable could come to pass, we would put him in prison. Why then should we excuse God for causing such undeserved pain, no matter how wonderful the ultimate result may be?" [2]

Explaining away the suffering of the innocent in terms of some divine design just does not seem to be consistent with our belief in a good God. Likewise, Kushner finds fault with another commonly held theory. This is the view that suffering and evil are God's means of putting us to the test, with of course, its frequent corollary that God never tests us beyond our endurance. This is a theory, he reasons, that just does not stand up:

> "If God is testing us, He must know by now that many of us fail the test. If He is only giving us burdens that we can bear, I have seen Him miscalculate too often."[3]

Such miscalculations include those friends or relatives many of us have seen collapse beneath depression, find a loss just too much to bear, or endure to the utter distress of everyone around them, a prolonged and painful death. Apparently then, if we were to accept the theory that God puts us to the test, it is better to be weak, in the face of illness, pain and suffering of any kind, than to be strong, because, logically, God will have to ask us to endure less.[4] What virtue then resides in patience, forbearance and dignified endurance.

Kushner says of the loss of his own young son that he does not in any way feel privileged in having had to experience such grief, nor does this strange view of unbearable burden as divine gift help him understand why God visits upon hundreds of thousands of families a year a disabled baby. True, caring for the child will be a supreme test for the parents but the question is could a good God willfully intend it as such and what of the baby who is, manifestly, innocent? [5].

That the disabled child may very well, and often does, bring out wonderful qualities in the parents raises a variation on the theory that God puts us to the test and it comes with the suggestion that suffering and evil are, in some way, God's attempt at ennobling us. Kushner quotes Rabbi Joseph B. Soloveitchik who proposes this position as follows:

> " 'Suffering comes to ennoble man, to purge his thoughts of pride and superficiality, to expand his

horizons. In sum, the purpose of suffering is to repair that which is faulty in man's personality.' " [6]

In his searing contemplation of his wife's death, the great C. S. Lewis allows himself a rather more rueful expression of this same approach. He says:

> "The tortures occur. If they are unnecessary, then there is no God or a bad one. If there is a good God, then these tortures are necessary. For no moderately good Being could inflict them if they weren't. Either way, we're for it." [7]

In one of his early works, Lewis had also referred to pain as God's "megaphone" used to "rouse a deaf world" [8]. So, numbed by our inexplicable experience of suffering and now deafened by a contemporary culture that is defined by noise, our pain remains unprocessed.

In any event, Kushner's objection made above to the idea of suffering as a test still applies to this variation on that theme. As an explanation of the suffering of those who are young and innocent it is just inadequate and feeble in the extreme. Taking the example of the birth of a disabled child, we cannot simply disregard the child's innocence for the sake of any theory, or in some inappropriate defence of our own inadequate image of God. Who would want to believe in a God that uses the innocent as pawns in a pitiless pedagogy?

Yet, there are no atheists in the trenches, it is said. When we are in danger, we instinctively turn to God. This is also the case when we are vulnerable or sick. At the same time, we can be angry with God and blame God, even when our suffering is caused by fellow human beings. Rationality, it seems, does not have a lot to do with things.

At a purely intellectual level, we may know that God does not wish suffering upon us and does not send suffering our way, but, when suffering does come our way, we can still have the feeling that we are being tested by God. How is it, we wonder, that those who were closest to God invariably endured great suffering? Now, perhaps to some extent we are going back over ground just covered here, but the point I am making is that our understanding of suffering is one thing, yet how we actually feel within ourselves when we are in the grip of suffering is quite another.

Here we must be careful. We must be gentle and patient with ourselves. We would never, I hope, try to rationalize away suffering endured by someone else, so we should not be tempted to rationalize away our own. In calm seas, we can always prepare the ship for the storm, but when the storm strikes, all we may be able to do is to hang on for dear life. It may even help to rail at God when doing so, if we cannot otherwise bring ourselves to pray.

But, let us look at just one more attempt to explain suffering. This attempt is popularly framed in the belief, that God will put everything right when we get to heaven. The big reckoning, we are convinced, will sort things out and everyone will be rewarded, or dealt with as they deserve, when the time comes. An attractive notion, perhaps, but it is one that smacks a little of the all too human and even childish idea that life, or, at the very least, everlasting life, has to be premised upon fairness. Not that there is anything wrong with fairness but it is a rather simple concept with which to approach something as intractably complicated as the problem of suffering. C. S. Lewis, anyway, undermines this view with a rather unnerving observation. He writes:

> "If God's goodness is inconsistent with hurting us then either God is not good or there is no God......If it is consistent with hurting us, then He may hurt us after death as unendurably as before it."[9]

It is hard to resist this logic and this, in itself, is a point worth noting. Logic does not seem to get us very far when it comes to making sense of suffering because there is no making sense of suffering. In saying this, I am not trying to take refuge in some age-old recourse to mystery. That option is as insensitive as any of the ideas just considered. No, I am only saying that, as unpalatable as it may be to admit it, we have over the centuries, failed to come up with a satisfactory response to human suffering. There is, however, more to be said on the issue, but before any attempt to do that, let us look as the question of human evil.

Human Evil and the Absence of Good

There is in Tibetan Buddhism a fearsome female figure called Palden Lhamo.[10] She rides into battle astride her war-horse and cuts a grotesque, macabre and utterly terrifying figure. Her mission is to protect those who follow the Buddhist path from all manner of evil. She is a Dharma-Protector. She is also a liberator because those who do evil are seen as being trapped in delusion and moral under-development. Evil itself, therefore, derives from misinformation, stunted growth and a warped perspective on life. So, the fearsome Palden Lhamo thunders forth to free bandits, outlaws, gangsters and the rest of us from shackles fashioned by our own misguided ways.

Now, interestingly, there is in traditional Christianity something of an echo to this explanation of evil as delusion and under-development. It finds expression in the assertion that evil is the absence of good - a teaching termed the *privatio boni*. No less a person than Augustine puts the case in this way:

> "God is not the author of evil. For how can He who is the cause of the being of all things be at the same time the cause of their not being – that is of the falling off from essence and tending to nonexistence? For this is what reason plainly declares to be the definition of evil." [11]

Here, Augustine sees evil as a departure from essence and a tendency towards nonexistence. It is a corruption of an original goodness of being. In the bible, the early chapters of Genesis teach us that God's creation, human beings included, is good and that evil results when there is separation from God. Thomas Aquinas writes:

"Evil cannot exist but in good; sheer evil is impossible."[12]

Yet, even given that Aquinas is speaking in ultimate terms, the statement that sheer evil is impossible leaves us gasping. The history of the last hundred years has been, by and large, a catalogue of sheer evil. How can we explain, for example, the horrors of the Nazi concentration camps, the massacres in Cambodia and Rwanda, the mindless killing that bloodied the streets of Beirut, Belfast and Derry and the hate that guided two passenger planes into the twin towers in New York except in terms of sheer evil? And, in this context, is it enough to say that that evil is merely the absence of good? I really do not think so.

Ann Belford Ulanov also points out that Carl Jung makes a similar and related point in maintaining that the *privatio boni*, for him, means that evil does not have quite the same kind of force as does good. She rejects Jung's idea with some eloquence:

"...I find the privatio boni a sophisticated idea, both psychologically and theologically. Evil does exist as an existential force, real, effective, but it does not exist as does good. It exists as making absence where there is presence; as a howling mood of resentment, unbudging in the face of anyone's attempt to reach us; as a refusal to recognize the presence of this person in front of us as a person. It demotes; subtracts; abstracts; chooses void over substance, goneness over being here, now facing the task." [13]

Certainly, Ulanov's argument convinces but on a personal, individual, almost domestic scale. Now, undoubtedly, this is the level at which human evil begins but, having said that and leaving aside momentarily, philosophy, psychology and theology, the terrifying autonomy, pervasiveness and relentlessness of evil on the truly grand scale is hardly explained for us with any degree of emotional satisfaction as the absence of good.

Again, Carl Jung, in his extraordinary book, *"An Answer to Job"*, a very individual and subjective treatment of evil [14], says that the *privatio boni* is a "nonsensical doctrine" [15] because it starts with the assumption that God is good. As an explanation of evil in itself, therefore, he sees it as lacking and his observation does bring the whole question of ultimate responsibility for evil back again to a question of God. Pain and evil may be awful realities for the atheist but they are not problems for him or her, theologically or even philosophically. They are only problems for the believer in God, [16] and in a good God at that, says Conn quoting C. S. Lewis.

Learning from Job

In the Book of Job[17], in the Old Testament, Job is a truly virtuous man and he is also a believer in a good God, or at least, he starts out as a believer in a good God. Life, which had been very good to Job, takes a different turn and everything changes for him after God accepts a challenge from Satan to test Job's devotion by taking away his wealth and his wonderful family. So, Job's world falls dramatically apart and he is left a broken man whose misery is only compounded by the pious attempts his friends make to comfort him. Job eventually rounds on them, rebutting their suggestions that somehow he himself must ultimately be to blame for his sorry plight because God could not be to blame. God, they assert would not allow such misfortune to befall a totally innocent man. Job, however, refuses to believe that he has perpetrated any wrong and, eventually, directly challenges God on the issue. God responds but not by addressing the issue of Job's guilt or innocence. Instead, He demands of poor Job what he could possibly know about what was involved in holding all of creation in being. Job, suitably awestruck and realizing he is out of his depth, humbly and unequivocally retracts. The story then has a happy ending as God reprimands Job's friends and, in response to Job's prayers on behalf of his friends, restores with interest, as it were, Job's fortunes.

Kushner offers a brilliant summary of the flow of argument in the Book of Job when he reduces its complex rhetoric around Job's sufferings to the futile attempt to hold in balance three irreconcilable stances. They are, first of all, that God is all-powerful, secondly, that God is good, just and fair and thirdly, that Job is a good person. These three stances, Kushner maintains, simply cannot be held all at once. Only two of the three can, logically, be held at any one time. So, if Job's less than comforting friends want to insist that God is indeed both an all-powerful God and also a good God, they have no alternative but to seriously doubt that Job is, in fact, a good person. Similarly, if Job wants to maintain his innocence and is convinced only of God's power, then, he has to consider letting go of his belief that God is good, just and fair. That means that the third and final option available is to hold on to the belief that God is good, just and fair, to acknowledge Job as a good person but to let go of the insistence that God is all-powerful.

So, these options are inclusive of the very quandary that that we have been struggling with here as we have tried to keep in balance, God's goodness and God's power. Kushner is saying that we really have to let one of these insistences go, especially in the face of the fact that all of the common and traditional explanations of evil and suffering have, as we have seen, proved inadequate. Furthermore, he sees the writer of the Book of Job as taking the last option and letting go of an unqualified insistence that God is all-powerful. Therefore, he interprets chapter 40 of the Book of Job as God saying to Job that containment of evil is not as easy as Job might imagine.[18] The author of the book has God, in effect, engage Job in a thought experiment specifically on the question of human evil:

> "Have you an arm like God,
> and can you thunder with a voice like his?
> Deck yourself with majesty and dignity;
> clothe yourself with glory and splendour,
> Pour out the overflowings of your anger;
> and look on all who are proud and abase them.
> Look on all who are proud and bring them low;
> tread down the wicked where they stand.
> Hide them all in the dust together;
> bind their faces in the world below.
> Then I will also acknowledge to you
> that your own right hand can give you victory."
> (Job: 40.9-14)

If we think of it, there is a particular difficulty with the containment of human evil, because of the fact that God has given us freedom to choose between good or evil and will not interfere with that freedom. This is not just a matter of God being able to displace responsibility for human evil onto the human conscience, it is an irreversible consequence of God's creation of humanity accepted by God as a limitation of his power. Nor is it the only such limitation. God also invites us into a relationship of love with Him and we can reject Him. We can deny the otherwise all-powerful God our affection and even God cannot heal us if, deep down, we do not really want to be healed.[19]

These limitations relate to the question of human evil, but, likewise, God is limited in relation to the pain and suffering that occurs within nature. He will not, for example, alter the laws of nature, even should we ask. [20] In the epilogue to the Book of Job, God turns to one of the three friends and says that He, burns with anger against the three, "for you have not spoken of me what is right as my servant Job has." (Job: 42.7) What does God mean?

The three friends after all had tried to defend God while Job had accused Him and challenged Him. What I think is being suggested is that we actually meet and engage with God when we engage meaningfully with the reality of our lives, however painful that reality may be. When we deny that reality, we miss the opportunity to engage with God. The three friends may have wanted to engage with a God who was good, fair, just and all-powerful but they could only do so by denying the reality of the experience of the man who was sitting in front of them clothed in suffering. To engage compassionately with the innocent Job they had to let go of a God who was all-powerful and this they were not prepared to do.

Living with Randomness and the Vulnerability of God

Some of us are more at home, I think, with an all-powerful God. It guarantees us at least a conceptual certainty in our world and someone other than ourselves and other people to blame. Admitting that God may not be all-powerful, on the other hand, brings us back to the uncomfortable consideration of a world characterized by randomness within nature and within human interaction and that we do not want. We do not want a world in which there is no particular reason why a member of my family should unexpectedly contract terminal cancer or one of my closest friends should meet one night, with fatal consequences, a drunken driver on the way home. We do not want a world in which the very young and radiant sometimes die and the old fade away, their once sharp minds dulled by dementia, their spirit, generosity and achievement already almost a distant memory.

Yet, that is the world that we have and that is the world in which the writer of Job reminds us that we meet God. So, when we face suffering and evil, we constantly find ourselves asking with the Hebrews in the desert if God is among us or not. How each one of us answers that question is crucially important. We can answer it in a negative or a positive manner. If we answer in the negative and do not look for God in our pain and suffering, we further torment ourselves, continue to seek a kind of order that is not there in creation and we push away from a vulnerable God. If we answer positively and continue to search for God in our pain and suffering, we acknowledge the randomness that seems to define our universe and open our arms to embrace the vulnerability of Christ on the cross.

It is an amazing thing about Christianity that, for the most part, we no longer seem to be able to see that ubiquitous and most dramatic of all Christian symbols, the crucifix. How is it that we can sit in a room struggling with the devastation of an appalling tragedy or a violent bereavement and our eyes do not wander to the crucifix on the wall opposite? Part of the answer, I think, is the way we have understood the crucifixion. We have seen it as atonement to the Father for the evils of humanity. It has been seen as a price paid, a sacrifice on our behalf to buy back our innocence. We have reverenced, rather than identified with, the suffering figure portrayed. The depiction of God as a Father who demands the bloody death of His own Son has not, for some strange reason, seemed to disturb us unduly.

What we have not often seen and what might have raised our eyes to the wall opposite, is the crucifixion as an at-one-ment, a further sharing by Christ in the pain and suffering of humanity. This was an inevitable consequence of His refusal to back down from His vision of God as a loving Father, wishing only to set us free to be truly and spectacularly human. It was love not duty that led Jesus to the cross and His suffering there is also our suffering. Here, once again, we have to return to the incarnation for its meaning to be made clear. The promises of the Old Testament and God's offer of relationship reach breathtaking eloquence and poignancy and are given flesh in the person of a suffering Jesus Christ. The cross is the sign of Jesus' love for the Father and for humanity past, present and future. The resurrection is the Father's return of that love because the Father, as Jesus knew, is love.

Passion, death and resurrection are one moment, one all-embracing reality. Jesus' outstretched arms enfold all of creation. He is a cosmic Christ and in him, death and evil, pain and suffering are overcome on the cross, if not explained. Even so, we are left awestruck and speechless, just as Job was.

Mute we may be, but, Calvary is the, "meaning, the one event of all history [21]" and we are drawn into that event in our baptism and in our celebration of the eucharist. Our lives as Christians are a participation in Calvary and a further unfolding of its meaning. As Merton puts it: "... my suffering is not my own. It is the Passion of Christ." [22] We believe that our suffering is a sharing in Christ's suffering and that it is overcome, along with all evil, both archetypal and personal, in his resurrection. In this context, then, it is not just evil on the grand scale that is in question. It is also the thousands and the hundreds of thousands of individual and sometimes private acts of evil that produce evil on the grand scale. M. Scott Peck that reminds us of the importance of our personal struggle against the evil each one of us perpetrates:

"For the moment, then, God tormented, waits upon us through one holocaust after another. And it may seem to us that we are doomed by this strange God who reigns in weakness. But there is a dénouement to Christian doctrine: God in his weakness will win the battle against evil. In fact, the battle is already won. The resurrection symbolizes not only that Christ overcame the evil of his day two millennia ago but that he overcame it for all time. Christ impotently nailed upon the cross is God's ultimate weapon. Through it the defeat of evil is utterly assured. It is vitally necessary that we struggle against evil with all the power at our command. But the crucial victory occurred almost two thousand years ago. Necessary and even dangerous and devastating though our own personal battles may be, unknown to us they are but mopping-up operations against a retreating enemy who has long since lost the war."[23]

Ann Ulanov adds her voice:

"God has come and entered our long day's dying, our being dust and to dust we return; God has taken up into God's self the suffering that human life entails, which we magnify by inflicting it upon each other. God has taken responsibility for creating us free creatures who can refuse God, taking the consequences onto the cross, where the Holy One suffers as if guilty. The logic of evil stops here."[24]

Evil is reduced to silence by the cross. It has no answer to love. Love confounds its logic. Death now owns, "a wasted kingdom."[25] In the home, in the workplace, in the international forum only love can break the self-perpetuating cycles of accusation, counter-accusation, bitterness and recrimination. Only love can make the leap to reconciliation and healing. The great symbol of such love is the cross. It is the very same love which holds us in being and which is continually on offer to us.

It is extraordinary that when so much comes to us by way of life, love, goodness and gift, we take it for granted and, instead, allow ourselves to be fascinated, paralysed and bound by the mystery of suffering and evil. This can sometimes even happen on a very personal level when, tragedy aside, there is a preoccupation in life with the wrongs that inevitably have been done to us and the inexplicable misfortune that has occasionally befallen us.

Lazarus entered the tomb, bound by death and mourned by his family and friends. Responding to the call of Jesus, he leaves behind entombment and casts off his bonds to enjoy again the gift of life. Within a few hours, Jesus himself, is designated for death by the Jewish authorities (cf Jn:11.53). But, the theme of new life is taken up again with the Evangelist placing Jesus in the house of the resurrected Lazarus. There Mary anoints the feet of Jesus (cf

Jn:12.3ff). Mary fully understands that life and resurrection are to be found in Jesus, so she now boldly anoints Jesus, in a way which really only befits those who have already died. Evil, suffering and death are already overcome. To be healthy and honest, we will always have much grieving to do and in our struggle with evil we must, in Christ, be unremitting, but it is time to let go of any personal fascination or disproportionate, philosophical preoccupation with solving the question of evil. Those bonds we must cast off, if we are to live life to the full.

Summary

The gift of free-will is the source of human evil and, therefore, much suffering. Jesus rejected the notion that such suffering or any natural disaster was a punishment from God. Instead, Jesus, the great healer, always gave hope that suffering and evil could be overcome.

Inadequate explanations of suffering include the notions: that it is part of some grand, divine tapestry; that it is God testing us; that God sends it to ennoble us; that it is okay as God will sort it all out in heaven. As for explaining evil, it is not enough to say that on the personal or the grand scale, it is just the absence of good. So, evil remains a problem for those who believe in God.

Reflecting on the Book of Job, Harold S. Kushner says we cannot hold in balance these three statements: God is good; God is all-powerful; Job is a good and blameless person. One, at least, must be incorrect. Job's comforters doubt Job, of course, and Job himself is left to juggle God's goodness and his power. Poor Job is reduced to silence. At the end of the Book of Job, God rounds on the three friends who loudly sang His praises but in doing so denied Job's suffering was undeserved. The lesson seems to be that we must engage with both our idea of God and with the reality of human suffering. So, as we do this, which are we more comfortable with , a good God who is not all-powerful, or, a powerful God who is not always good? Accepting the latter seems outrageous; accepting the former means accepting a vulnerable God and the randomness of suffering in life and this we are reluctant to do.

Do we see Jesus' suffering on the cross as an *atonement for* humanity or is it an *at-one-ment with* humanity? What led Jesus to the cross, love or duty? Evil and suffering may reduce us to silence, but, as Christians we believe that all evil and all human suffering are overcome in Jesus' death and resurrection?

Quotation for Discussion

"The promises of the Old Testament and God's offer of relationship reach breathtaking eloquence and poignancy and are given flesh in the person of a suffering Jesus Christ. The cross is the sign of Jesus' love for the Father and for humanity past, present and future. The resurrection is the Father's return of that love because the Father, as Jesus knew, is love. Passion, death and resurrection are one moment, one all-embracing reality. Jesus' outstretched arms enfold all of creation. He is a cosmic Christ and in him, death and evil, pain and suffering are overcome on the cross, if not explained. Even so, we are left awestruck and speechless, just as Job was."

Questions for Discussion

- What has been my response when I have been faced with suffering or with evil and how adequate do I think that response has been?
- How do I understand Calvary and the cross and can I really see them as a triumph of love over evil and suffering in which I am invited to participate?

1. "C. S. Lewis and Human Suffering", Marie A. Conn, Hidden Spring Books, (2008) p42.
2. "When Bad Things Happen to Good People", Harold S. Kushner, Pan Books, (2002) p17.
3. Ibid p25.
4. Ibid cf. p24.
5. Ibid p24.
6. Ibid p18.
7. "A Grief Observed" C. S. Lewis, Faber and Faber (1966) p38.
8. Quoted from "The Problem of Pain" by Marie A. Conn, Op. cit. cf p45
9. Lewis, Op. cit p25.
10. "The Transcendent Fury of Palden Lhamo" Miranda Shaw, "Parabola" Volume 24 Number 4 November 1999 p40ff.
11. "On the Morals of the Manichaeans" Augustine, quoted in "Fruits of Knowledge" Rama P Coomaraswamy, "Parabola" Volume 24 Number 4 November 1999 p76ff.
12. "ARCS", "Parabola" Volume 24 Number 4 November 1999 p70ff
13. "The Living God and Our Living Psyche" by Ann Belford Ulanov and Alvin Dueck, Eerdmans Publishing (2008) p64.
14. "An Answer to Job" by Carl Gustav Jung, Routledge Classics (2002) cf p2.
15. Ibid p24 note 13.
16. Conn, Op. cit, cf reference to C. S. Lewis pXI
17. Kushner op. cit. cf p33ff.
18. Ibid p46ff.
19. "The People of the Lie" by M. Scott Peck, Arrow Books (1998), cf p225.
20. Kushner op. cit. cf p136.
21. "St. John", by John Marsh, Penguin (1976), p71.
22. "No Man is an Island" by Thomas Merton, Shambhala (2005) p86.
23. M. Scott Peck, op. cit. p235.
24. Ann Ulanov, op. cit. p62.
25. "Thomas Merton: A Book of Hours" edited by Kathleen Deignan, Sorin Books (2007) p165, excerpted from the Merton's collected poems.

5. Reframing the Sacredness of Scripture

How do I understand the sacredness of the scriptures? What assumptions do I make when I pick up the bible? Is my familiarity with scripture flawed? How explain apparent contradictions in biblical books? How many languages and literary genres are represented? How did our modern bible evolve?

Let me make a confession – well, a confession of sorts! I am a person who picks up the daily newspaper and turns first to the sports pages. There are, of course, more serious things than sport happening around the world but perhaps I reason that a little play before all that seriousness may be no bad thing. In any event, I do turn first to the sports pages and read the headlines and a paragraph here and there. I also cast an eye towards the sports in brief section which usually runs down the side of the page as these snippets can be a fund of entertaining if, more or less, useless information.

Every now and again, however, these distilled reports drive me to distraction because you read about a person or a team doing well and you are told how tense and finely balanced the action was and how the finale unfolded spectacularly. What you are not inadvertently sometimes told, though, is what sport is actually being described. Is it basketball, or some kind of football, or hurling, or field hockey, or ice hockey, or something else? So, you retrace your steps and read the paragraph again – this time more carefully – and try to find some hint or reference that will solve the mystery. Needless to say, this is not what we expect of any newspaper article. We expect all the information to be laid out clearly for us, without the need to fill in any gaps in the story and we are, or at least I am, often hugely frustrated when that, unintentionally, is not the case.

Now, it is my belief that too often we bring the same kind of expectation to the reading of the bible and that is not helpful. In fact, the attitude that we bring to the reading of the bible can have further levels of complication. I cannot imagine that anyone after

Unbinding Christian Faith: Free to Be   Denis Gleeson

reading Jonathan Swift's "Gulliver's Travels" would set out to discover Lilliput, because we as readers understand that the novel is a satire set in imaginary lands. Likewise, readers of Tolkien's fantasy "The Lord of the Rings" may decide to visit New Zealand to see the spectacular scenery used in the filming of the trilogy but they do not expect to find themselves in Middle Earth. The explanation is that when we open a book containing a poem, a novel, a play, a myth, a fairy-tale or a fantasy, we make allowance for the type of literature we have to hand. This ability though, for some strange reason, seems to desert us when we pick up the scriptures. We actually expect, it seems, to be able to read them as if we were reading a newspaper. Why is this, I wonder?

The problem in part may be that we have not been taught how to read the scriptures. It may also be that because we may consider the scriptures to be inspired and to be God's sacred revelation, we may really see them as beyond human influence and to be deserving of reverence just as we find them. This, however, is to do the scriptures an injustice and to deprive ourselves of their richness. It is, once again, to restrict ourselves and to bind ourselves with bonds that squeeze the life out of our Christianity and prevent us from breathing freely. Jesus calls us to throw off such bonds and to savour the scriptures because they are, after all, foundational to our faith.

A Flawed Familiarity

Sometimes we assume a familiarity with the scriptures that we do not really have. With this assumption can come cursory re-readings of texts we have read many times before, followed by careless consideration of those same texts. We still, for example, routinely refer to Eve plucking an apple in the Garden of Eden whereas modern translations tend to translate the original Hebrew term with the word "fruit". Early translations of the bible into English account for the apple becoming established in our consciousness and contemporary texts have failed to remove that impression. [1] Writers, artists and illustrators still present us with an apple. Similarly, in our minds the talking serpent in the garden story is usually identified with Satan, yet, nowhere in the bible story itself is such an association made. That particular link was made later by readers of this very ancient story. [2]

Our reading of the New Testament can suffer from the same type of assumption. Believe it or not, I once had to survive a homily on the fourth wise man. Unsurprisingly, he was even named without any fear of contradiction. Now, the vast majority of us are happy enough to concede that there were actually only three wise men, but close reading of Matthew's narrative reveals that no number at all is given. The number three comes from the fact that the newborn was said to have received three gifts namely, gold, frankincense and myrrh (cf Mt: 2.11), hence, our assumption.

Let me add one further example from the Acts of the Apostles. If asked to recount the story of Paul's conversion (cf Acts: 9), most of us might say that Saul, as he was then known, was on his way to persecute Christians in Damascus when he was struck down from his horse by a great light from heaven. The text of the story, however, makes no mention of a horse. That detail probably arises from several renowned paintings of that momentous incident including works by no less than Michelangelo, Rubens and Caravaggio. Once again, we can see that cultural influences can cloud our take on matters religious, and in this instance, scriptural.

Now, in a way, it makes little difference whether Saul was struck down from a horse or was struck down while walking. The point I am making is that we can be careless in our approach to the scriptures and we can also make assumptions. Some of these assumptions may indeed be on matters that are trivial but others may be on matters that are key to the meaning of scripture itself. Crucially, for example, we can assume we are reading one type of literature when we are, in fact, reading a completely different type of literature, or, we can take literally what was meant to be figurative, or, we can take at face value what was deliberately exaggerated for effect. Furthermore, if we do hold the scriptures to be sacred, then, they certainly deserve an open mind, our fullest attention and some guidance as to how best to approach what are ancient, culturally obscure and very complicated texts.

Now, even a reasonably careful reading of some of the most famous passages of scripture throws up obvious examples of what appear to us to be anomalies and apparent contradictions. In the first three chapters of Genesis, for example, there are two accounts of creation and two accounts of how humanity came into existence. There is no attempt to reconcile them, they are simply placed end to end and readers are left to their own reflection. Apparent contradiction was not a problem for the minds that compiled Genesis, but seems to be a problem for some contemporary minds and a cue for fundamentalist wriggling for others.

Certainly, the editor of these three chapters, as we have them, never envisaged that millennia later some readers might attempt a factual reconciliation. His concern - given the times, it was presumably a man – was to communicate essential truths held about God and about creation. These were that God created all that exists; that God's creation was good; that humankind's masculine and feminine complementarity somehow reflects the Godhead; that the Sabbath is to be observed and that the world as we experience it, and the world as God wants it to be, are two different realities.

Similarly, in chapter fourteen of the Book of Exodus, we read about the Hebrews' escape from the Egyptians by crossing the Sea of Reeds. Again, a careful reading of the text makes it clear that there are actually two accounts of this key event being offered, though they are interwoven into one story. One strand of the story appears entirely feasible. The marshy land is sufficiently dried up overnight for Moses to lead the people on foot to safety. As the Egyptian soldiers with their heavy armour, horses and chariots get bogged down in pursuit, the escape is made good. So, the timing of the crossing is perfect and the escape dramatic, though not spectacular. The alternative strand, however, is pure Hollywood. There are towering walls of water either side of the Hebrews as they flee in terror. The Egyptians are fatally stubborn in their refusal to call off the chase and catastrophe results. They are wiped out by the returning sea. There are no survivors. The contrast in these two accounts could not be starker but this was not a problem for the compiler. They could be presented together [3] partly because of the reverence in which the community held these two accounts which had come down to them through generations and partly because it was the action of God that mattered rather than the detail of the action.

To illustrate further what reasonably careful reading of scripture throws up let us look to the Gospels and a story beloved by all Christians, the story of the nativity. I say "story", but the story we recount, dramatise and artistically present as the Christmas story is actually a combination of two very different renderings, one in the Gospel of Matthew and the other in the Gospel of Luke. Matthew offers us drama, with Joseph, Mary's husband, troubled by dark dreams. We have strange travellers coming from the East, a scheming and bloodthirsty King Herod and, amazingly, a life-saving escape by Joseph, Mary and the newborn child into, of all places, Egypt!

Luke offers us the alternative. His is a story of domestic bliss beginning with Mary visiting her cousin Elizabeth who is expecting a child. There follows lyrical and timeless prayers from Mary and from Elizabeth's husband, Zechariah. Then, when the time comes for Mary herself to give birth, angels appear and nearby shepherds come to visit and to share in the joy of the happy event. The two accounts could hardly be more different but in our psyche we have fused them into one Christmas story. It is a story that remains undiluted and untroubled even when we read one or other original account in Church.

As I have already mentioned, we seem to have a facility for filling in the gaps and mentally airbrushing a narrative if it jars with the story we were brought up with. The collateral damage, of course, is that we miss the direct and audacious challenge the two infancy narratives represented to the dominant and extremely oppressive religious and political system of the time. This surrounded the Roman cult of a divine Emperor. [4] The gospel writers, though, are making the point that Jesus, not the Roman emperor, is the "Son of God" (cf Lk: 1.35).

If it is true, then, that our familiarity with scripture can, at times, be flawed, where can we look for guidance and what have we learned about the bible that will help us to read it with more understanding?

What we have learned about the Bible

Even though the bible sits on our shelves as a book, the first thing to be said about it is that it is not a book in any usual meaning of that word. It is rather a library, [5] a collection of books of all different sorts. It is a compendium. More correctly, it is a collection of ancient manuscripts all of which date back to times long before books, as we know them today, ever came into existence. These manuscripts arose out of an oral tradition that itself was an expression of the religious experience of a community over countless generations. The experience was not that of an individual. Richard F. Smith writes:

> "It is now an established certainty that at least a great many books of the bible were the products of a long period of gestation, involving at times even centuries of previous written and oral traditions." [6]

In fact, not often have any of these manuscripts even come down to us as one complete document. Consider the famous and incomparable Dead Sea Scrolls [7] that were found in caves near

Qumran between 1947 and 1956. Apart from the Book of Esther, they include at least a fragment of every book of the Hebrew Bible. The Scrolls do include some almost complete manuscripts but only one complete copy of any book of the bible. That is the Book of Isaiah. The Dead Sea Scrolls, nevertheless, are the most spectacular ever find of bible manuscripts, or, more correctly, bible fragments.

So, most of the books we include in our bible have been pieced together from fragments of manuscripts and owe their integrity to comparison with manuscripts that are more complete and were pieced together from other fragments. Originally, and prior to fragmentation due to the ravages of time and climate, these manuscripts were often the work of compilers or editors who brought together different sources and materials to produce one text, fashioned for a specific reason. They chose whatever literary genre suited their purpose. This means that all kinds of literature are represented in our bible including some types of writing, such as apocalyptic literature, that are unknown in the literature of today. It follows that to make sense of any particular book of the bible, we must, at the very least, be aware of the type of writing with which we are dealing. As well as that, we should have some understanding of the conventions surrounding that style of writing and we must have an appreciation of the social, cultural and political circumstances of the time.

Turning, then, to the question of language, it is important to remember that there is no one original language for the bible. The people of the Exodus spoke and wrote in Hebrew. However, about 250 years before the birth of Jesus, a famous translation into Greek was made of the first five biblical books for the Egyptian ruler, Ptolemy II. This translation became known as the Septuagint (LXX) because legend had it that it took seventy-two scholars seventy-two days to complete the task. [8] Then, though the Jewish people at the time of Jesus spoke Aramaic, the Christian scriptures were written not in Aramaic but in a common version of Greek. So, the words of Jesus, in so far as we can identify them, are only available to us in translation.

Finally, when the Hebrew and the Christian scriptures were eventually brought together in one volume by St. Jerome, about 360 years after the time of Jesus, the presenting language was Latin. St. Jerome's bible was referred to as the Vulgate. This means that arriving at the exact meaning of words as they were written, and even more so as they may have been spoken, is an extremely difficult challenge at times. The bible scholar today, therefore, has to be familiar with all of these languages and even with variations of them.

Moreover, there was disagreement in ancient times as to what writings were to be recognized as properly belonging to the Hebrew bible, or the Old Testament, as it was called in the Christian bible, and what scriptures were to be recognized as properly belonging to the Christian scriptures, or the New Testament. In due time, a level of agreement was reached within Christianity and also within Judaism as to what books were to be held as belonging to their respective bibles, but, around some books, disagreement remains unresolved to the present day. [9]

Our bible, therefore, is an ancient, complex, brilliant and unique "book", if we wish to use that term. In itself it is challenge enough but we have further complicated matters for ourselves because sadly, and scandalously, the bible was a battleground within Christianity for more than four hundred years and up until quite recently. The conflict was unedifying. But, there were advances and where our understanding of the bible was concerned, Protestant scholarship led the way and eventually Catholic scholarship also weighed in with its contribution. Angles of approach continued to differ but, happily, we find ourselves in a very different place today with regard to our overall attitudes towards the scriptures.

The modern bible journey really began with scholars like Richard Simon in the seventeenth century. The standard position at the time was that the first five books of the bible, called the Pentateuch, had actually been written by Moses himself and handed down by him to the people of Israel. Simon, however,

"...drew attention to the doublets, discrepancies in content, and differences of style observable in the Pentateuch – discoveries not easy to reconcile with the attribution of the entire text to Moses as a single author." [10]

Obvious as these things were, and still are, attention had not often been drawn to them possibly because printed bibles were still not a commonplace but, more importantly, because people only began to approach the bible with a literal mindset as late as the nineteenth century. Up to that, the first chapter of Genesis, for instance, was never taken as factual and the general approach to the reading of the scriptures was a highly allegorical one. [11] Symbolic, creative and poetic interpretations of the scriptures had held sway since the emergence of the New Testament which is itself full of symbolic re-interpretation of the Old Testament in the light of Christian belief in the resurrected Jesus. He is, for example, the new Adam (cf Rom: 5.12ff) and the new High Priest (cf Heb: 6.19ff). So, within Christianity, spiritual and allegorical reading of the sacred scriptures was the norm for those who had access to them.

By the nineteenth century, however, the "documentary hypothesis" had emerged. It held that there were four major influences across the five books of the Pentateuch and that these influences, sources, narratives or documents, had been interwoven to give us the texts we have today. The documents were distinguished from one another by their written styles and themes and the names they used for God. The four authors, or groups of editors, or scholarly schools, came to be known as the Yahwist, Elohist, Deuteronomist and Priestly, or J, E, D and P sources respectively. Though the four-document theory[12] was later seen by

Julius Wellhausen (1844-1918), its chief architect, as a bit too simplistic, literary analysis and criticism of biblical texts had begun. The methods employed were classically scientific and the general approach was referred to as the historical-critical method. For our understanding of the ancient and sacred texts today, this method is now seen as an "indispensable" [13] aid.

Just as the historical-critical method transformed our reading of a book like Genesis in the Old Testament, so too it transformed our reading of the Gospels in the New Testament. Scrutiny of the Pentateuch, had given rise to a four-document theory and scrutiny of the four Gospels gave rise to a two-document theory. According to this theory, the writers of Matthew and Luke made use of the Gospel of Mark along with a collection of the sayings of Jesus that we no longer have. This mysterious collection of sayings was given the name "Q" from the German word *quelle,* which means, "source".[14] As the Gospels of Matthew, Mark and Luke, therefore, could be compared, or seen together in parallel, they became known as the Synoptic Gospels. The Gospel of John was viewed as very different in style to these three.

In all of this, it is vital to emphasize again that, as with the Old Testament, the New Testament has its origins not just in documentary sources but also in the oral traditions that gave rise to those sources. Each of the Gospels emerged from a particular Christian community that had done its own reflection on the Good News of Jesus against the religious, social and political circumstances that challenged its very existence as a community. Each of the Gospels, consequently, is an interpretation of that Good News and reflects a purpose of that community. But, much of the background that there is to a particular Gospel or to any book of the bible can only be a matter of historical uncertainty and educated surmise. And strange as it may appear to us, it was also an accepted convention simply to attach the name of a revered figure from the past to the title of a manuscript to give the document added authority. [15] Consider the tentativeness with which John Marsh writes in the introduction to his commentary on the Gospel of St. John:

"When all is said and done, then, it is difficult if not impossible to achieve anything more than probability about the various 'critical' introductory problems about John. The present writer believes that it is not impossible to hold, and quite possible to be true, that during the last decade of the first century A.D. a certain John, possibly John Mark, with access to a large amount of material about Jesus, and knowing probably one and possibly more of our synoptic gospels, wrote down a new form of the story of Jesus for his own community, which was both cosmopolitan and affected by the presence of disciples of John the Baptist. He was … able to fuse together … the various sources, materials and ideas he gathered, and transmit them to his world, and ours, in a way which could speak equally well to Jew or Greek, pagan and follower of John the Baptist alike." [16]

Such scholarly and well-researched hesitancy serves as a reminder that we have far to go in our study of the bible and the establishment of fact surrounding even one of the very latest of the sacred writings is no easy matter. The bible and what the modern mind thinks of as history are not always compatible companions. In fact, at this stage, a word about history and how the bible itself considers history may be opportune.

Summary

Reading any piece of writing, we have to make allowance for the type of literature it represents. Is it poetry, prose, fact, fiction, or drama? We also have to allow for cultural assumptions we may have. There are many types of literature in the bible and some that we are not too familiar with today.

Reverence for oral tradition often results, in the bible, in two apparently contradictory accounts existing side by side. The story of the crossing of the Sea of Reeds during the exodus from Egypt and our popular version of the Christmas story are good examples of this. Centuries of oral tradition, the collection and editing of a variety of fragments and manuscripts, all combined to give us the compendium of writings we call the bible today.

Our bible represents offerings in many languages and considerable argument surrounded what was to be included and what was to be left out in both the Hebrew bible and the Christian bible. With the arrival of the printing press in the 15th century, the bible became available to those who could read. A spiritual and allegorical approach to reading the scriptures was the tradition within Christianity and it was only in the 19th century that some began to read them in a literal and factual way.

However, it was also in the 19th century that we began to understand how the bible evolved. The historical-critical method gave us, for example, insight into the origins of the Pentateuch in the Old Testament (the four document theory) and the gospels in the New Testament (the two document theory). In addition, the long held suspicion that the attribution of authorship to books in the bible was often simply an accepted and useful convention, was confirmed.

Quotation for Discussion

".....the first chapter of Genesis, for instance, was never taken as factual and the general approach to the reading of the scriptures was a highly allegorical one. [(11)] *Symbolic, creative and poetic interpretations of the scriptures had held sway since the emergence of the New Testament which is itself full of symbolic re-interpretation of the Old Testament in the light of Christian belief*

in the resurrected Jesus. He is, for example, the new Adam (cf Rom: 5.12ff) and the new High Priest (cf Heb: 6.19ff). So, within Christianity, spiritual and allegorical reading of the sacred scriptures was the norm for those who had access to them."

Questions for Discussion

- What approach to the bible were you raised with and does it differ from your approach now?
- What do you think are the advantages and disadvantages of an allegorical approach to a passage from the bible?

1. "Bible Babel" by Kristin Swenson. Harper Perennial (2011) cf p.190
2. Ibid. cf p.188
3. Cf "The Bible: The Biography" by Karen Armstrong, Atlantic Books (2007) p4 and "The Interpretation of the Bible in the Church" by The Pontifical Biblical Commission. Published by the United States Catholic Conference (1996) p26.
4. "Jesus" by Marcus J. Borg. HarperOne Publications (2006) cf p66.
5. Swenson, op. cit cf p.1.
6. "Inspiration and Inerrancy" by Richard F. Smith. Article in "The Jerome Biblical Commentary" (1968) Published by Geoffrey Chapman. (66: 42).
7. Cf Swenson op. cit. p57-58.
8. Ibid cf p.12ff and Karen Armstrong op. cit. p.48.
9. Note: There are seven books (Tobias [Tobit], Judith, 1-2 Maccabees, Wisdom, Ecclesiasticus, Baruch) and additions to two other books (Esther and Daniel) that are included in the Old Testament in Catholic Bibles but are not included in the Old Testament in most Protestant Bibles and in the original Hebrew Bible (Masoretic Text). Cf Swenson op. cit. Appendix 1 and "The Jerome Biblical Commentary" op cit. (67:21-47)
10. The Pontifical Biblical Commission. Op. cit. p5.
11. Karen Armstrong, op. cit. p3.
12. Ibid cf p194 on Julius Wellhausen (1844-1918); also "Modern Old Testament Criticism" by Alexa Suelzer, article in "The Jerome Biblical Commentary" op. cit (70:18-36) and Kristin Swenson op. cit p44ff.

13. Pontifical Biblical Commission op. cit. p5.
14. Cf Ibid p5; also Karen Armstrong, op. cit. p66. Kristin Swenson, op. cit. p51.
15. Cf Kristin Swenson, op. cit p49; also Karen Armstrong, op. cit. p21 and "How to Read the Bible" by Steven L. McKenzie, Oxford University Press (2005) cf. p154.
16. "Saint John" by John Marsh, Penguin Books (1979) p81.

6. Reading and Interpreting the Scriptures Today

Is the bible a book of history? How do we understand history in the bible? What was the intention of the writers of the scriptures? What types of literature does the bible contain? How can we read scripture today? Can we interpret scripture passages in any meaningful way?

The Bible and History

To celebrate the New Year's night that brought in the new millennium, I made the short journey from Dublin across the Sally Gap and into the Wicklow Mountains to the valley of the two lakes, Glendalough. I went there because amongst the ruins of the monastic city associated with St. Kevin stands a complete round tower that is about thirty metres high. The tower is thought to date back almost a thousand years, so it was for me a link with the last millennium. However, standing there in the dark at midnight, I found it difficult to really grasp the passing of the thousand years since the tower had been built and to make a connection with all the eyes that had marveled at it, all the hands that had touched its stones and all the joy that had been experienced and the villainy that had taken place in the valley where the tower cast its shadow.

Yet, the sweep of bible history [1] is such that its timescale is even harder to take in. A thousand years further back than the tower in Glendalough, Jesus stood on the Mount of Olives and wept over Jerusalem. A thousand years before Jesus, Jerusalem became King David's city. The oldest verse [2] in the bible, the Song of Miriam (cf Ex: 15.21) may have been composed orally about two hundred years before David and then some six hundred and fifty years before that, Abraham had herded his flocks on the plains of the Fertile Crescent.

That is a long span of time to try and digest and given that one generation today can often have difficulty even identifying

Unbinding Christian Faith: Free to Be   Denis Gleeson

with the generation that follows it, understanding events in the bible really stretches our powers of imagination and comprehension. Then, in recounting the past, the Hebrew people were not interested in history as we conceive of it. That is, they were not interested in dry factuality, exact dates, geographical precision and clear chronology. They were interested in the significance of what happened and defined that significance in terms of their relationship with God and the impact not on individuals but on them as the people of God. This makes the cross-referencing and verification of events with other independent, non-biblical sources problematic.

Take Joseph, [3] the favourite son of Jacob (Gn: 37.1-50.26). He is sold into slavery by his jealous brothers and ends up in Egypt. This is hugely important because, ultimately the scene is being set for the Exodus when Moses will be dispatched by God to lead the People of Israel to the Promised Land after their stay in Egypt had taken several turns for the worse and descended into misery and slavery. Yet, even though the bible says that Joseph had risen to be second only to the Pharaoh himself (Gn: 41.39-40), there is no definite reference to him in Egyptian accounts of the time. Even more startling is the fact that there is no reference in Egyptian records to the Exodus itself, when such a migration would have cut the population of the country by perhaps a third and was also said to have been accompanied by a military disaster of at least some significant scale. Furthermore, the subsequent invasion and conquest of Canaan, the Promised Land, is not supported by archaeological or cultural evidence.

Steven L. McKenzie tells us that history in the bible is, "more of a creative activity than modern readers typically assume".[4] So, the problem lies not with the bible itself but with the expectations that we bring to it. He adds:

"The Joseph-Exodus-Conquest complex makes perfect sense when one recognizes the nature and techniques of ancient history writing. The story of the flight of the

Hebrews from Egypt and their defeat of Canaanite cities may contain genuine historical elements. * But to focus on these is to miss the intent of the story, which is to account for how Israel gained possession of the land of Canaan. Its explanation is theological: God chose Israel, rescued the people and gave them the land of Canaan."[5]

The application for today is that God is present, his presence changes things, he chooses to be in relationship with us, he gifts us with freedom and promises to bring us home. That message is more important than detailed historical accuracy. The intent of the story is always the key. Kristin Swenson puts it this way:

"In the Bible's 'history', God's relationship to people is in, under, over, and behind it all, making it unapologetically unverifiable. That is bringing God into the equation necessarily takes the stories out of the realm of disinterested, historical reporting, making them instead faith-based interpretations of events." [6]

In this instance, what is true of the Old Testament is also true of the New Testament. The writer of St. John's Gospel tells us towards the end of the Gospel (cf Jn: 20.31) that his purpose in writing is that the reader will come to believe in Jesus and may have life. It is not his purpose merely to record history. It is his purpose to offer us, and through us all people, transformation in Christ. Compared to this purpose, writing accurate historical accounts is understandably inconsequential.

Distinguishing the biblical approach to the writing of history from the modern approach to the writing of history is only one of the issues faced by the unwary reader of the bible. A quite different issue arises when we try to read as history, something that was not written as history at all, a book that was intended as an entirely different genre. A case in point is the Book of Jonah.

Learning from Jonah

To allow oneself debate whether Jonah could possibly have lived for three days in the belly of some great fish is to allow the mind to hover between the silly and the surreal. It is to misunderstand the nature of the book and to try to read the book on a factual level. Yet, it was never the intention that the book was to be read in that fashion. Steven L. McKenzie observes:

> "A careful reading of the book of Jonah suggests that ... misunderstanding arises from attempts to make it something that it is not. The story is full of humor, exaggeration, irony and ridicule. These features indicate that the book was never intended to be read as history but was written as a kind of satire. No wonder it has been misunderstood." [7]

McKenzie explains that Jonah cuts a "ridiculous figure" [8] in the book with an irrational attempt to run away from God rather than be a good and obedient prophet and go, as commanded, to the city of Nineveh to warn the citizens about their behaviour. Now, Nineveh is a symbol of everything that Jonah loathes. It stands for all those who oppress the people of Israel and it typifies a religious practice and a cultural milieu that are, in his opinion, to be shunned and rejected. Consequently, Jonah has no intention of doing what a good and obedient prophet should do.

Of course, eventually and with the help of a great fish, God has his way and Jonah delivers God's message in one brief, surly and reluctant sentence:

> "Forty days more and Nineveh shall be overthrown!" (Jonah: 3.4).

Then, much to his annoyance, the people of Nineveh respond in an unambiguous and an unprecedented fashion, turning to God and humbly begging his mercy and forgiveness. Jonah is unimpressed and his annoyance turns to anger when God hears the prayers of the people of Nineveh and decides not to destroy them and their city. Jonah surpasses himself at this stage, openly admitting to God that he knew God was merciful, compassionate and loving and that this was the very reason he had tried to avoid fulfilling his mission. Such was Jonah's distaste for the people of Nineveh that he wanted to see them destroyed even if it meant trying to thwart God's mercy.

So, while Jonah fumes, God has a plant with broad leaves grow up to give Jonah some shade. Jonah is grateful but when a worm causes the plant to die, Jonah once again over-reacts and calls on God to let him die. He has had enough. However, God challenges Jonah on his reaction to the loss of one plant and asks simply if he, as God, should not be much more concerned at the possible loss of 120,000 people and their animals? This time, there is no answer from Jonah. McKenzie spells out the lesson of the book for us:

"Jonah would rather die than have God be merciful to other people. His attitude of prejudice and hatred toward non-Israelites is what the book satirizes. The ludicrous features of the story ridicule this attitude of bigotry. Ideally, the humor and exaggeration help the audience to perceive in Jonah the silliness of their own attitudes and the ridiculous lengths to which arrogance and prejudice can lead them."[9]

So, the Book of Jonah is a brilliantly executed satirical treatise on racial and ethnic prejudice. It is entirely relevant to our times. What a tragedy were the point to be missed today as we preoccupied ourselves with debates about whether or not a person could fit into the belly of a great fish!

Fitting it all together

In order to avoid misreading biblical books entirely, therefore, we need to have some sense of the kind of literature that is in question in any specific instance. Walter Brueggemann offers us "an introductory scheme for orientation" [10] in this regard and although he warns that his scheme will not be robust enough to survive rigorous scrutiny, it still lends a very useful overview.

At the centre of his scheme, Brueggemann places the primal narratives. By this he means the, "most simple, elemental, and nonnegotiable" [11] texts that lie at the heart of the Old Testament and the New Testament. Having their origins in the oral tradition, these are the oldest and most primitive statements of belief providing the foundation stones for both Judaism and Christianity respectively. In a way, the rest of scripture simply provides elaboration.

Brueggemann cites three passages identified by the great scholar Gerhard Von Rad as primal narratives. Two are in the Book of Deuteronomy (6:20-24 and 26:5-9) and one is in the Book of Joshua (24:1-13). He notes that other scholars are convinced that a passage in Exodus (15:1-18) provides a more likely example. All four of these passages, however, share the one assertion. It is that God delivered the people of Israel from slavery in Egypt and gave them, as their own, the land in which they now live. This is the heart of Judaism. Everything else in the Old Testament rests on this core memory and, in a way, serves as commentary upon it:

"When your children ask you in time to come, 'What is the meaning of the decrees and the statutes and the ordinances that the LORD our God has commanded you?' then you shall say to your children, 'We were Pharaoh's slaves in Egypt, but the LORD brought us out of Egypt with a mighty hand. The LORD displayed before our eyes great and awesome signs and wonders against Egypt, against Pharaoh and all his household.

He brought us out from there in order to bring us in, to give us the land he promised on oath to our ancestors. Then the LORD commanded us to observes all these statutes, to fear the LORD our God, for our lasting good, so as to keep us alive, as is now the case.' " (Deut. 6:20-24)

Similarly, in the New Testament, we find primal narratives that articulate the core Christian memory that lies at the heart of Christianity. This time, Brueggemann looks to the work of New Testament scholar C. H. Dodd and lists three passages taken from Paul's first letter to the Corinthians (1:23; 3:11 and 15:3-8). Paul writes:

"For I handed on to you as of first importance what I in turn had received; that Christ died for our sins in accordance with the scriptures, and that he was buried, and that he was raised on the third day in accordance with the scriptures, and that he appeared to Cephas, then to the twelve. Then he appeared to more than five hundred brothers and sisters at one time, most of whom are still alive, though some have died. Then he appeared to James, then to all the apostles. Last of all, as to someone untimely born, he appeared also to me." (1 Cor. 15:3-8)

Now, as can be seen from the above, these primal narratives do not come as stand alone texts. They come as part of much longer texts. Sometimes these longer texts are an actual expansion of the primal narrative. This is the case with the Book of Exodus (1-15). These chapters give us the "fulsome story" [12] of the deliverance from Egypt. Likewise, the memory of the years spent in the wilderness is also expanded upon in the Book of Exodus (16-18). But the expanded narrative can come elsewhere and we find another account of the wilderness sojourn in the Book of Numbers (10-24). As for elaboration on how the people of Israel took possession of the land promised to them, that comes in the Book of Joshua (1-12).

Turning to the New Testament, the primal narrative is expanded upon in the Gospels. There, the core memory is supplemented with memories of the ministry of Jesus and other material such as the infancy narratives, but all are seen, as Brueggemann puts it, "...through the prism of the dominant theme of crucifixion and resurrection..." [13]

Spinning our scriptural web ever further outwards, there are what Brueggemann calls derivative narratives. [14] Derivative narratives differ from expanded narratives in that they are not an expansion of the primal narrative. Rather, they are an extension of it to include the sacred memory of what happened after the core event as the community developed and an ongoing tradition began to emerge. In other words, derivative narratives deal with what happened after the days of Moses and Joshua and what happened after the ascension of Jesus.

In the Old Testament, the story of the emerging community and the transformation from refugee status in the desert to sovereign nationhood is captured in the Book of Judges, the first and second Book of Samuel, the first and second Book of Kings, the first and second Book of Chronicles and the Book of Ezra and the Book of Nehemiah. These are all derivative narratives. In the New Testament, we are dealing with the Acts of the Apostles. Here, once again, we need to remind ourselves of the nature of bible history. In both parts of our Christian bible, we are talking about reports that are more concerned to capture the significance of past events rather than to communicate accurate and informative, but ultimately lifeless, chronology. We are talking about, "...how the spirit of God ruled the history of this people, the bearers of a new presence in history." [15] The real stories, the stories really worth telling, are the stories of how the ongoing power of the primal event of the Exodus was later used by God to shape a nation and how the ongoing power of the primal event of Christ's death and resurrection was later used by God's spirit to shape a Church community.

The formation of a new nation and the formation of a new community of faith were both inevitably followed by institutionalization. Not surprisingly, then, some of the literature of institutionalization is included in the sacred scriptures. Understandably, and probably among the least read of the books of the bible, are these dry treatises on law, rules, regulations and procedures. They include the last fifteen chapters of Exodus, the Book of Leviticus and most of the Book of Numbers (1-10 and 25-36) in the Old Testament. In the New Testament the two letters of Paul to Timothy and the letter to Titus, are examples.

Finally, at the same remove from the primal narratives as the literature of institutionalization, Brueggemann[16] places other types of literature such as that concerned with theological reflection, or with instruction and vocation. The Book of Deuteronomy and the Letter to the Romans are viewed as providing "mature theological reflection." [17] And included as books of instruction and vocation in the Old Testament are all of the prophetic books and books that capture some of the wisdom, poetry and inspiration of their times. These are such books as the Book of Job, the Book of Psalms, the Book of Proverbs and the Book of Ecclesiastes and apart from the Letter to the Romans, mentioned above, all of the other letters in the New Testament could be included in this category.

Brueggemann looks upon this long list of works as providing a "catchall" category that is "essentially *instructional* in character"[18] and he would even see apocalyptic works such as the Book of Daniel and the Book of Revelation as included here. He writes:

"…. functionally, this literature is the same, for it seeks to assert the primal narrative in a way of power and authority for a special circumstance. Out of all these times and in these various ways (instructional, lyrical, visionary), these materials are presented with the passion of those who consider this faith the only option."[19]

It is their relationship to the original core experiences of the presence of God that give all of the books of scripture their focus and their authority and it is that relationship that makes them relevant for us on our journey.

Reading Scripture Today

Relevant the bible may be but from what has been said it will be clear that we need to be wary of approaching it without some level of preparation. Good news in this regard is that we have never had a wider range of quality resources and translations. The first thing to do, I would suggest, is to abandon the copy of the bible that you have treasured now for some years and to arm yourself with at least two modern editions and to be prepared to do a little research before doing so. Whatever translation you choose, it is worthwhile buying a study edition that will give you at the very least good footnotes and a brief introduction at the beginning of each book. This will probably be a bulky volume so you will also need a portable bible. You can stick with the same translation, or for the sake of variety and to enable comparison, choose a different one. You will be spoilt for choice.

Brueggemann's categories will help as you begin to read but he also warns us that to read the bible "intelligently" [20] we do need to have some basic background knowledge. We need, for example, some sense of the chronology involved and to be able to fit individual books of the bible into the sweep of Israel's history. Some editions of the scriptures helpfully include a timeline. Then you will need to have a grasp of the geography that you are reading about and where cultures, peoples and empires fit into that geography. Again some editions include excellent maps. Finally, you will need an understanding of the major events and crises undergone by Israel herself and an insight into her psyche and how this expressed itself in institutions, laws, religious ritual and daily life. To get all of this, you will probably have to purchase a small commentary.

When settling down to read, imagination, Brueggemann suggests, provides the final part of the jigsaw. [21] Imagination allows us to bring metaphor, allegory and symbolism into play and balances out any obsession we may have with the literal. We realize that scripture can be layered and open to multiple meanings. We see that the Exodus journey, or the journey of Jesus from Galilee to Jerusalem, is in every way a contemporary journey. We recognise ourselves in Moses, David, Peter and Pilate and everyday familiar things like bread, water and fire can take on deepening dimensions of meaning.

A traditional form of meditation in Ignatian spirituality, for example, involves choosing a passage, let us say, from the gospels and then using the imagination to enter into the passage. The person meditating puts themselves into the picture, as it were, sees the sights, smells the air, brushes up against those beside them and relates personally to Jesus as the action unfolds. The experience can be a powerful one, accessing the unconscious, engaging the emotions and inviting a holistic response.

An even older method of praying with scripture is lectio divina, or, holy reading. This has its origins within Judaism itself where the scripture scholar's interpretation of the text, "was wholly informed by prayer" and his interaction with scripture "transformed him and made him a force for good in the world."[22] Similar experience and practice emerged with the rise of monasticism in the early centuries of Christianity. The monk, having prayed the psalms in choir and listened to readings from scripture would take with him a thought, or a phrase or two, that would sustain him as he mulled over it throughout the day, or at least until the next hour of the divine office. Monks and nuns, therefore, lived with and breathed in the scriptures in the course of the day. For them, as for the scholars before them, the scriptures were an ongoing, living and vibrant communication with the Divine and as a communication with the Divine they held the promise of personal transformation.

Lectio divina today can be undertaken privately or with a group. A simple approach to it is to read slowly through the chosen passage twice. Then, pause and permit words or phrases from the passage to catch the attention. After a period of time read the passage again and let thoughts, questions or observations rise to the surface. Having reflected, or meditated in this way for a while, the person, or the group, now allows prayers of adoration, thanks or intercession to be voiced spontaneously. Finally, as these subside, there is a movement into simple silence and quiet, inviting the gift of contemplation. So, the four phases of lectio divina are the reading of the sacred scriptures (lectio), reflection on what has been read (meditatio), the articulation of vocal prayers (oratio) and the movement into silence (contemplatio). [23] This last phase of silence, it should be said, is a non-verbal, non-conceptual waiting on God and whether it is actually accompanied by the gift of contemplation itself is God's prerogative entirely.

Now, given that the God who communicates with us through the sacred scriptures is a God of love and compassion, it follows that our interpretation of what we read has to be guided by love and compassion. The story [24] goes that the great Jewish Rabbi Hillel was approached one day and challenged by a pagan to summarize the Books of the Law, the Torah, whilst standing on one leg. The man promised to convert to Judaism if Hillel was equal to his bizarre request. So, Hillel, standing on one leg is said to have replied:

"What is hateful to yourself, do not to your fellow man. That is the whole of the Torah and the remainder is but commentary. Go study it."

We are reminded, of course, of the so-called Golden Rule quoted in the Gospel and which is probably just a version of the saying attributed to Hillel: [25]

"In everything do to others, as you would have them do to you; for this is the law and the prophets." (Mt.7: 12)

We are also reminded of the incident in the Gospel of Luke when Jesus is challenged and another summary of the law is given:

"Just then a lawyer stood up to test Jesus. 'Teacher,' he said, ' what must I do to inherit eternal life?' He said to him, 'What is written in the law? What do you read there?' He answered, 'You shall love the LORD your God with all your heart, and with all your soul, and with all your strength, and with all your mind; and your neighbour as yourself.' And he said to him, 'You have given the right answer; do this and you will live.' " (Lk.10: 25-28)

The lawyer feels he has to save face and comes back at Jesus asking him to define who could be classified as a neighbour and Jesus' response is the great parable of compassion, the Parable of the Good Samaritan.

According to Hillel and Jesus, therefore, love and compassion lie at the heart of the law, and by extension, the bible. The Golden Rule provides not just a guideline for our general behaviour, because as a summary of the bible itself, it provides an outline of the spirit in which we should approach our interpretation of the sacred writings. Nothing we find there should lead us in the direction of ill treatment of another person and if it does we should revisit our interpretation along with our reading of the context of the passage concerned and our understanding of the limitations of the images of God that are being utilized. Karen Armstrong writes:

"Augustine … arrived at the same conclusion as Hillel and the rabbis. Charity was the central principle of

Torah and everything else was commentary. Whatever else Moses had written, his chief purpose was to preach the dual commandment: love of God and love of neighbour. This had also been the central message of Jesus."[26]

Both Armstrong and Stephen L. McKenzie note a quote from Augustine used by other authors:

"Whoever, therefore, thinks that he understands the divine Scriptures or any part of them so that it does not build the double love of God and of our neighbor does not understand it at all."[27]

Augustine, McKenzie remarks, was recalling Matthew's version (cf Mt.22: 34-40) of the incident between Jesus and the lawyer.

Using love and compassion as our point of reference may not salve our perplexity around all of the passages we come across in our reading of the sacred scriptures but it will keep us pointed in the right direction. As for the rest, it is important to remember that an open mind is not enough. Our reading has to be done with an open heart and an invitation to the Spirit to reach into our hearts through the written word and to transform our lives. Transformation is ultimately what we seek from the sacred scriptures not information. A transformational experience of God's presence in our own lives today is what we look for, not knowledge of God's presence in a distant past.

Summary

The books of the bible cover a vast swathe of time. What is thought to be the oldest verse, the Song of Miriam (cf. Ex: 15.21), was orally composed over three thousand years ago. Abraham, the most ancient historical character in the bible lived well over half a millennium again before that.

Hebrew writers were not concerned with historical accuracy but with the significance of events in the relationship between God and the people of Israel. Independent verification of biblical events is very often problematic. The bible, therefore, is more theology than history.

The intent of the Exodus story, for example, is to show us that God is present, God's presence changes things and God sets us free and brings us home. Similarly, the purpose of the gospels is to bring us to belief in Jesus as the Christ. Then, take the Book of Jonah. It was written as satire, so efforts to work out if Jonah could have survived in the belly of a great fish rather miss the point. The book is a masterpiece on racial and ethnic prejudice.

Bible scholars have divided biblical writing into primal narratives, expanded narratives, derivative narratives, treatises on law, rules, regulations and procedures and, finally, books that are essentially instructional.

To read the bible today it is helpful to have two modern translations for comparison. One can be a portable edition and the other a study edition. Use your imagination when reading and bring metaphor, allegory and symbolism into play. Engage the emotions. The practice of lectio divina is helpful.

Interpret biblical passages only with love and compassion, remembering the Golden Rule attributed to Hillel and Jesus' reminder that love of God and love of neighbour summarise the law. No bible interpretation can contradict these.

Quotation for Discussion

"Using love and compassion as our point of reference may not salve our perplexity around all of the passages we come across in our reading of the sacred scriptures but it will keep us pointed in the right direction. As for the rest, it is important to remember that an open mind is not enough. Our reading has to be done with an open heart and an invitation to the Spirit to reach into our hearts

through the written word and to transform our lives. Transformation is ultimately what we seek from the sacred scriptures not information. A transformational experience of God's presence in our own lives today is what we look for not knowledge of God's presence in a distant past."

Questions for Discussion

- What are your favourite Old Testament and New Testament passages and where do they fit into Brueggemann's categories?
- What one step is it possible for you to take in order to improve your understanding of, and familiarity with, the bible?

1. Cf Kristin Swenson op. cit. Appendix 3.
2. Ibid cf Appendix 4, also
    "The Jerome Biblical Commentary" (3:36), op. cit. Commentary by John E. Huesman S.J. on Exodus 15:1-21.
3. Steven L. McKenzie, op. cit. cf. p62-64. Also Karen Armstrong op. cit p15.
4. Steven L. McKenzie op. cit. p62.
5. Ibid p63. McKenzie here adds this note (* See Redford, *Egypt, Canaan and Israel*, esp. 408-22. Redford thinks that the biblical story is a mythologised and elaborated faint memory composed in the Saite period [7-6th century BCE] of the expulsion of the Hyskos from Egypt which took place a thousand years earlier.)
6. Kristin Swenson op. cit. p25.
7. Steven L. McKenzie op. cit p2.
8. Ibid p5.
9. Ibid p13.
10. "The Bible Makes Sense" by Walter Brueggemann, published by St. Anthony Messenger Press (2003) p48.
11. Ibid p39.

12. Ibid p44.
13. Ibid p44.
14. Ibid p45.
15. Ibid p45.
16. Ibid cf p47-50.
17. Ibid p47.
18. Ibid p48.
19. Ibid p48.
20. Ibid cf p26.
21. Ibid p27.
22. Karen Armstrong op. cit. p39.
23. To download a free pamphlet on Lectio Divina go to www.contemplativeoutreach.ie and click on Practices or go to www.contemplativeoutreach.org and click on Lectio Divina.
24. Karen Armstrong op. cit. cf p82 and reference to B. Shabbat, 31a in A. Cohen (ed.), *Everyman's Talmud,* New York, 1975, p65.
25. "The Jerome Biblical Commentary", op. cit. Commentary by John L. McKenzie S.J. on Mt. 7:12 in "The Gospel According to Matthew" (Article 43.51).
26. Karen Armstrong op. cit. p123.
27. Stephen L. McKenzie op. cit. p175. (The quotation from Augustine is from *On Christian Doctrine* 1.35.40) cf also Karen Armstrong op. cit. p.124 and p263 (note 71).

7. Rediscovering the Kingdom of God

Why does the gospel story so often fail to enthuse us? Is it just a backdrop to Western culture? What part did early Christian communities play in bringing us the gospels? How can we separate memory and metaphor? Who is Jesus for me? How did the early Christians see Jesus after the resurrection? What is the kingdom that Jesus spoke of?

Now, we have already used broad brushstrokes to look at some aspects of the New Testament but it is time to look in greater detail at the gospels, which tell us the story of Jesus of Nazareth, his preaching of the Kingdom of God and his passion, death and resurrection. To do this, we need again to return to the image of Lazarus that I have been using, to try to throw off some of the bonds that tend to restrict us. The most obvious of these for those born into Christianity is a lifelong acquaintance with the gospel. We think we know the story. This fact, says Bourgeault is, perhaps, "the most deadening aspect of our Christianity". We are just too used to it and Bourgeault adds that the story of the gospel really has evolved in our society into no more than a kind of "cultural backdrop".[1] Certainly, we would struggle for evidence that the gospels are actually more than a mere backdrop to our Western culture and, I imagine, that few would argue that they inform society in any significant way even in those countries that like to think of themselves as Christian. Have we managed, in other words, to reduce Jesus and the gospels to cultural footnotes to Western civilization – however important we may deem those footnotes to be? This is an uncomfortable question for anyone who wants to take the gospel seriously.

However, there is another difficulty to add to that of our easy, or should I say, uneasy aquaintance with the message of Jesus and, after the previous chapter, it should come as no surprise that it is one of interpretation. Now many people unambiguously embrace the message of Jesus and live heroic Christian lives, so I am not going to suggest that all of us have simply failed to understand the message to date. Our failure to be Christian is more complex than that, as we have seen in earlier chapters. What I am saying is that accurate interpretation of the message is most definitely at the heart of our acceptance of the message and also lessens the likelihood of corruption, or self-interested manipulation, of that message. History attests to the fact, after all, that much evil has been prepetrated in the name of the gospel. So, if we are to live the message with integrity, we have to be able to understand the message and interpret it correctly.

The gospels are a particular kind of literature. As has previously been noted, they are not biographical in the usual sense of the term and they are full of symbolic re-interpretation of the Old Testament. Nor are they history, as we expect history to be today, because the early Christian communities produced each gospel to meet a specific purpose and, like the Hebrew contributors to the Hebrew Scriptures, they were more interested by far in the significance of events than in their chronology. So, when the primal narrative, which consisted of the story of Jesus' passion, death and resurrection, was expanded into the narratives we now know as the gospels, it was done by looking back through the lens provided by those tumultuous last days in Jerusalem in an attempt to understand them. To understand those last days was to understand who Jesus was and why his message of the Kingdom of God was good news.

Modern Jesus Scholarship

For Marcus Borg, the foundation of "modern Jesus scholarship" [2] is the acceptance that the understanding of Jesus presented in the gospels is an understanding that developed within particular Christian communities over a period of time. Supported by this foundation are what he calls three "pillars". The first pillar is that the gospels combine an authentic memory of Jesus with testimony regarding how the early Christian community came to regard Jesus as it developed after Pentecost. The second pillar follows on from this and is the necessity, when reading the gospels, to keep in mind the distinction between the "pre-Easter Jesus and the post-Easter Jesus" [3] because they are quite different. The third pillar is to recognise that metaphor[4] plays a big part in the gospels and is used both by Jesus himself and by the gospel writers as they write about him.

All of this means that the Jesus who speaks in the gospels is sometimes the carpenter's son from Nazareth and sometimes the resurrected Christ. The words that he speaks are sometimes the actual words of the carpenter's son and sometimes they are words containing the treasured reflections of an early Christian commmunity. In both instances, that is, when it is Jesus himself who is speaking and also when it is the early Christian community speaking through him, metaphor is much used as a vehicle for the truth that is imparted. So, it is not true to say that Jesus was a shepherd, but, it is certainly true that early Christians spoke of Jesus as a shepherd. They did this to capture the reality of their experience of Jesus and to cross-reference that reality with metaphor as used in the Hebrew scriptures.

Now, our understanding of how the gospels came about, clearly impacts upon our way of actually reading the gospels. Those who see Jesus as the focus of their doctrinal beliefs may be more inclined to take a quite literal interpretation of gospel stories and those who see Jesus as the focus of their way of life may be more inclined to take a more metaphorical interpretation of the gospel stories.[5] This distinction requires explanation and once again, we find that we come back to issues of memory and of metaphor and we have to remind ourselves of Brueggemann's advice to use not just our intellects but our imaginations.

We may readily accept that the gospels articulate the treasured memory of Jesus held by the early Christian communities along with their testimony about Jesus, but what are we to make of their use of metaphor? We would be mistaken, Borg observes, to regard metaphor as "*only*" metaphor for, "...metaphor is about a surplus of meaning, not a deficiency of meaning." [6] Metaphor, therefore, can call forth layers of symbolism, the richness of image, the dynamism of story and the creativity of imagination. It points towards truth that rises above the strict meaning of words and the limiting parameters of factuality.

Jesus himself is the master of metaphor and in delivering his message, he frequently makes use of metaphor to add emphasis, drama and colour to what he has to say. So, he speaks of trying to strain out a gnat but swallowing a camel (cf. Mt.23:24). He imagines someone with a log in their eye (cf. Mt.7:3) and warns against false prophets who are really wolves but come disguised as sheep (cf. Mt.7:15).

Of course, Jesus' favourite method of teaching was through parables and though the Good Samaritan (cf. Lk.10:30-35) may never actually have set out from Jerusalem and the Prodigal Son (cf. Lk.15:11-32) may never have travelled to a distant country, these stories will speak the truth to us timelessly, even though that truth has nothing whatsoever to do with the factuality of the events recounted. Metaphor and memory interplay because the metaphor keeps the memory alive and fresh for us and allows us to carry the memory in our minds as we ponder it and explore it. Likewise, the early Christian community used metaphor in writing what was true for them about Jesus and probable examples of this are when Jesus speaks of himself in the gospel of John as the light of the world (cf. Jn.8:12), or the good shepherd (cf. Jn.10:11), or the true vine (cf. Jn.15:1). [7] Jesus himself may have used metaphors such as these but it is more likely that they are the metaphors of the early Christians.

But, memory and metaphor are not always discrete and readily distinguishable in the gospels, nor do they need to be, maintains Borg. He uses the example, from the gospel of Mark, of the journey that Jesus makes from Galilee to Jerusalem. [8] This journey (cf. Mk.8:22 – 10.52) connects the early activity of Jesus in territory familiar to him, to his last days in Jerusalem. Now, we cannot actually say how long the ministry of Jesus lasted or how often he actually visited Jerusalem but for Mark these details are of no consequence. He weaves together the historical memory of Jesus' journey and the well established biblical metaphor of journey and his resulting tapestry is a means of presenting us with Jesus, the message of Jesus and a Christ who was crucified. Skillfully interwoven, memory and metaphor elegantly enhance each other to provide a structure for the gospel.

This raises for our Western minds, of course, questions in relation to individual sections of the gospel. How we can draw any semblance of a line as to where either memory or metaphor may begin or end in a gospel narrative. Are we able to know? The purpose of a story and what a story means is always key in trying to separate memory and metaphor but, once again, it is Borg who offers us two common sense guidelines.[9] The first is that if a story is verified by two different sources then there is a good chance that it is an authentic memory. Now remember that Matthew and Luke rely on Mark as a source, so the synoptic gospels, at times, can count as only one source though, obviously, there are stories that are unique to Matthew or to Luke. "Q" would constitute a second source as would the gospel of John.

The second guideline is that the story must be consistent with the image of Jesus established by the first guideline. The best examples of this are parables. Parables are clearly characteristic of Jesus' method of teaching. So, parables that are found only in Matthew (e.g. The Unforgiving Servant, The Labourers in the Vineyard and The Talents) or in Luke (e.g. The Good Samaritan, The Prodigal Son and The Dishonest Manager) can be taken to be an authentic memory of Jesus even if, as is the case with these parables, they appear only in one source.

There are other considerations. For example, language asserting that Jesus is the Son of God, for example, is more likely to be from an early Christian community than from Jesus himself. The same applies to little sayings that are tagged on to the end of a parable.[10] At the end of the parable of the Labourers in the Vineyard, we read, "So, the last will be first, and the first will be last" (Mt.20:16). This does not really seem to fit as the parable is a tale about unexpected generosity, so, more than likely it is a saying that was in use in the early Church. However, we can never definitively say that it was not a saying which fell from the lips of Jesus and was just slotted into the gospel narrative at this point by the writer.

More significantly, the creative combination of memory and metaphor also helps us make better sense of those incidents in the gospels which are both strange and spectacular. We have already looked at the infancy narratives in Matthew and Luke but Borg would also list such stories as the healing of the Gerasene demoniac (cf. Mk.5:1-20), the changing of the water into wine (cf.Jn.2:1-11) and Peter being invited to walk on water (cf.Mt.14:28-31). Among other stories that readily spring to mind are the raising of Lazarus (cf.Jn.11:38-44), the transfiguration (cf.Mt.17:1-8), the calming of the storm (cf.Mk.4:37-41) and any of the various accounts of the feeding of the multitudes (cf.Mk.6:31-44). We may well ponder how we can begin to take in these very strange and spectacular events?

It is perhaps not a difficulty to accept that some of these stories hold a memory of Jesus as, for example, a wonderful healer and even a performer of exorcisms. [11] And in the light of our discussion to date, it is not unreasonable to accept that the gospel writers would not have considered it in any way strange to overlay these memories with metaphor in order to further establish that Jesus was, in fact, the Christ. So, Borg says, we are never wrong giving these stories a metaphorical reading and setting aside the question of memory. In addition, he advises that we should always acknowledge our own sense of the probable.[12] He writes of Jesus:

"I do think he performed healings and exorcisms, but I am skeptical that he walked on the sea or fed a multitude with a small amount of food or changed water into wine. I could be wrong, of course; historical judgments are always probability judgments... I conclude by emphasizing once again that metaphorical narratives can be powerfully truthful, even though not literally factual." [13]

Not everyone will be comfortable with this approach, but it does still focus on the truth that the gospel writers wish to convey about Jesus. This truth is twofold. It concerns who Jesus was and what he means by his message about the kingdom of God.

Who do you say that I am?

The synoptic gospels tell us that Jesus himself raises the question of his identity with his disciples (cf. Mt.16:13-20, Mk.8:27-30 and Lk.9:18-20). He first asks them, "Who do people say that I am?" and the answers given by the disciples are that Jesus is seen as either John the Baptist, Elijah or Jeremiah. There is, in other words confusion over the identity of Jesus. There is a debate. Jesus, however, follows up with a further question, a question which truly echoes down the ages, "But who do you say that I am?". It is Peter who speaks up and the answer that he gives is that Jesus is the Messiah, or, the Christ. It is a central moment in the gospel story and today everyone who reads or hears the gospel story is challenged to come up with their own answer. So, whether the exchange as related is a genuine memory, or, whether it is a question phrased by the early Christian community matters little. The question put by Jesus stands, "But who do you say that I am?".

Appropriately, then, when dealing with the resurrection stories where the followers of Jesus have difficulty recognising him, Cynthia Bourgeault speaks of a "drama of recognition". [14] She makes the point that be it because of overwhelming grief, trauma, disillusionment, anger, self-pity or nostalgia, all the people in these stories create their own obstacles to recognising Jesus. He, however, gently leads them around the barriers they have erected and overcomes their resistance until their eyes are opened, their hearts burn within them and they gain the courage to go forward. Interestingly, in the case of the two disciples on the road to Emmaus, he does this by explaining the scriptures to them in so far as they apply to himself (cf Lk: 24.27). Let us keep in mind though that these post-Easter stories reflect the belief, experience and practice of the early Christian communities. The truth expressed is their truth, it is their recognition of the risen Jesus.

But, let us return to Peter's declaration to Jesus. Borg[15] points out developmental changes in the story as it is related by each of the three synoptic writers. In the gospel of Mark, Peter calls Jesus the "Messiah", in Luke, Peter says that Jesus is the "Messiah of God" and, finally, in Matthew, Peter proclaims that Jesus is the "Messiah, the Son of the living God." So, while Luke elaborates just a little on Peter's answer as given in Mark, Matthew turns his answer into a much more unambiguous confession of faith in Jesus as the Son of the living God. It is worth quoting what Borg has to say about this in full:

> "What we see in these texts reflects a general tendency that can be seen in the gospels. As they develop, they add christological language to their story of Jesus, with John's gospel doing so most overtly and frequently. They are not to be faulted for this, as if they should not have done so. Rather, this language expressed their communities' most central conviction: the Jesus whom they remembered is the decisive revelation of God. He is the Messiah, God's Son, the Light of the World, the Bread of Life, the Living Water, the Word Become Flesh; indeed, he is Lord. In their experience and devotion, he was all of these. This language is their testimony to him. It is gospel." [16]

Significantly, Borg gives John's gospel specific mention in this context and uses the famous last supper discourses by way of simple but very effective illustration. These discourses are unashamedly christological and contain two[17] of the "I am" sayings of Jesus – " 'I am the way, and the truth, and the life. No one comes to the Father except through me.' " (Jn: 14.6) and " 'I am the true vine and my Father is the vine-grower.' " (Jn: 15.1). As far as Borg is concerned, though, the salient point is that these lengthy and poetic discourses are not recorded by any of the synoptic writers. Now, had they been delivered by Jesus at the last supper as John reports, with all of the closest disciples of Jesus present, it hardly seems credible that any gospel writer would forget them, or just decide to omit them, if they were part of the historical memory of Jesus. The only logical alternative that we are left with is that at the last supper:

"Jesus did not speak of himself as he does in John. Rather, this language is the post-Easter testimony of John and his community." [18]

Again, that it is the language of John and his community does not make it any less true. It is their truth and describes their experience of Jesus after the resurrection. Jesus was for them, the way, the truth and life. Jesus was the true vine and so much more as well.

So, even if we cannot say with absolute certainty whether any particular phrase or title used of Jesus in the gospels goes back to Jesus himself, or is inserted as a statement of belief by the first Christians, we can form opinion around how those first Christians came to regard Jesus. They saw him as the fullest revelation of what God himself is like. [19] They saw him as God's final, exquisitely eloquent Word. They saw him as filled with God's own Spirit. They saw him as being the fullest possible expression of the divine in human form. In other words, they saw him as the Son of God. In later centuries such a title would be refined and the doctrine of the dual nature would be articulated, declaring Jesus to be both fully human and fully divine. This would not be done without crisis and bitter division with a succession of factions wanting to change the balance, as it were, and to place emphasis either on Jesus' human nature or on his divine nature. This discussion has actually been revived today and some writers are prepared to nuance or take clear issue with what has been maintstream Christian belief for the best part of two millenia. In the modern quest for the historic, or pre-Easter, Jesus various degrees of distinction are being made with the post-Easter Jesus.

Whilst declaring that there is no need for a sharp distinction between the two and that both matter in our portrayal of Jesus, [20] even a scholar like Borg, for example, maintains that the pre-Easter Jesus is not God.[21] Yet, as we have seen, he acknowledges without hesitation that the early Christian communities saw Jesus as both human and divine and clearly portrayed him as such in writing of his earthly life.

Again, though brilliant and inspirational and with much to teach us, a writer like Robin R. Meyers goes further and rejects the divinity of Jesus altogether. His cry is that we need to become followers of Jesus rather than just worshippers and that we must leave aside the pursuit of individual salvation which allows us distance ourselves from Jesus' message. We can, of course, both worship Jesus as the Son of God and be followers of him as well – as numberless thousands have demonstrated over generations. So, while acknowledging the point that Meyers makes about the need to be followers of Jesus, we do not have to depart, as he does, from long established, traditional Christian belief.

Just as in our approach to God, in approaching the person of Jesus, there is a crucial difference between looking at him as a figure portrayed in history and looking at him as a living person, who is present to me in my life and with whom I have a relationship. Now, to those of us who profess to be Christian, this may seem entirely unnecessary as an observation, but, I wonder is it? Let us think about it! If Jesus is a person who has little impact on my life but about whom I believe certain things and to whom I ascribe certain points of view, then Jesus, for me, is really a figure in history. On the other hand, if Jesus is a person to whom I relate daily and who has an ongoing, transformational and sometimes challenging influence on my life, then Jesus is indeed a living person with whom I have a real relationship. So, which Jesus do I relate to, the Jesus who was or the Jesus who is? At the beginning of the twenty-first century, even if I accept the traditional doctrinal position of the dual nature of Christ, I still have to answer Jesus' question for myself: "But who do you say that I am?" Then, there follows the question of the message that Jesus taught and the weight that I allow that message in my own life. What then did Jesus mean when he spoke of the kingdom of God?

The Kingdom of God

The kingdom of God is a new order of existence. The old order is to be turned on its head and things are to be radically different. At the beginning of the gospel of Luke, Mary in her song of praise sets out the agenda, as it were, and says of God that:

> "He has shown strength with
> his arm;
> he has scattered the proud in the
> thoughts of their hearts.
> He has brought down the powerful
> from their thrones,
> and lifted up the lowly;
> He has filled the hungry with
> good things,
> and sent the rich away empty."
> (Lk: 1.51-53)

The new world order would be about lifting up the lowly, feeding the hungry and scattering the rich, the proud and the powerful. At the beginning of the gospel of Matthew, Jesus says:

"Repent for the kingdom of heaven has come near" (Mt: 4.17)

Matthew uses the term the kingdom of heaven for this new order rather than the kingdom of God, a common explanation for this being that as a Jew, he shared the traditional reluctance to use the divine name. In any event, the two terms can be taken as interchangeable. What Jesus is doing is calling on people to turn over a new leaf, to change their mindset, to see things differently, to alter their perspective, to see the big picture. The reason Jesus gives for his call is that the kingdom of heaven is near, it is at hand. The kingdom is, in fact, among us and within us [22] and a response is demanded.

The kingdom demands a new consciousness[23]. This new consciousness will be based on positive relationship as distinct from self-interest, conflict and confrontation. It will be unitive with a focus on acceptance and wholeness, rather than divisive with a focus on exclusion and fragmentation. Jesus comes to assure us that nothing need separate us from each other or from God. The poor, the oppressed, the incapacitated, the captives and the marginalised are not separated from God, though they may perceive themsleves to be so and may even be told that they are so. Likewise, those who are declared unclean, or who are not in a position to fulfill the requirements of the law are not separated from God. When, for their own sake, John the Baptist sends some of his followers to Jesus with instructions to ask if Jesus is the one all have been waiting for, Jesus says to them:

"Go and tell John what you have seen and heard: the blind receive their sight, the lame walk, the lepers are cleansed, the deaf hear, the dead are raised, the poor have good news brought to them. And blessed is anyone who takes no offence at me." (Lk: 7.22-24)

Jesus defines his own mission in terms of freeing people from the burdens that crush them and bringing people the good news that God is available to them and accessible to them whoever they are and whatever their circumstances. Jesus knew that the political oppression that the Roman Empire represented was not the main problem that people faced. Their real problem was that they thought themselves to be separated from God and that, in many respects, this misconception was underscored by the religious practice and religious leadership of the day. The good news that Jesus brought was that separation from God was not the case. God was close, God was available to all and his kingdom, which was everything that God wished for humanity, was where true human freedom and fulfillment were to be found.

The kingdom, therefore, was about the present moment, the here and now. It was not primarily about an afterlife. It was not just a heavenly realm defined in terms of a reward for a good life, or a compensation for a life of hardship and suffering. It was not a spiritualised kingdom though it was a kingdom of the spirit and of the heart. Jesus was not, primarily, interested in changing political or religious structures, he was interested in changing hearts and minds, for if that happened everything would change. Bourgeault [24] says that the kingdom is a life lived out of a transformed consciousness. The kingdom, she says, is no mere metaphor, it is a world we can bring into being, a world that actually exists. Borg [25] agrees and quotes the following verse from the Gospel of John:

""And this is eternal life, that they may know you, the only true God, and Jesus Christ whom you have sent." (Jn: 17.3)

Knowing God now, in the present, is salvation. It is an experience of the life to come and a dawning of a new world order. Jesus, the ultimate revelation of God, the fullest possible expression of the divine in human form, came that all of humanity might have life and know what it truly means to be human. The kingdom is humanity in harmony with itself, breathing in sync with the rest of creation and with the divine. Jesus does not teach his disciples to pray that they will attain the kingdom when they get to God's kingdom in heaven, he teaches them to pray that God's kingdom in heaven will come upon the earth. [26] The kingdom is "....about the transformation of life in this world."[27] It is about life in this world of ours as God wishes it to be. It is about God's will. It is about love, peace, justice, forgiveness, reconciliation, compassion and fullness of being. [28]

And if the kingdom is about all of these, it must also be about the choices that we make. If we choose total openness to God and to others in life, we choose the kingdom. If instead, we choose for ourselves safety, security, reputation, esteem, power, control and wealth in life, we reject the kingdom. To choose the kingdom perspective is to discover the treasure hidden in the field (cf. Mt: 13.44), it is to find the one pearl of great value (cf. Mt:13.45-46). It is to sow a mustard seed and see it become a tree (cf Mt: 13.31-32), or to add yeast to the flour so that the flour is leavened (cf Mt: 13.33).

To choose the kingdom perspective is to choose love and compassion for, "....the character of God as known in Jesus is love." [29] Jesus leaves us in no doubt about this. Peter McVerry selects three passages to illustrate the point.[30] They are two parables, The Rich Man and Lazarus and The Good Samaritan, taken from the gospel of Luke, along with The Judgment of the Nations, taken from the gospel of Matthew. The rich man fails in compassion (cf Lk: 16.19-31) by his indifference to poor Lazarus, or, perhaps, his inability to even see him. Similarly, the priest and the Levite fail in compassion (cf Lk: 10.25-37) by passing by the man beaten up by the robbers. In this case, they certainly see him, though they still do nothing. Whatever the reason or rationale that may be used by way of excuse, indifference and inaction are what is condemned in the judgment passage in Matthew (cf Mt: 25.31-46). When the hungry, the thirsty, the sick, the naked, the stranger and the prisoner are ignored, it is the Son of Man himself who has been ignored. Conversely, when compassion is shown to the hungry, the thirsty, the sick, the naked, the stranger and the prisoner, it is shown to the Son of Man himself and the consequence is eternal life.

The challenging thing here, of course, is that those who are judged to be lacking are those who are lacking in compassion. It is not as we might expect, those who have committed obvious and outrageous crimes. Wrong doing of that nature scarcely needs condemnation and is a judgment on itself. To lack compassion, however, is to allow ourselves become submersed in the daily demands of a more comfortable and self-centred existence. We take the wide gate and the easy road (cf Mt: 7.13-14) when our social prejudices and cultural assumptions remain unexamined in the light of the gospel. It is then that our house is built upon sand (cf Mt: 7.24-27). When we are blind to the needs around us and to the injustice and oppression of our world, then we have eyes but fail to see and we have ears but fail to hear (cf Mk: 8.18).[31] Borg observes that Jesus:

> "...saw his contemporaries as preoccupied with their concerns, limited in their vision, captive to their convictions, and embedded in convention. What was true then seems still to be the way things are for most of us most of the time."[32]

What was needed, therefore, in the time of Jesus was a change of heart, just as it is what is needed today. We tend to think of the heart as the centre of the affections but in the wisdom tradition and in the bible the heart is also the inner self, the deepest self and the place of spiritual perception.[33] Furthermore, the heart is the place of transformation,[34] where real change begins. For Jesus, purification is not a matter of washing your hands at prescribed times, cleaning cups, pots and bronze kettles and avoiding foods that are held to be unclean (cf Mk: 7.1-23). Rather, it is a matter of cleansing the heart, or, allowing the heart to be cleansed:

"And he said, 'It is what comes out of a person that defiles. For it is from within, from the human heart, that evil intentions come: fornication, theft, murder, adultery, avarice, wickedness, deceit, licentiousness, envy, slander, pride, folly. All these evil things come from within, and they defile a person.' " (Mk: 7.20-23)

Such thorough cleansing, such a total transformation of the heart can only be brought about by God himself and signals in the individual, the dawn of the kingdom. It is symbolised in the gospel every time Jesus cleanses of disease, heals the crippled, or restores sight or hearing. It is enacted every time he calls someone to look into their heart and every time he offers forgiveness.

In the New Testament, as in the Old Testament, to be in relationship with God is to open one's heart to God, trusting in him alone. It is to show mercy and compassion to the least among his people and to those who are most vulnerable. Trusting in God and showing compassion stand in stark contrast to the deification of the Emperor and the cruelty, violence and exploitation of Roman rule. They also stand in contrast to the complicated and exacting religious regulations and highly controlled sacrifical rituals of the Jewish temple aristocracy. Compassion places personal sacrifice and service of others above self-interest, power and privilege. The message of Jesus was a radical message. The kingdom he proclaimed belonged to those who were poor and not to those who were held to be righteous because of religious observance. Compassion, along with being open to God's call to relationship present in all of the reality of life, positive and negative, provided entry to the kingdom.[35] This stance, inevitably would bring Jesus into deadly conflict with the authorities of his day and he knew this, as we will now see.

Summary

Each gospel communicates the understanding of Jesus in a particular early Christian community. Reading the gospel we should also keep in mind the distinction between the "pre-Easter" Jesus and the "post-Easter" Jesus. Then, there is the fact that both Jesus himself and the evangelists make so much use of metaphor. Those who see Jesus as a focus of doctrinal belief tend to read the gospel more literally than those who see Jesus as a focus for a way of life.

Metaphor and actual memory interplay in the gospels and it is not always easy to distinguish them. If there are two sources for a story, or it fits the image of Jesus established by multiple sources then it might be an authentic memory of Jesus. Any parable is an example of the latter. On the other hand, claims that Jesus is the Son of God are more likely to come from the Christian community than from Jesus himself. The more strange and spectacular a story the more we may wonder if the truth it holds is held in metaphor.

The big question Jesus puts to all of us is the question of his identity. In fact, the recognition of Jesus is an issue in some of the resurrection stories. It is to be expected that the conviction of early communities around who Jesus was would have been expressed in these stories and in passages such as John's last supper discourses. It took centuries to articulate the dual nature of Jesus Christ with which we are familiar today.

The kingdom of God that Jesus proclaimed is a new order of existence. It is a new consciousness that calls for a response from us. No one and no thing is separated from God. God is close but our minds and hearts need to change to embrace the fullness of life. Indifference, inaction, preoccupation need to be replaced by compassion, service and self-sacrifice in our lives.

Quotation for Discussion

"Let us think about it! If Jesus is a person who has little impact on my life but about whom I believe certain things and to whom I ascribe certain points of view, then Jesus, for me, is really a figure in history. On the other hand, if Jesus is person to whom I relate daily and who has an ongoing, transformational and sometimes challenging influence on my life then Jesus is indeed a living person with whom I have a real relationship. So, which Jesus do I relate to, the Jesus who was or the Jesus who is? At the beginning of the twenty-first century, even if I accept the traditional doctrinal position of the dual nature of Christ, I still have to answer Jesus' question for myself: 'But who do you say that I am?'"

Questions for Discussion

- When we read of water being changed into wine (cf Jn.2:1-11), or Peter being invited to walk across the stormy sea (cf Mt.14:28-31), how can we understand the contributions of memory and of metaphor to these accounts?
- What understanding of the kingdom holds most meaning for you and what understanding of the kingdom is most likely to engage young people?

1. "The Wisdom Jesus" by Cynthia Bourgeault, p2. Shambhala (2008).
2. "Jesus" by Marcus J. Borg, cf. p42. HarperOne (2006).
3. Ibid p44.
4. Ibid cf. p51ff.
5. Ibid p15.
6. Ibid p52.
7. Ibid p53.
8. Ibid cf. p54ff.

9. Ibid cf. p70ff.
10. Ibid cf. p71.
11. Ibid cf. p56-57 and Borg's comment on the Jesus Seminar's acceptance of Jesus as an exorcist.
12. Ibid cf. p73.
13. Ibid p75.
14. Bourgeault, op. cit. p129 (Shambhala 2008).
15. Borg op. cit. p42.
16. Borg op. cit. p42.
17. There are seven "I am" sayings in John: cf. Jn: 6.35 ("I am the bread of life"); 8.12 ("I am the light of the world"); 10.7 ("I am the gate for the sheep");10.11 ("I am the good shepherd"); 11.25 ("I am the resurrection and the life"); 14.6 ("I am the way, and the truth, and the life") and 15.1 ("I am the true vine").
18. "Jesus", Borg op. cit. p47.
19. "The Heart of Christianity" by Marcus J. Borg, cf. p.88 (Harper 2003).
20. "Jesus", Borg op. cit. cf. p304.
21. Ibid cf. p109 and p136.
22. In its translation of Lk. 17:21 the NRSV offers the word "within" as an alternative for the word "among" which is used in the text.
23. Cf. Bourgeault op. cit. p31ff expansion of reference to Jim Marion's equation of the kingdom with a *state of consciousness.*
24. Ibid cf. p32-33.
25. "The Heart of Christianity" by Marcus J. Borg, cf. p174-175. (Harper 2003). Cf also his book, "Jesus" op. cit. p144.
26. "Simply Jesus" by Tom Wright, cf p146. (SPCK 2011)
27. "Jesus", Borg op. cit. p144
28. Ibid. See Borg's explanation of the Hebrew for peace, "shalom".
29. Tom Wright op. cit. p185.
30. "Jesus: Social Revolutionary?" by Peter McVerry, cf p27ff for his treatment of these three passages. (Veritas 2007).
31. "Jesus", Borg op. cit. cf p194-195 and p219.
32. Ibid. p217.
33. Cf Bourgeault, op. cit. p35; Borg's, "The Heart of Christianity" p149. And Borg's "Jesus" p210.
34. Tom Wright op. cit. cf p98ff,
35. Peter McVerry op. cit. p40.

8. Inevitability and the Cross, Vindication and Resurrection

Why was Jesus different? What is the significance of Jesus' death? What is the significance of his incarnation? Why did Jesus cleanse the temple and why did this make his death inevitable? What does it mean for us to take up our cross today? What does the resurrection mean?

Where Jesus was present, the kingdom was present, a new world order was coming into being. He entrusted his life completely to the Father. He embodied the Father's love and compassion for his people. He was incapable of doing otherwise. For Jesus it was inconceivable not to be open to the reality of God in life and he could not but live to proclaim God's kingdom. When this proclamation ran counter to the vested religious and civil interests of the day, a violent and bloody response could be anticipated. In his passion for God and the kingdom, Jesus was fully aware that he would, sooner or later, embrace an altogether different passion for he knew he could not compromise on who he was and what his message was.

In this sense, Jesus death is a literal atonement. It is being "at one" with his Father and what the Father wills for humanity and being "at one" with humanity in its suffering and its search for meaning and for freedom. This sits more easily than the dominant traditional theological interpretation of the death of Jesus as the Father's demand for atonement for the "Fall" of Adam and Eve in the garden and for the all the subsequent sins of humanity. Jesus did not die because the Father demanded his blood, Jesus died because to compromise on who he was and what his message was would have done greater violence to himself than any crucifixion. His death was indeed a sacrifice but a willing sacrifice of love rather than a blood atonement. Jesus' embrace of the inevitable on the cross is an embrace of love. His outstretched arms embrace the

Father, humanity and all of created reality. The generosity of his embrace is timeless, incarnational and cosmic.

Embracing the Inevitable

Bourgeault writes that the incarnation of Jesus:

"....is not about fall, guilt, or blame, but about goodness, solidarity, and our own intimate participation in the mystery of love at the heart of all creation." [1]

The incarnation is not a response to wrong doing or the initiation of reparation for an affront to the Divine. It is a further step in the creation and formation of humankind. It is the most spectacular outpouring of divine energy and love. Borg takes a similar view to Bourgeault, commenting on one of the best known of all gospel verses:

" 'For God so loved the world that he gave his only Son, so that everyone who believes in him may not perish but may have eternal life.' " (Jn: 3.16)

Focusing on the phrase, "that he gave his only Son", he says:

"In John, this phrase does not refer to Jesus' death on the cross as substitutionary atonement for sin, but to the incarnation as a whole. God loves the world so much that God incarnate in Jesus became part of it, vulnerable to it, partaking of it. To love the world means to love the world as God in Jesus loved the world, to give one's life for it." [2]

That life which begins in the dark seclusion of Mary's womb and ends in the nightmarish public humiliation of the cross is not a contrived response to disobedience, it is a magnificent, unambiguous and yet still mysterious affirmation of all that God looked upon and saw to be good.

The journey to the cross that begins in Nazareth with the annunciation enters its final phase with Jesus' entry into Jerusalem on the day we have come to commemorate as Palm Sunday. The Jews are gathering for the most sacred festival of the Jewish calendar, Passover. The roads into the city are choked with pilgrims. The priests are preparing the temple, the royalty are gathering in their palaces, the Roman garrison is on high alert, ready to shed blood at the slightest sign of trouble. The excitement, as always, is heightened by the usual raft of rumours and gossip some of which, no doubt, surround the man of the moment, Jesus the Nazarene.

The stage is set for something truly extraordinary and Jesus does not disappoint. He carefully plans his arrangements, sending two of his disciples ahead. He eventually approaches the city riding on a young donkey (cf Mt:21.1-9; Mk:11.1-10; Lk:19.28-38; Jn:12.12-19). The symbolism, alluding to a passage in the book of Zechariah (cf Zech: 9.9-10), is calculated. Jesus is a king. Jerusalem can rejoice. But, Jesus is a humble king and his kingdom is a kingdom of peace.[3] The people acclaim him wildly. We can imagine how this would have contrasted with the barely contained resentment and the sullen reception which probably greeted Pilate's display of military pagentry and power as he entered the city, perhaps by another gate at that very same moment.[4]

However, Jesus the great communicator was not finished. Having wordlessly, though eloquently, denounced civil oppression, he heads for the temple to denounce religious oppression and to nominate yet again, as the citizens of his kingdom, not the Sadducees or the Pharisees, but the impoverished, the powerless, the traumatised and the forgotten. The temple stood at the very heart of Judaism at the time. This was the temple that the Jews had returned from exile in Babylon to build. The sacrifices that were offered in the temple defined Jewish religious life and were central to all the great festivals. The temple housed the Holy of Holies, the sacred place of God's very presence. The splendour of the temple building itself was the people's pride and joy. There were, however, other dimensions to the temple. As well as having become the centre for the collection of Roman taxes,[5] it was the place where a record was kept of people's debts. Almost inevitably, therefore, the temple was not free of the whiff of financial corruption. In addition, and by way of contrast, it was also a potent symbol of an often violent nationalism.[6]

So, when Jesus enters the temple (cf Mt: 21.12-17; Mk: 11.15-19; Lk: 19.45-48; Jn: 2.14-22) and begins to overturn the tables of those who changed money and sold doves, he is making more than just a pious point about being quiet in Church, as it were, and not carrying on business in a sacred space. He is challenging aspects, at least, of the system of sacrifice itself. For Borg the cleansing of the temple is an "indictment of the temple".[7] He explains:

> "The theology that developed around the temple claimed for it an institutional monoply on access to God. Not only did the temple theology affirm that God dwelled there and nowhere else, but the temple was the one and only place of sacrifice. Only there could sacrifices be offered for certain kinds of sins, and only there could certain kinds of impurities be dealt with. Doing so was the prerequisite for access to God, for entering the place of God's presence."

The anger of Jesus is not challenging a perceived desecration but the control over God's mercy and forgiveness[8] that the priests purported to exercise through the rituals of sacrifice. He also challenges the tax and commercial arrangements that kept people in poverty and debt and he challenges a violent national political ambition. Then, still within the temple compound, he points again to the kingdom, curing those who come to him because they could not see or were crippled (cf Mt: 21.14). And when the children sing out his praise, naming him as the Son of David, he accepts their praise (cf Mt: 21.15). The people are enthralled. The priests are incensed and look for a way to kill him (cf Mk:11.18). Before that can happen, Jesus is to celebrate Passover with the disciples.

According to the synoptic gospels, Jesus' final meal with his closest friends is a Passover meal. In John's gospel, things are arranged a little differently, with the final meal taking place before the Passover (cf Jn: 13.1) and Jesus being condemned (cf Jn: 19.14) and dying on the cross on the day of Preparation for Passover (cf Jn: 19.31) - the actual day when the sacrificial lamb would have been slaughtered. Whatever the timing, the symbolism is the same for all the gospel writers and Jesus' death is associated with the great Jewish celebration of freedom and of the beginning of the journey towards nationhood. Just as Jesus preached a kingdom of freedom, of wholeness and of unity with God and each other, so the meal by which he asks to be remembered and his very death itself celebrate these same things. The Passover lamb was eaten standing, with walking staff in hand, dressed for the journey, ready to depart, ready to walk away from slavery and oppression. The lamb, therefore, was not a substitution sacrifice, it was "food for the journey".[9] So too, the eucharistic meal by which the Christian community commemorates Jesus provides us with food for the journey, the journey we are on as a community and as individuals.

Jesus promises us nourishement along the way as he invites us to journey with him as his disciples. He asks us to take up his cross on a daily basis and follow him (cf Mk: 8.43-9.1; Mt: 16.24-28; Lk: 9.23-27). This means that in our living of life, in our everyday interaction with others, he wants us to embody the Father's love and compassion just as he did. He wants us to be open to the fulness of the reality of God in our lives, as he was. Jesus wants us to be at one with the Father and with those around us. At the last meal in the gospel of John, Jesus prays to the Father for his disciples: "I am asking on their behalf.....(17.9), and for their sakes I sanctify myself....(17.19), that they may all be one.....(17.21), that they may be completely one....(17.23), so that

111   Unbinding Christian Faith: Free to Be   Denis Gleeson

the love with which you loved me may be in them, and I in them (17.26)."

Jesus is asking us to accept the kingdom which is all that God wishes for us personally and communally as well as what God wishes for humanity. He tells us that to do this, we must be prepared to lose our present lives, open our minds and hearts to a greater reality and then we will learn to truly live. Taking up the cross as Jesus did is our readiness to grow and change and to be transformed in God given all the circumstances of our lives. It is our readiness to allow God replace our old attitudes and mindset with a fresh and enlivening perspective.

Jesus refused to step back from his choice of God in life and when that meant running foul of those with authority, influence and even power over life and death, then he was prepared to embrace the inevitable. As followers of Jesus, we are to be equally committed in our life choices day to day. This is the type of sacrifice that Jesus asks of us. [10] To be filled with God we are asked to empty ourselves. Introducing the great hymn of "kenosis", of self-emptying, in the letter to the Philippians, Paul encourages us to be of the "same mind" as Christ Jesus (cf Ph: 2.5-11). We too are to empty ourselves so as to be filled with God. There is hardly a more exacting passage in all of scripture and the courage to open ourselves to the transformation needed can itself only come as a gift from God and as part of a conscious spiritual search.

But the death of Jesus does more than model for us an attitude and a mindset required for establishing the kingdom of God on earth. It also, in fact, establishes the kingdom of God by breaking the power of all that is counter to God in the world and in history. The ministry of Jesus consisted of doing battle with all the forms of evil manifest both in creation and through the mindlessness, selfishness and, at times, evil intent of humanity. In his acceptance of his death, Jesus allows himself become the focus of all that evil can do, confident of the fact that evil will be overcome and the will of God will triumph. This is the meaning of his triple prayer of acceptance in the Garden of Gethsemane (cf Mt:26.36-46). The suffering and the hardship endured by humankind, along with the estrangement between God and humanity which is acknowledged in the magnificent myth of the Garden of Eden, will be overcome in this garden on the Mount of Olives outside Jerusalem. God's will is not that Jesus die, but that the power of all evil be broken, that the kingdom be established and that hope be given new foundation. With the power of evil broken and the kingdom inaugurated, humanity, through Jesus, responds to God as never before. Israel's depressing story of serial unfaithfulness will not be repeated. Now we can understand the words written in Jeremiah:

> "But this is the covenant that I will make with the house of Israel after those days, says the Lord: I will put my law within them, and I will write it on their hearts; and I will be their God, and they shall be my people." (Jer: 31.33)

This new covenant that cannot fail is a new Exodus, a new return from exile. The vision outlined in the Sermon on the Mount is taking root.[11] Mary's words in her Magnificat are being fulfilled. The message sent by Jesus to John the Baptist is being realised. By way of contrast, Jesus has rejected Peter's option for violence (cf Jn: 18.11), the judgement on his message by the high priests (cf Jn:18.19-24) and the authority and power of Rome invested in Pilate (cf Jn: 19.11). Surprisingly, however, Jesus does reveal to Pilate, a gentile and unlike the high priests an unbeliever, the nature of the kingdom and of his own kingship. It is one of truth and Jesus himself is the Truth (cf Jn: 14.6 and 18.33-38). Jesus is the truth and declares the truth surrounding the reality of God as love and the reality of full human existence that lies in our readiness to be open to God in life. Jesus tells Pilate that his kingdom is not from this world. Wright says that the confrontation between Jesus and Pilate:

"......... lies at the heart of both the political and theological meaning of the kingdom of God. Jesus has announced God's kingdom and has also embodied it in what he has been doing. But it is a different sort of kingdom from anything that Pilate has heard of or imagined: a kingdom without violence (18.36), a kingdom not *from* this world, but emphatically, through the work of Jesus, *for* this world. (The routine misunderstanding of the kingdom as 'other-worldly' has been generated by the translation 'My kingdom is not *of* this world'; but that is certainly not what John means, and it isn't what Jesus meant either.)" [12]

And now, as Jesus faces Calvary, the kingdom of God *for* this world is unfolding, though it unfolds as no one expected. The cross, in fact, is a judgement not on Jesus but on our estrangement from God. It is also a judgement on all kinds of evil. Jesus proclaims:

" 'Now is the judgement of this world; now the ruler of this world will be driven out. And I, when I am lifted up from the earth, will draw all people to myself.' " (Jn: 12.31-32)

John, in his gospel, has Jesus go to this death bearing his cross by himself (cf 19.17). He goes without help. There is no mention of Simon of Cyrene. Jesus' physical ability to carry his cross, having already suffered terribly, becomes a parable of his spiritual ability to establish the kingdom, despite what has proved to be ruthless and ferocious opposition.[13] The crucifixion takes place with Jesus positioned between two others (cf.19.18). The "King of the Jews" is, unknowingly, being granted an ironic and macabre place of honour (cf. 19.19). Though all four gospels report the inscription above the cross, only John mentions "Nazareth" as an inclusion. Its mention echoes Pilate's question to Jesus earlier in the day, "Where are you from?" (19.9) and resonates with the Synoptic question, dealt with earlier, of the identity of Jesus.

The Hebrew, Latin and Greek of the inscription (cf 19.20) denote both the Jewish setting of the event and its universal character and application. Everyone is being asked to take note. The kingdom of God that is being ushered in is not just for Israel but for all nations. In this context, Jesus' seamless robe may allude to similar attire proper to a high priest (cf. Lev: 16.4), or, it may be a reference to the casting of lots for clothing in the messianic Psalm 22 (cf. v18). [14] Again, all four gospel writers mention the garment so it was clearly held to be of significance, just as with the inscription. The three synoptics mention that Jesus is mocked on the cross but John, who stands at the bottom of the cross with Mary, the mother of Jesus, does not mention it. The mocking of Jesus on the cross further confirms that everyone will not subscribe to Jesus' message of the kingdom of God. Some will not be convinced. Some will persist with their familiar mindset and will not find in God the meaning and inspiration for their lives. Some will not empty themselves to be filled with God. Those who trust in God can expect to be mocked as Jesus himself was (cf Mt: 27.43) and some will even face forms of crucifixion.

In their exploration of the crucifixion of Jesus and his embrace of the inevitability of his death, the gospel writers are content to report different sayings of Jesus on the cross. There are seven last sayings in all. Matthew and Mark are at one on Jesus' last words. They make further reference to Psalm 22 with Jesus quoting its first verse as his last utterance: "My God, my God, why have you forsaken me?" (cf Mt: 27.46; Mk: 15.34). Luke and John both have three sayings but three different sayings. In Luke, Jesus asks forgiveness for his torturers (cf 23.34), promises Paradise to one of the criminals crucified with him (cf 23.43) and cries out, "Father into your hands I commend my spirit." (23.46) as he breathes his last. In John, Jesus provides for his mother, Mary, (19.26-27) says that he is thirsty (19.28) and dies having said, "It is finished." (19.30) In this latter phrase, Wright[15] finds an echo of God's completion of his work of creation in Genesis (cf 2.2). The suggestion is that the inauguration of the kingdom of God, the new creation is complete. The resurrection comes as confirmation.

Embracing a New Creation

What a roller-coaster of emotion the apostles and disciples of Jesus must have experienced over these few days! On Friday they are traumatised by overwhelming grief, disillusionment, shame and denial. On Monday they are in a different kind of denial, unable to believe what their ears have heard and their very eyes have seen. They must have gasped for breath as paralysing sorrow gave way to shocked confusion and their hold on sanity hung by a thread. They must have looked to each other for confirmation, again and again, as the horror of death by crucifixion was gradually replaced by a fearful joy. Jesus was still with them. Somehow he was alive. He was present. What could it all possibly mean?

What it means most immediately is that the kingdom of God spoken of by Jesus has not been rendered a hollow reality by the cross. In fact, all the utterances of Jesus now vibrate as never before. As the disciples recall his words, those words now hum, even more than before, with freshness and vitality. His vision of a world alive with the presence of a loving God inviting us into relationship and encouraging us in promoting peace, justice, reconciliation and compassion, beckons as never before. The main thing to know about the resurrection, says Wright, is that when Jesus rises on Easter Sunday morning, he rises, "...as the beginning of the new world that Israel's God had always intended...".[16] Borg adds that the resurrection, therefore, is God the Father's vindication[17] of Jesus, his rejection of the theology of exclusion held by the Jewish priestly class and his rejection of the oppression and imperialism of the Romans. Such is that vindication, he says, that the followers of Jesus now experience his presence with them as a divine presence. Jesus is one with the Father and Peter is the first to give witness to this after Pentecost

"Therefore let the entire house of Israel know with certainity that God has made him both Lord and Messiah, this Jesus whom you crucified." (Acts: 2.36)

Jesus is Lord and a new world order has been inaugurated. His refusal, even in the face of death, to see life other than as rooted in the Father, and as defined by the Father, has resulted in the launch [18] of the kingdom.

The kingdom of God, the new creation, straddles heaven and earth. Jesus is equally "at home" [19] in either, as the ascension confirms. Assuredly, Jesus after the resurrection, therefore, is somehow different. Mary Magdalene thinks at first that he is the gardener (Jn: 20.15-16). The two disciples do not recognise him, or are prevented somehow from recognising him, on the road to Emmaus (cf Lk: 24.16) and Peter and those with him by the lake also fail to identify him (cf Jn: 21.4). Sometimes when he appears, he is mistaken for a ghost (cf Lk: 24.37). Jesus, however, insists he is the same person, showing them the wounds of his crucifixion (cf Lk: 24.36; Jn: 20.27) and he underlines the reality of his presence by eating and sharing food (cf Lk: 24.42-43; Jn: 21.9-13). To help them make sense of his presence, he refers them to the scriptures (cf Lk: 24.44-47). Failure to understand the scriptures is offered as a reason for failure to understand the resurrection itself:

"Then the other disciple, who reached the tomb first, also went in, and he saw and believed, for as yet they did not understand the scripture, that he must rise from the dead." (Jn: 20.8-9).

Having been inaugurated, the good news of the kingdom has to be announced far and wide, so Jesus commissions his followers to do just that having breathed on them and given them the Holy Spirit (cf Lk: 24.49; Jn: 20.22). The message that they bring is that of Jesus of Nazareth who was crucified and who was raised from the dead (cf Acts: 2.22-24).

Today that message is unchanged though it is not uncommon now for debate to flow back and forth around the factuality of the resurrection itself and the details of the resurrection stories. To some extent that kind of debate brings us back to the oppositional and relational mindsets that we discussed in Chapter Two and so the issue of factuality is unlikely ever to be resolved. Borg notes that the spectacular miracle stories and the Easter stories are presented not just as episodes in the life of Jesus but for their "more-than-literal meaning" [20] and that their truth as metaphor is not contingent upon their factuality. Leave aside the question of historical memory, for the moment, he suggests. Whether or not they happened exactly as recounted in not immediately the point. The point is what they actually mean. Why are we being told these stories? What is the truth that they hold for us? For Borg,

> "The truth of the Easter stories is grounded in the ongoing experience of Jesus as a figure of the present who is one with God and therefore 'Lord'." [21]

So, rather than endlessly debate the scriptural, theological and metaphysical imponderables surrounding the empty tomb and the resurrection stories, each Christian has to ask whether they experience Jesus as a living person today. Christian spirituality must always be incarnational spirituality. It is always about experiencing Jesus in the events of life and in each other. That is why the gospel of the Kingdom of God is a gospel that is grounded in justice and in how we treat those around us. Indeed, in the world we now live in, it is about how we treat those who are on the far side of the globe. Christian spirituality is less about securing a place in heaven, having earned a share in the resurrection of Christ, than it is about being in Christ and accepting Christ right now in the circumstances of my life whatever they may be:

".... and it is no longer I who live, but it is Christ who lives in me."
(Gal: 2.20)

The challenge is to leave aside the illusion that we have a life separate from Christ, that we can be fully human and reach our potential as human beings without Christ.

Bourgeault accepts that Jesus rose from the dead but wonders if we ask the right questions around Jesus' resurrection and around his divine sonship. She says:

"The real point is this: what Jesus does so profoundly demonstrate to us in his passage from death to life is that the walls between the realms are paper thin. Along the entire ray of creation, the 'mansions' are interpenetrating and mutually permeable by love. The death of our physical form is not the death of our individal personhood. Our personhood remains alive and well, 'hidden with Christ in God' (to use Paul's beautiful phrase in Colossians 3:3) and here and now we can draw strength from it (and him) to live our temporal lives with all the fullness of eternity. If we can simply keep our hearts wrapped around this core point, the rest of the Christian path begins to fall into place."
(22)

The new creation put in place by Jesus is an acknowledgment of the world as it exists in God. It is, therefore, not an alternative world, nor is it "other worldly". So, for example, when Paul exhorts us to choose the "things that are above" rather than the things that are "on earth" (cf Col: 3.2), he is simply encouraging us to see everyday life, human existence and even suffering through eyes that are also lifted towards God rather than through eyes that are veiled by the everyday and, as it were, earthbound. To see with the eyes of Christ we must allow our narrow, limited, earthbound vision to fade, to die and to be replaced by eyes that look through a much wider lens. We will then be new people and experience a new self (cf Col: 3.10). The world around us may not necessarily have changed but when we fix our gaze on others we will not see Greek or Jew, circumcised or uncircumcised, slave or free, but we will see all in Christ (cf Col: 3.11) and the world that we see will certainly have changed. The marks of this new world, this new creation, will be love, compassion, kindness, humility, meekness, patience, peace and forgiveness (cf Col: 3.12-15).

Summary

With Jesus the kingdom was present, the opportunity was there for life to be different. This was because Jesus was totally open to the reality of God in life. Jesus was at one with the Father and at one with suffering humanity. Jesus' death was a willing sacrifice of love rather than payment of a debt owed to God to eradicate guilt. The incarnation is not a response to wrong doing. It is a further step in God's outpouring of love and the continuing affirmation of his creation.

Jesus enters Jerusalem on Palm Sunday as a humble king, a bringer of peace. He rejects the religious and political repression around him. He also rejects the temple's rituals of exclusion along with its symbolism of violent national ambition. The priestly class are incensed and look to kill him. Jesus knows this and realises that his death is inevitable. All the gospels associate the death of Jesus with the great Jewish celebration of freedom, the feast of Passover. Jesus, the new Paschal lamb, provides us with food for the journey. However, if we are to embody God's passion for humanity, we too must take up our cross, we too must be open to the fullness of the reality of God in our lives. The cross we have to take up is our readiness to replace old attitudes and be transformed by God. We have to be prepared to empty ourselves, as it were, if we are to be filled with God.

But, Jesus' death is more than a challenge to the evils of his day. It breaks the power of evil for all ages. It establishes the kingdom, a new order of existence and spans the estrangement between the human and the divine acknowledged in the great myth of the Garden of Eden. It declares the truth of God as love and asserts that the truth of our humanity is found in openness to God. The resurrection of Jesus vindicates his vision of a world alive with the presence of God. His disciples now experience Jesus' presence as a divine presence. His ascension confirms that the new creation straddles heaven and earth. Each Christian today must ask how they experience the presence of Jesus in life. We have to leave aside the illusion that we have a life separate from Christ.

Quotation for Discussion

"For Jesus it was inconceivable not to be open to the reality of God in life and he could not but live to proclaim God's kingdom. When this proclamation ran counter to the vested religious and civil interests of the day, a violent and bloody response could be anticipated. In his passion for God and the kingdom, Jesus was fully aware that he would, sooner or later, embrace an altogether different passion for he knew he could not compromise on who he was and what his message was."

Questions for Discussion

* How would you explain the mystery of the incarnation to someone who is not a Christian?
* How would you explain the significance of Jesus death and resurrection to someone who is not a Christian?

1. "The Wisdom Jesus" by Cynthia Bourgeault, p103. Shambhala (2008).
2. "Jesus" by Marcus J. Borg, cf. p306-307, HarperOne (2006).
3. "Simply Jesus" by Tom Wright, cf p125-126. (SPCK 2011).
4. "Jesus", Borg op. cit. cf p232.
5. Ibid. cf. p91.
6. Tom Wright op. cit. cf p132-133.
7. "Jesus", Borg op. cit. p233 and p106.
8. Ibid, cf Borg on John's antitemple preaching of baptism for the forgiveness of sins.
9. Ibid. p269.
10. Ibid. cf Borg p268-269 on the history of substitution theology and on New Testament uses of sacrifical imagery. Cf also "The Bible" by Karen Armstrong (Atlantic Books 2007) p136-137 and p120 on atonement and the incarnation.
11. Tom Wright op. cit. cf p176.
12. Ibid. p179.
13. "St. John" by John Marsh (Penguin 1976) cf. p613.
14. Ibid. cf. p615. Marsh attributes an observation surrounding a High Priest's garments to Josephus.
15. Tom Wright op. cit. cf p180.
16. Ibid p187.
17. "Jesus", Borg op. cit. cfp276.
18. Tom Wright op. cit. cf p189.
19. Tom Wright op. cit. p188.
20. "Jesus", Borg op. cit. cf p60 and on the question of historical memory, cf p73-75.
21. "The Heart of Christianity" by Marcus J. Borg, p55. (Harper 2003).
22. Bourgeault op. cit. p133-134.

9. Exchanging Paradise for the Kingdom?

How can we understand the new creation? Is it regaining paradise? Is there an alternative to understanding the garden story in the Book of Genesis as, "The Story of the Fall"? What truths about human existence does the garden story hold for us? How has the garden story influenced the practice of faith? Why is the mystery of the incarnation so central?

Despite the scriptures, the precise nature of the kingdom and the new creation put in place by Jesus has been subject to much interpretation. In fact, a wide variety of interpretations has never been lacking within Christianity. Key disagreements began early. Unsurprisingly perhaps, in view of what has already been said earlier in this book, some of these disagreements rest, in part, on beliefs around the beginnings of creation that were taken for granted at the time.

The great myth of creation recounted in chapter 2 of the book of Genesis along with the garden story and "The Fall" in chapter 3 have been at the centre of much of the past and current misunderstanding concerning the nature of the kingdom. In the minds of some, for example, the kingdom came to be equated with being readmitted, in a manner of speaking, to the garden of Eden as our heavenly reward after death. And, as the well known Marian prayer, the Salve Regina (Hail Holy Queen) puts it, this reward comes after a life spent "mourning and weeping" in a fallen world that it darkly defines as a "valley of tears."[1] This world is apparently devoid of Christian joy and celebration and, depressing though such an outlook may be, we do not have to look very far to locate its origins. Any news broadcast, after all, provides plenty of support material for such a gloomy perspective on life. At the same time, the initial chapters of Genesis do allow us alternatives.

A Paradise Lost?

Traditonal and fundamentalist interpretations of the early chapters of Genesis have been difficult to shake off and are still subscribed to by many Christians today. Such interpretations hold that the world created by God was initially perfect and was a paradise. Humanity, however, contrived through disobedience to spoil this perfection and paradise was lost. God, though he knew it would happen, had not intended this to happen. So, he had to adjust his plans and, in his love, send us his Son. This meant that the situation could be retrieved and paradise, or, heaven, could be regained at the end of their lives by those who believed in his Son and had lived accordingly.

However, the theory of evolution and scientific insight into the origins of our universe have made possible alternative interpretations to the one just outlined. These interpretations posit that paradise is offered to us as something to aspire to, as an ideal to be aimed at. The story sequence is reversed in other words, with the garden paradise offered as destination rather than beginning. God's creation was never actually perfected and the fallen state described in Genesis is just a description of life as we know it to be. Humanity, therefore, is being called by God to collaborate in an ongoing creative process that beckons us forward as life and history unfold. The coming of the Son is not an afterthought but the key stage, always intended, [2] in the great drama. Paradise is not lost, but becomes, as it were, a vision and a consequence of our life and of our loving, as enabled by Christ.

Kess Frey refers to traditional, fundamental, literal, disaster consequence approaches as tragic approaches. The more contemporary, non-literal, open-ended approaches, he refers to as evolutionary approaches. I find this terminology helpful and I will make use of it here. Interestingly, Frey not only outlines the disparities between the two approaches, he also seeks some resolution of them. The parameters of human existence thrown up by the bible story of the garden, to start with, do not change. Whatever your angle of interpretation, the four issues addressed in the biblical myth and the truth enshrined by the myth surround the following: the realities of change and death as part of human life; our struggle with desire and sexuality; our inevitable facing up to choices between good and evil and the deep aloneness and incompleteness we feel as consequence of our separation from God. Tragic interpretations of the garden story, Frey observes, at least correctly identify these dimensions of human existence and evolutionary interpretations allow us to view them as offering developmental possibility.[3] So, to some small degree, the two approaches to interpretation can be resolved.

Religious Faith Lost?

Let us now look at developmental possibility, for it stands not just at the heart of our approach to the interpretation of the garden story, it also stands at the heart of our approach to religion itself at the beginning of the twenty-first century. This is, in part, because the importance of the garden story is such that it culturally and theologically influences our understanding of death and change, sexuality and desire, our choice of good or evil and our need for God. As a consequence, our interpretative approach to the story also influences our image of God, our understanding of our own humanity and our attitude to religious faith itself. In general terms, then, our choice of a tragic interpretation of the garden story, tends to cover life's canvas with heavy, dark, brooding hues and our choice of an evolutionary interpretation invariably offers a canvas covered with warmer, more vivid and vibrant splashes of colour.

Growing up as a Catholic in the second half of the last century, the religion [4] I was introduced to was strongly founded upon faithful, religious practice, religious belief based upon creeds and dogma, a theology of redemptive atonement and clear moral demands based upon the ten commandments. Devotional rigidity

Unbinding Christian Faith: Free to Be   Denis Gleeson

was often the hallmark of spirituality with prescribed and formal prayer exercises and much repetition. Spiritual growth was framed in terms of a disciplined and determined, personal cultivation of the virtues. Liturgy was mainly a matter of attendance and passive observation. Hierarchical and clerical power and presence were the most obvious and immediate characteristics of Church. When people referred to the Church, they were really referring to the bishops. As a consequence, developmental possiblity was, to say the least, limited. And as they were often grounded in fear, the protective bonds that enwrapped and bound Christianity did bring stability, but they were also suffocating.

This style of religious understanding has, for quite a while now, been tired and dated and for this and other reasons there is a steady drift away from regular practice, a search for new spiritualities and a disenchantment with Church. So, at the beginning of the twenty-first century, for our own sake and for the sake of our children in particular, we must look to other approaches. We must seek to unbind the bonds that restrict us and allow ourselves be called forward to a religious living that constantly evolves, engages and unfolds and is much more dynamic than has been the case in the past.

To begin the process, we need to acknowledge that our faith is experiential. The focus of our faith, therefore, is a personal God, a God who communicates with us and with whom we are in relationship, a God of unconditional love - a love that is not conditional upon our moral behaviour. [5] This God of unconditional love offers us life, pleading only that we treat each other justly and with compassion. The gospel has displaced dogma in importance. The study of scripture has displaced theology in importance. The heart of the Church, its essence, is Jesus of Nazareth. [6] Called to be non-violent not just with others but with ourselves, spirituality is defined by growth. Our task is simple. It is to prayerfully allow God into our lives to transform us. The hallmarks of liturgical celebration are inclusivity and active participation. The most obvious and immediate characteristics of Church are community and collaboration. Christianity is identified with freedom and stability has been displaced by openness to growth and developmental possibility.

The Kingdom and the New Creation

Ultimately, the building up of the kingdom is God's work and will not be a human achievement. This does not mean we are to be passive, it simply means that we have to retain perspective. No matter how positive and enlightened our attitudes and actions are, within and outside of the community of religious believers, it is in God's action deep within the human heart that the hope of humanity lies. It is still precisely within the human heart and through human actions that God is at work to bring about the kingdom. Tom Wright puts it this way:

> "The crucial factor in Jesus' kingdom-project picks up the crucial factor in God's creation project. God intended to rule the world *through human beings.* Jesus picks up this principle, rescues it and transforms it."[7]

Jesus may have modelled the work of the kingdom but never envisaged, Wright says, that he would complete the work on his own. What Jesus rescues, refreshes and reminds us of then, is the thrust of those early chapters of Genesis which place humankind at God's side as his collaborators.

The reason God has for doing this is the trinitarian nature of God as love[8] – a love constantly seeking out the Other in creative relationship. Jesus understood this because this was his experience of God. It was his experience of the Father. In preaching the kingdom and in inviting his disciples to follow him, he is challenging the disciples to open up to and to explore their own experience of God. They are to set about this by being open to the experience of God within their own hearts and in their neighbour, in creation and in the events of life.

The new creation will be nurtured as love is expressed through service, as creative relationship allows others to grow, as we embrace the painful demands of growth in ourselves and as we enrich our perspective on all dimensions of those attitudes described by Jesus in the beatitudes. The beatitudes provide the "agenda for the kingdom-people" [9] according to Wright. He adds:

> "The Beatitudes are much more than a 'new rule of life', as though one could practise them in private, away from the world. Jesus rules the world through those who launch new initiatives that radically challenge the accepted ways of doing things: jubilee projects to remit ridiculous and unpayable debt, housing trusts that provide accommodation for low-income families or homeless people, local and sustainable agricultural projects that care for creation instead of destroying it in the hope of a quick profit, and so on." [10]

So, there are practical things that need to be done. Even where education is provided for all and health and social welfare services are firmly established, the well of human suffering never runs dry. Homelessness, poverty, addiction, suicide, marginalisation and violence of all kinds are commonplace in our most affluent societies. A collective mindset shaped by the beatitudes would certainly be a step in the right direction. Wright speaks of the need to radically challenge existing practice but Peter McVerry is not by any means overstating the case when he says that what we really need is a revolution that strikes at the very heart of our established structures:

> "The passion of Christians for a new world, a world in which the dignity and humanity of each human being is respected, requires a revolution in the economic, social

and political relationships that are currently characteristic of our societies and of our globalised capitalist structures. To challenge those structures, by our words and by our actions, is to invite the criticism, hostility and opposition of many in those societies." [11]

It would be naive, however, to think that a collective realignment with the beatitudes is very likely any time soon. Despite the oratorical insistence and the eloquence of politicans and others, we simply do not seem to have the appetite, or imagination, required for such revolution. Sadly, this also seems to be the case among those who hold institutional leadership within the Christian community itself. Yet, within those same Christian communities Borg senses a shift from being communities characterised by "convention" to being communities characterised by Christian "intention." [12] Let us hope that he is right.

Like McVerry, Borg also acknowledges that confrontation with vested interests, in the spirit of the gospel, will be inevitable. This is the cross that we must take up if Jesus' passion for the kingdom of God is to be our passion for the kingdom of God. It means that Christians cannot but be political in that their opinions and actions will have political consequences and will, at times, run counter to popular culture. Pondering, for example, what the reign of God would look like, he writes:

"It is the world that the prophets dreamed of – a world of distributive justice in which everybody has enough, in which war is no more, and in which nobody need be afraid. It is not simply a political dream, but God's dream, a dream that can be realized only by our being grounded ever more deeply in the God whose heart is justice. Jesus' passion got him killed. But God has vindicated Jesus. This is the political meaning of Good Friday and Easter."[13]

Some might think that though it is encouraging to talk about dreams of the kingdom and developmental possibility, dreams are all too often linked with impossibility and impracticality. For this reason, they can be dismissed. Yet, Martin Luther King's famous proclamation of his dream would surely be accepted as having made a major contribution to resisting racism in the United States of his day. Racism, of course, remains with us but its power is certainly diminished and attitudes appear to be changing. Dreams of the kingdom can certainly be realised - if slowly.

But what of something like humanity's dream of world peace? Can we really hope for a world without war? Our planet is torn apart by conflict, constantly convulsed by new outbreaks of international and civil violence and threats of further violence. There is, in addition, the abiding fear that sometime, someone possessed, as Merton puts it, of a "perfectly calm dementia"[14] and with access to nuclear capability will decide to resort to use of that capability, thereby bringing us all to the brink of extinction. Given this contemporary context, dare we dream of anything beyond mere survival?

However, acknowledging our lack of disposition and the absence of any logic to support hope, Merton does situate our hope for us:

"Because there is love in the world, and because Christ has taken our nature to Himself, there remains always hope that man will finally, after many mistakes and even disasters, learn to disarm and to make peace, recognising that he must live at peace with his brother (sic)." [15]

Once again, we are reminded that ultimately the kingdom is God's work and not ours, though we are called to collaborate passionately. I lived in Northern Ireland throughout the Troubles. I dreamt of peace and prayed for it daily but did not expect to see it in my lifetime. I also grew up during the cold war and like most people never expected the Berlin wall to fall. Who can evaluate God's creative ability to use for good even our feeblest and most timid efforts? Veronica Littleton, asks the question in a different way, but, more eloquently and profoundly:

"Jesus spoke of reality as the Kingdom of God: Is this reality ours to build or to realize? Is the call of our humanity to worship or to give thanks; to make things holy or to recognize the holy; to create a drama, or to ritualize our understanding of Divinity at the heart of life; to do good or to discover compassion?"[16]

Each day of our lives God goes about the work of building up the kingdom with us, within us and often despite us. That work is grounded in the reality of ordinary life as we experience it and live it out. The ordinary is, in fact, the extraordinary cloaked merely by familiarity. It is developmental possibility awaiting a spark to enflame it. Building the kingdom has nothing to do, therefore, with heaven or heavenly reward. It has nothing to do with earning affirmation in the after-life. It is incarnational growth. It is the slow, evolutionary, coming to consciousness of humanity. It is a collective phenomenon brought to life over centuries by countless individuals as, again and again, the spiritual search all are called to is embraced. It is a contemporary fire of awareness, relationship and service, fuelled by and choreographing a communal dance of solitary sparks as they dazzle briefly before flaming upwards. That dance begins and continues with a painful and gradual, personal transformation. Collective transformation is even more slow burning. The kingdom, a new creation enacted only by and in Christ, always consists of existing reality as well as developmental possibility.

"So if anyone is in Christ, there is a new creation: everything old has passed away; see everything has become new." (2 Cor. 5:17)

Summary

The story of the Garden of Eden is traditionally known as the story of "The Fall." It is seen as the story of a paradise lost. God the Father then had to send his Son so that obedience could cancel disobedience and the promise of paradise could be regained. By way of contrast, an evolutionary interpretation of the garden story sees it just as a description of life as we know it. The Father's sending of the Son, therefore, becomes a great, and always intended, leap forward in the work of creation.

So, there are traditional interpretations and evolutionary interpretations but they struggle with the same human realities. The parameters of human existence identified by the garden story are: death and change; choosing between good and evil; desire and sexuality; our incompleteness without God.

Twentieth Century Catholicism was founded on dogma, practice, clear moral demands and a theology of atonement for the sin of Adam and Eve and all sin. Stability and suffocation resulted. Twenty-first Century Catholicism needs to see faith as experiential, inclusive, based on relationship, justice and compassion. Openness to growth and communal development will, hopefully, and in time, be the result.

The kingdom as a new creation is always ultimately God's work but our collaboration is absolutely essential. God's trinitarian nature means God constantly seeks us out in love. The beatitudes are Jesus' description of the response called for. They call us to revolutionise our thinking in both Church and society and to challenge popular culture. It is only the incarnation that gives us hope. In Jesus, God embraces all of human reality and all of creation in the continuing dance of personal and communal transformation.

Quotation for Discussion

"The ordinary is, in fact, the extraordinary cloaked merely by familiarity. It is developmental possibility awaiting a spark to enflame it. Building the kingdom has nothing to do, therefore, with heaven or heavenly reward. It has nothing to do with earning affirmation in the after-life. It is incarnational growth. It is the slow, evolutionary, coming to consciousness of humanity. It is a collective phenomenon brought to life over centuries by countless individuals as, again and again, the spiritual search all are called to is embraced. It is a contemporary fire of awareness, relationship and service, fuelled by and choreographing a communal dance of solitary sparks as they dazzle briefly before flaming upwards."

Questions for Discussion

- What do you see as the causes of the transition that is taking place in our attitude towards religious belief today?
- When you pray the words, "Thy Kingdom come" in the "Our Father", how do you understand your prayer?

1. Cf. "Eternal Music" by Veronica Littleton, publised by the author (2009) p40.
2. Cf. Kess Frey's reference to "Memories, Dreams and Reflections" p38, by C. G. Jung, in "Human Ground Spiritual Ground", Portal Books (2012) p12.
3. Ibid: cf p29.
4. Unfortunately, I cannot source where first I came upon the type of comparison I am outlining here but Marcus Borg, for example, certainly treats of it. In "Jesus" p16ff and 295ff, HarperOne (2006), he contrasts "an emerging Christian paradigm" with "an earlier Christian paradigm". Veronica Littleton offers her observations in chapter 8 (op. cit). Other authors also offer their own analysis of the transition we are experiencing.

5. "Jesus: Social Revolutionary?" by Peter McVerry, cf p126 (Veritas 2007).
6. Littleton op. cit. cf p146.
7. "Simply Jesus" by Tom Wright, p209. (SPCK 2011)
8. Ibid cf p210.
9. Ibid p216.
10. Ibid p217.
11. McVerry op. cit. p119.
12. Borg op. cit. cf p302.
13. Ibid cf p291-292.
14. "Conjectures of a Guilty Bystander" by Thomas Merton, An Image Book (1989) p209.
15. Ibid p214.
16. Veronica Littleton, op. cit. p170.

10. The Kingdom and Consciousness

How conscious am I of the reality of the divine within and around me? What, truly, is my deepest yearning? What is the point of my life? What really drives and motivates me? How well do I know myself? What is the human condition? What is sin? Am I aware of my false self? Can I say that I believe totally in God's love for me?

The Kingdom of God, as has been said, declares the truth surrounding the reality of God as love and the reality of full human existence that lies in our readiness to be open to God in each other, in creation and in the everyday circumstances of our lives. Having discussed our response to this reality from a social perspective, I want now to look at that response from the perspective of the change it demands in our personal lives. Social change, after all, takes root in the hearts of individuals. Before delving into the nature of personal transformation, though, let us consider the question of our consciousness of the reality of the divine in us and around us

Consciousness of the Divine

One of my favourite passages in the Psalms, and one which I never tire of, consists of the first four verses of Psalm 19:

" The heavens are telling the glory of
God;
and the firmament proclaims his
handiwork.
Day to day pours forth speech,
and night to night declares
knowledge.
There is no speech, nor are there
words;
their voice is not heard;

yet their voice goes out through all
the earth,
and their words to the end of the
world."

David, to whom the psalm is attributed, marvels at the
voiceless and wordless articulation of God in the world that
surrounds him. He is clearly conscious of God's presence in
creation and his consciousness seems to go beyond the fleeting awe
that can follow a few hurried moments taken to gaze up at the stars,
or in our day, a once in a lifetime trip to the Grand Canyon. For
David, God communicates through creation and creation, therefore,
is a revelation of God. Creation pours forth in acknowledging
God's boundless creativity. It proclaims God's magnificence. It
declares God's love. Yet, for most of us, this is simply not the case.
God may be in the beauty that surrounds us, in the people that we
meet and in the events of our lives, but we struggle to remind
ourselves of the fact. Our awareness, our level of consciousness is
certainly not such that God's presence wordlessly proclaims itself
to us throughout the day. This is so, however much we might
wistfully desire the opposite. Our limiting preoccupation is normal,
but, it does not actually have to be the case. Despite our
separateness from God, our estrangement from God, we are invited
to a greater depth of awareness. We are invited to grow in and into
consciousness.

Irrespective of our present level of consciousness, the
invitation to develop deeper consciousness stands. It can be like the
kingdom of God that Jesus compares to the tiny mustard seed that
grows up into a tree (cf Mt. 13:31-32). It can be like a hidden
treasure, or, a magnificent pearl buried deep within us and once we
are aware of its presence, we are prepared to give everything to
have access to it (cf Mt. 13:44-46). We may never be gifted with
the kind of experience Thomas Merton had at the corner of 4th and
Walnut Street, but our lives can increasingly and consistently be
blessed with "thin" moments, "thin" encounters and "thin" places

where the presence of God shines through, because shine through it does. Veronica Littleton writes:

"Ultimately Revelation is an awakening. It has nothing to do with a God who speaks. As human beings, we awaken to the mystery of existence within the Universe, as the Universe presents itself to our understanding. In the last one hundred years we have awakened to the awesome reality of an evolutionary Universe – in this sense the Universe is revelatory. It reveals itself to the <u>probing</u> of human beings. It is also revelatory on another level – on the level of mystical experience of human beings. It was such mystical experiences that gave birth to the major religions of our time. Thus the revelation of the earth and the revelation of the human within the earth complement one another." [1]

All of creation is a call to consciousness of the Divine. All of life is a call to consciousness of the Divine. Achievement of our full potential as human beings lies in our ever deepening awareness of the Divine within us. Made in the image and likeness of God, we are called collectively to express that image and individually we are called to express that image in an absolutely unique and irreplaceable way. Humanity, many believe today, is the universe conscious of its own evolution and complexity, reflecting upon it and capable of responding to it.[2] Yet, it is not so much the nature of consciousness that is important, it is the nurture of it.

Littleton says that some five or six centuries before the time of Christ, humanity made a breakthrough that carried it beyond rational consciousness and beyond preoccupation with the ego into the realm of transpersonal consciousness. She explains:

"This is the supreme achievement of the human race, when beyond the ego we opened ourselves to the deeper reality in which we are immersed. This is where the human/earth/divine relationship becomes one, and the human experiences identification, not with the ego, but with the deeper reality itself." [3]

This breakthrough, she says, was what was experienced by the great mystics, by the Buddha and later by Jesus and was what gave birth to the great religions. The breakthrough, however, was not understood, or embraced by all, as the story of Jesus illustrates. That remains the situation today. We resist change and we resist it stubbornly and what is so new about that?

For all of us, our natural and initial sense of consciousness and identity is with our mother. As emotional consciousness develops, we identify with the extended family. Cultural consciousness brings with it identification with a larger group still. This can be an ethnic group, a sect, a nation or a religion. Then comes rational consciousness where we identify with our individual ego. As we progress, we do not leave behind earlier stages, we integrate them into an ever widening concern until eventually the developmental possibility is that our conscious focus is on the broadest reality. Our identification, at this stage, is not with ourselves or with our group but with all that is, with the fullness of existence, with being itself and with God. The movement is an evolutionary "movement of love" and of "human emergence". [4] So, with the prospect of such promise, what is it that feeds our resistance?

The Ego and Consciousness

Thinking once again of the garden story, we remember that one of the tragic consequences of The Fall was our sense of being separated from God, of being incomplete apart from the Divine. We are left with a separate sense of ourselves compounded by a deep, if ill-defined yearning, that can express itself sometimes in the most inappropriate and even destructive ways. Frey sees this yearning as the life force [5] within us reaching out in its search for reunion with God. Interestingly, he interprets the serpent in the garden story as a symbol of the life force energy of creation.

Infancy and childhood are marked by a certain innocence [6] where the life force and sexuality are concerned and, therefore, they lie dormant within us just as with Adam and Eve in their state of initial innocence. With us, adolescence brings a dramatic change physically and spiritually and the search for completeness and wholeness and what we sense is lacking in ourselves, begins in earnest. There is no rest from this search. Sexuality and desire are experienced in the context [7] of our aloneness, our yearning and the longing which will eat away at us for the rest of our lives. The invitation of the serpent, understood as the life force energy, is to move progressively beyond our existing level of consciousness in respect of this longing. This invitation is also a call from God. It is as relentless as much as it is misunderstood when we experience it. For at its very deepest level, our sexual desire is not merely sexual attraction or the urge for genital satisfaction, it is "a symbolic expression" [8] of our more fundamental longing for God in whom the Masculine and Feminine Principles are one [9]. This is a fact that is routinely disregarded by counsellors and therapists and is ill served even in the world of spiritual guidance. In popular parlance it is reduced to the little three letter word, "sex" and as such it is commercially exploited in every conceivable way.

This interpretation of the serpent can be seen as hugely ironic given some literal, tragic consequence approaches to the garden story but not so from the evolutionary perspectives. Frey writes:

> "Our separate-self sense, together with its transcendence into progressively higher, more integrated states of conscious wholeness, is central to the evolutionary theory of human spiritual development."[10]

His understanding of the eyes of Adam and Eve being "opened" (cf Gen. 3:7) is that this was the moment when they came to ego-consciousness, experienced the duality of separating consciousness and had a sense of their own separate-self identity. From this moment on, duality rather than oneness is their interpretation of reality around them and the foundation upon which ego is based. For each one of us, the ego is the excluding and assertive personality and the irrepressible "I" that is close to our lips in every conversation and that engages in incessant internal dialogue. In the face of the ego, God becomes distant and estrangement is experienced with the rest of creation. Innocence has come to an abrupt end and, as the serpent promised, they now possess knowledge of good and evil. The process of evolution has surely begun.

The serpent remains the symbol of the energy that drives evolution, motivates us and forms the basis of our desire to have and to be more. This is the same energy that drives our search for happiness, freedom and fulfillment, however they may be perceived by us. [11] And herein lies a problem. Driven we may be for happiness, freedom and fulfillment, but we tend to look for them in all the wrong places. In trying to deal with the parameters of human existence laid out in the garden story, we rely on our own understanding, unexamined assumptions and the demands and imposition of our own will. In other words, in facing the realities of change and death as part of human life, our struggle with desire and sexuality, our inevitable facing up to choices between good and evil and the deep aloneness and incompleteness we feel as the consequence of our separation from God, we still instinctively look to ourselves rather than to God who is the Creator of all that is.

Thomas Merton once posed to himself the question of what he feared most. [12] His answer was that he would live in ignorance of his true being, that he would be wrapped up in what was not the truth about himself. He feared that he would be carried away by all the external impressions that imposed themselves on him and that he would misguidedly accept an understanding of himself that was pure illusion. His fear was that he would make:

"..... the decision to regard my ego as my full complete, real self and to *work to maintain* this illusion *against* the call of secret truth that rises up within me, that is evoked within me by others, by love, by vocation, by providence, by suffering, by God."

Would any of us like to feel that our lives were inauthentic, that we were even to some extent living at a superficial level, that we were, if not missing the whole point of life itself, experiencing ourselves falling significantly short in our understanding of what our lives are truly about? Yet, if we know that we are made for God and that our humanity is rooted in God, and we still consciously decide to ignore God, there is every possibility that this is the case. But, what is our level of consciousness around our aloneness and incompleteness apart from God? Is it similar to our consciousness around the unity of all people and things? Is it something that is familiar enough as an idea but remains vague and intangible?

All the major religions attest to the fact that the human race is afflicted in some way, ill at ease with itself and - personal dysfunction aside - is seriously and universally dysfunctional as a species. [13] Within Christianity, we rather awkwardly labelled this in the past as, "original sin" and the term has much to do with literal, tragic consequence interpretations of the garden story. Keating says that:

"The term *original sin* is a way of describing the universal experience of coming to full reflective self-consciousness without the certitude of personal union with God." [14]

He himself prefers to use the term, "the human condition" [15] and he defines the human condition as having to do without the true source of human happiness which is the presence of God. This happiness, which we have lost, is what we blindly but desperately search for in all the wrong places. What we fail to realise is that the spiritual search for the presence of God is, at the same time, our search for ourselves[16] We conduct this search through prayer which is how we build our relationship with God. Specifically, we conduct it by taking a contemplative stance and being open to God's gift of contemplation. Now this is fair enough as far as it goes but the religious upbringing that I received was firmly of the view that contemplative prayer was rare and for the few. So, where does that leave the rest of us on our spiritual search?

Consciousness, the False Self and the True Self.

The spiritual journey is a journey towards ever greater consciousness and awareness. We begin the journey by looking at ourselves. The great spiritual writers invariably tell us to know ourselves first, if we expect to know God. Honest self-reflection and self-observation are necessary if we are to develop insight into what drives us in life and discover what are our compulsive behaviours, dominating influences and real motivations. We need too to be able to accurately name our woundedness if we are to have any hope of bringing it to healing. Necessary as our awareness of all of these things is, it does not mean that we ourselves are going to be able to do much about them, however. I very much doubt if New Year resolutions ever really effected much change in any of us. St. Paul says in a much quoted passage:

> "I do not understand my own actions. For I do not do what I want, but I do the very thing I hate." (Rom. 7:15)

So, change for the better, spiritual growth, is not a task of the ego, it is a task ultimately best left to God. We can inform ourselves, though, and try to comprehend what growth needs to take place in us and how we can actually allow that growth and healing to take place over time.

Drawing on his own experience of human nature, a profound knowledge of the great spiritual writers and the insights of contemporary psychology,[17] Thomas Keating concludes that our failure to understand our own motivations is one of our biggest difficulties. In early childhood, he explains, in addition to the obvious physical needs, we instinctively manifest psychological needs[18] that have to be met, at least to some basic degree, if we are to thrive. Every child needs love, affection and esteem. Every child needs to feel reasonably safe and secure. Every child needs an appropriate measure of power and control in their lives. When these three instinctive needs are met the child can grow into a healthy and balanced adult. When they are not met, or one of them is absent, there will be behavioural and pyschological consequences and a resulting level of dysfunction, neurosis or difficulty as an adult. When the demands of our instinctive needs, now become our programmes for happiness, are frustrated, "primitive emotions" will flare up to torment us as "afflictive emotions." [19]

All of this seems reasonable enough but a problem arises when we over invest in the satisfaction of these instinctive needs and they become insatiable demands. Then we expect everyone we come across to love us and hold us in the greatest esteem. We cannot tolerate anything that we feel threatens our safety and security and we look for power and control over every circumstance and even over the people around us. This, of course, is unrealistic and is simply not going to be the case. So, if this is what we expect and the total satisfaction of our instinctive needs becomes our programme for happiness in life, we are going to be severely disappointed. Emotional turmoil will set in, for the instinctive needs operate hand in hand with the emotions. Keating says:

"The emotions faithfully identify the value system that developed in early childhood to cope with unbearable situations. The emotional programs for happiness start out as needs, grow into demands, and finally become 'shoulds'. Others are then expected to respect our

Unbinding Christian Faith: Free to Be   Denis Gleeson

fantastic demands. People can grow up intellectually, physically, and even spiritually while their emotional lives remain fixated at the level of infancy, because they have never been able to integrate their emotions with the other values of their developing selves." [20]

Happiness is not to be found in blindly and relentlessly pursuing satisfaction of our instinctive needs. That pursuit merely feeds a misguided sense of who we are and the person we are meant to become. It cultivates a false self. It ignores the conscience, rights and needs of those around us and attempts a very poor substitute for a love, security and freedom that can only be found in God. [21]

The false self that arises from this kind of pursuit of happiness is the illusion and the illusory person that Merton feared. [22] It is the person that each one of us has convinced ourselves we have to be. It is the person who tries to exist apart from God's love and, therefore, apart from the true reality of life and the Kingdom. It is actually a rejection of my own person because the secret of my own deepest identity is to be found only in God's love and mercy. [23]

In his classic work on Thomas Merton, James Finley, a former novice of Merton, points out that Merton, in fact, ".....equates sin with the identity-giving structures of the false self." [24] We sin, therefore, not so much in what we do or do not do, we sin by choosing the false identity that we have chosen. Our sin, "..... is a fundamental stance of wanting to be what we are not." [25] And this stance does not arise just from our own investment in the emotional and motivational programmes for happiness. It is constantly affirmed by society and culture to the point where our every thought, feeling, emotion and reaction become manifestations of it. [26]

This does not mean, at all, that the false self is entirely bad or evil. Motivated by ego in one way or another, it can be responsible for great achievements, countless good deeds and acts of generosity and compassion. But, there is always a pay-off for the personality, a feeling good about ourselves and maybe even a feeling of superiority. The options [27] provided by the false self are a mixture of the positive and the negative but what is missing and what authenticity requires is the spiritual dimension, the connection with our deepest and truest self, the link with the Divine. Frey says:

> "Our false self is an incomplete self, a needy self, an unevolved self, and a temporary self. It's a spiritually ignorant self, trapped under the hypnotic spell and illusion of absolute ego-identity. This illusion of ego-identity is generally accepted as a given fact of human life and supported by cultural conditioning as 'consensus reality' in human society and relationships."
> (28)

The roots of the false self go so deep that it is pointless to harbour expectation that they can be addressed easily, or for that matter, by ourselves. The spiritual journey, Keating says, unfolds as neither a career nor a success story but as ".... a series of humiliations of the false self that become more and more profound." [29]

The spiritual journey is a journey from situating my identity in the false self to situating my identity in my true self and, therefore, in God. Made in the image and likeness of God, my deepest and truest self is an absolutely unique reflection of the Divine. Becoming myself, becoming the human person that I can be and was created to be is to allow expression of my true self. It is at the same time, to find and to relate to God as I never could have envisaged. Of myself I cannot do this. It is God's work, but I do have to stand aside and permit God to go about the task as it needs to be undertaken given my personal history, circumstances, abilities and woundedness. All I have to do is to consent to God's action and trust in God's love, which trust is itself a gift of God. In the acceptance of God's love I come to comprehend that nothing that I can do will bring God to love me more and nothing that I can do will bring God to love me less. God's love and the realisation of my own humanity are both related and are both pure gift. Again, Merton puts it succinctly:

"For me to be a saint means to be myself. Therefore the problem of sanctity and salvation is in fact the problem of finding out who I am and of discovering my true self." [30]

And he adds that his very existence, his peace and his happiness depend on this discovery of himself which comes about in his discovering God. [31] The God of unconditional love always has a hand, as it were, stretched out to us in invitation. When our level of trust is enough to allow us to reach for this hand, we are reaching for our own humanity. Religion can encourage us to develop this trust and accept God's invitation of love. Finley, relates the true self to the nature of religion when he says:

"For religious man, life is essentially a journey in which one sets out to quench a thirst, not simply to know that God exists but to drink directly from God's own life to which man is bonded (re-ligio) in the depths of his being. Religion is thus the intuitively known and symbolically expressed desire to become who we are in God. The fulfilling of this desire is the realization of the true self." [32]

So, we are left with the double question of how to facilitate the movement from the false self to the true self and given that I cannot bring about that movement by myself, how do I allow God go about this work? There are many answers but I am going to concentrate here on just one, Centering Prayer as described in the writings of Thomas Keating and, particularly, in his book *"Open Mind, Open Heart"* first published in 1986.

Summary

Creation pours forth God's presence and love but we are often too preoccupied to notice. Jesus, however, invites us to grow in consciousness and become acutely aware of God's presence and revelation in all of life. All the great religious traditions were founded by mystics who were brought beyond emotional, cultural and rational consciousness and fascination with the ego, to identification with the fullness of existence.

Our yearning and longing for God is an invitation to grow in consciousness. Our sexual yearning is an aspect of, and is symbolic of, this deeper yearning. The serpent, in the garden story, can be understood as the life force, or the energy, that carries us beyond our existing levels of consciousness. It is the serpent's promptings that drive this process of evolution and that opened the eyes of our first parents. But, in facing the realities of change, death, desire, sexuality and the choice between good and evil, we mistakenly look to ourselves rather than fix our gaze on the Creator God.

To miss the point of our lives, be ignorant of our true being and become wrapped up in an illusion would be such a tragedy. Yet, how accepting are we of our rootedness in God? What is our human condition? We need to recognise that our search for the presence of God is at the same time a search for ourselves and that this search is conducted through prayer.

We must also seek to know ourselves deeply. This means naming our woundedness, our compulsions, our true motivations. It means working with those emotions that afflict us and that result from the frustration of our insatiable, instinctive needs and our misguided programmes for happiness. Sin is our choice of a false self, of what we are not. It is the neglect of our deepest, truest self and our connectedness with the Divine. In contrast, the spiritual journey is the search for the true self and for the Divine. It requires acceptance of God's unconditional love and consent to God's action in my life.

Unbinding Christian Faith: Free to Be   Denis Gleeson

Quotation for Discussion

"In the acceptance of God's love I come to comprehend that nothing that I can do will bring God to love me more and nothing that I can do will bring God to love me less. God's love and the realisation of my own humanity are both related and are both pure gift."

Questions for Discussion

- How conscious are you of God's presence in life, of the spiritual search and of your own aloneness and incompleteness without God?
- How well do you really know yourself, your motivations in life and how much your desire for happiness is situated in the gratification of your instinctive needs?

1. "Eternal Music" by Veronica Littleton, publised by the author (2009) p43-44.
2. Ibid cf. p74.
3. Ibid p84-85.
4. Ibid p86.
5. "Human Ground Spiritual Ground" by Kess Frey, Portal Books (2012) cf. p13.
6. Ibid cf. p15.
7. Ibid cf. p28.
8. Ibid cf. p17.
9. Ibid cf. p33.
10. Ibid. p28-29 and following.
11. Ibid cf. p31.
12. "The Intimate Merton: His Life from His Journals", edited by Patrick Hart and Jonathan Montaldo. Lion Publishing 1999. Cf p358.
13. "Invitation to Love" by Thomas Keating in "Foundations for Centering Prayer and the Contemplative Life" by Continuum Publishing 2002. Cf p152.
14. Ibid p177.

15. "The Human Condition" by Thomas Keating. Paulist Press 1999. Cf p9.
16. Ibid cf p8.
17. Cf for example, "The Human Conditon" op. cit p11 and "Invitation to Love" op. cit p132.
18. Cf for example, "The Human Condition" op. cit cf p13 and p29 and "Invitation to Love" op. cit cf p136.
19. "The Human Condition" op. cit. cf p25.
20. "Invitation to Love" op. cit. p137.
21. Kess Frey op. cit cf p84.
22. "New Seeds of Contemplation" by Thomas Merton. Shambhala Books, 2003 cf p36.
23. Ibid cf. p37.
24. "Merton's Palace of Nowhere" by James Finley. Ave Maria Press, 2003. P31.
25. Ibid p31.
26. "Invitation to Love" op. cit. cf. p139.
27. Kess Frey op. cit. cf p85.
28. Ibid p85.
29. "The Human Condition" op. cit. p38.
30. "New Seeds of Contemplation" op. cit. p33.
31. Ibid cf. p38.
32. Finley op. cit. p63.

11. Centering Prayer and Transformation

What is Centering Prayer? How does it differ from other methods of prayer? Is it contemplation? What is the purpose of the sacred word that is used? What separates us from God in our lives? How did Jesus understand prayer? What are the benefits of a practice of Centering Prayer?

Based upon the anonymous fourteenth century English classic, "The Cloud of Unknowing", Centering Prayer is a non-verbal and non-conceptual method of prayer. It is a prayer of silence. You sit quietly, with your eyes closed, repeating silently a one or two syllable sacred word of your own choice as you disengage from the flow of thoughts in your mind. You do this for a predetermined period of twenty to thirty minutes, twice a day. As with all types of prayer, Centering Prayer is a means of developing our relationship with God. Relationship depends on communication. Without communication, any relationship is likely to wither and die. An advantage of Centering Prayer is that the prayer does not come out of our projected and inadequate image of God. Instead, we sit in silence before God and allow God communicate with us as God is. How we ourselves imagine God to be is of no consequence. We simply make ourselves present to the Mystery and are consciously willing to be mysteriously transformed. The ego has no part to play because Centering Prayer is a receptive method of prayer not a concentrative method. [1] So, if the ebb and flow of thoughts is such that the interior dialogue becomes still and with it the sacred word is stilled, then, that is allowed to happen. Indeed, that is *the* moment of Centering

Centering Prayer, Consciousness and Contemplation

Centering Prayer stands in the ancient and rich tradition of Christian contemplative prayer but Keating is clear that it is itself not contemplation but is best described as a preparation for contemplation. [2] He defines contemplation in terms of a most radical interior transformation and a restructuring of consciousness:

> "Contemplative prayer is a process of interior transformation, a conversation initiated by God and leading, if we consent, to divine union. One's way of seeing reality changes in this process. A restructuring of consciousness takes place which empowers one to perceive, relate and respond with increasing sensitivity to the divine presence in, through, and beyond everything that exists." [3]

Centering Prayer allows us to set out on a spiritual journey where this process of transformation and restructuring can begin. It may also lead, in time, to the gift of contemplation, but that is something that we can only leave to God. In that regard, our Centering practice is entirely without expectation. As a discipline, it is sustained only by love and a willingness to allow the Holy Spirit work unseen within us, purifying our faith by deepening our relationship of trust in God. In a wonderful passage identifying the task that the Spirit has to work upon, Keating writes:

> "The chief thing that separates us from God is the thought that we are separated from God. If we get rid of that thought, our troubles will be greatly reduced. We fail to believe that we are always with God and that God is part of every reality. The present moment, every object we see, our inmost nature are all rooted in God. But we hesitate to believe this until personal experience gives us the confidence to believe in it. This involves the gradual development of intimacy with God. God constantly speaks to us through each other as well as from within. The interior experience of God's presence activates our capacity to pervceive God in everything else - in people, in events, in nature." [4]

God is all around us, loving us, inviting us to love in return but too often we are oblivious to that love. Our spiritual senses are dulled. Lack of use and a cultural bias have blunted their edge. By sitting silently in God's presence during Centering Prayer, we permit God to act to restore that edge. The use of the sacred word signals our intent to be in God's presence and to consent to transformation in that presence. God's presence within us is the divine life dwelling within us, or, the divine indwelling. [5] That life is God's unconditional love and it affirms our core goodness. God's action within us is the ongoing process of bringing us to greater awareness of God's presence in every aspect of life and as this realisation grows we are transformed. The prayer, therefore, is a prayer of intention rather than a prayer of attention. [6] Once our intention is formed, it matters little what level of "distraction" we experience during the prayer. As we become aware that we are engaging with our thoughts, or with sensations, or feelings, we simply return again, very gently, to the sacred word. Keating says that:

> "....the sacred word is a way of letting go of all thoughts. This makes it possible for our spiritual faculities, which are attracted to interior silence, to move spontaneously in that direction. Such a movement does not require effort. It only requires the willingness to let go of our ordinary preoccupations." [7]

Our willingness is the key. The stream of thoughts, images and ideas will always flow but we can choose not to engage with it, at least for a short period of time. It is just a matter of not getting caught up, or hooked, by our internal chatter as it flows on by. Every inclination to do so can be regarded as an opportunity to revert back to God's presence. Even resistance itself would be a thought, so we let go of that as well as everything else. Again, we have no expectations of this prayer. God is allowed to work as God chooses and that is beyond our understanding. So, analysis of the prayer afterwards is pointless.

There is no such thing as a good period of Centering Prayer or a bad period of Centering Prayer. Who is to say what transformation, change or healing was worked within during our conscious choice to acknowledge and to be open to God's presence? We do not try to make the mind a blank or even to have no thoughts. Our sole activity, beyond sitting in silence, is to return to the gentle repitition of our sacred word when we notice we are engaged with our thoughts.

> "If you are aware of no thoughts, you are aware of something and that is a thought. If at that point you lose the awareness that you are aware of no thoughts, you will move into *pure consciousness*. In that state there is no consciousness of self. When your ordinary faculties come back together again there may be a sense of peaceful delight, a good sign that you were not asleep. It is important to realize that the place to which you are going is one in which the knower, the knowing, and that which is known are all one." [8]

The Benefits of Centering Prayer

Our sense of separation from God, our aloneness, our incompleteness apart from God are challenged and bridged every time we use Centering Prayer. What separates us from God is no secret. Our everyday preoccupation with life is an obvious factor even though it does not necessarily have to cause distance between ourselves and God. Then, there are culturally conditioned attitudes that we have towards God, religion, the spiritual and life itself along with our life circumstances. These attitudes come with largely unexamined assumptions as has been mentioned before. They also come with the multitude of feelings that they give rise to, so, there can be feelings of guilt, hurt, anger and fear, for example.

Finally, there is our own level of personal and spiritual development to take account of. Life may, or may not, have offered us opportunities to look honestly and in depth at ourselves, our life experience and our particular issues, in a safe and supportive setting and this fact too can contribute to our sense of separation from God.

We take the first steps in the spiritual journey when we come to some acceptance of ourselves as we really are, with our gifts, our limitations, our faults and our life story. We need, in addition, to attain some insight and understanding of the dynamics at play in our relationships, including our relationship with God. In other words, we need to accept the unadorned reality of ourselves, of the life that we have and of God as God is. There is certainly no shortage of raw material for the Holy Spirit to engage with during our Centering Prayer as She brings into clearer focus our core, true self, which is our potential in Christ.

The benefits [9] of our prayer are, then, to be seen in our daily life rather than during the prayer itself. Our core goodness begins to express itself in growing compassion for ourselves and for those around us. This is a core goodness that has been faithfully attested to by Christianity down through the ages despite much disturbing evidence to the contrary and tragic consequence interpretations of the garden story. Those we live with may be the first to notice subtle changes and nuances in temperament and behaviour. We may notice a greater appreciation of silence and an enhanced capacity to listen. We may become more comfortable with our own company and experience the slow and painful growth of self-knowledge. This will include an ability to let go, greater self-acceptance and greater acceptance of our given life circumstances. Finally, we may find ourselves reaching out to others in practical, non-judgmental and caring service reflecting the social justice message of the Gospel. Keating sums up the potential for us as follows:

"Contemplative prayer is the world in which God can do anything. To move into that realm is the greatest adventure. It is to be open to the infinite and hence to infinite possibilities. Our private self-made worlds come to an end; a new world appears within and without and around us and the impossible becomes an everyday experience." [10]

Centering Prayer is not a retreat into silence and self-absorption. It is an ongoing encounter with the God of silence that radically transforms us, redefines our life stance and our relationship with God and ultimately places us at the service of others. Jesus announced the kingdom and our openness to contemplative prayer provides a means by which the kingdom can further take hold in our lives. Contemplative prayer and Centering Prayer, as a predisposition, are, indeed, an adventure. They are the means by which we can allow ourselves and our world to actually change for the better.

How often we have seen the most wonderful projects and initiatives implode or come up short because of the human frailty of those involved! Neither the lack of resources nor invention nor imagination are the problems in our world. Our willingness to be changed is the problem. It is the problem for individuals and it is the problem for nations. But our resistance to change is not always evident to us. Our problem is, sometimes, a hidden problem. Thomas Keating outlines the purpose of Centering Prayer as follows:

"The purpose of Centering Prayer is not to experience peace but to evacuate the unconscious obstacles to a permanent abiding state of union with God. Not contemplative prayer but the contemplative state is the purpose of our practice; not experience, however exotic and reassuring, but the permanent and abiding awareness of God that comes through the mysterious restructuring of consciousness." [11]

We do not practise Centering Prayer, then, in order to experience peace, though that may well be an outcome. We do not practise Centering Prayer in order to feel good about ourselves, or to feel special and certainly not to feel superior. We practise Centering Prayer to allow God to work on us in silence, to calm our resistance to change, to temper our emotional preoccupations and to facilitate a measure of control over our incessant interior commentary and dialogue. We practise Centering Prayer in order to embrace the reality of a world that has its meaning in God and of a life that can only be fully lived in God. We practise Centering Prayer, in other words, to embrace the kingdom.

Jesus, the Kingdom and Prayer

In his teaching about the kingdom, Jesus had quite an amount to say about prayer and since prayer nurtures our relationship with God, how could it have been otherwise? He also taught by example and the Gospels record that, on occasion, Jesus withdrew from the crowds and from his disciples in order to pray alone (cf Mk:6.46 and Jn:6.15). At the very beginning of his ministry after the Spirit led him into the wilderness, we can be sure that he prayed when he was alone there and as he was tempted (cf Mt:4.1-11 and Lk:4.1-14). He attended the synagogue on the sabbath (cf Lk:4.16), went up to the temple for the Passover Festival (cf Jn:2.13ff) and was praying as the Spirit descended upon him as he was baptised in the Jordan (cf Lk:3.21-22). The transfiguration is framed as a moment of prayer with three of his disciples and with the same three disciples, he withdraws again to Gethsemane to pray and await arrest (cf Mt:26.36ff, Mk:14.32ff, Lk:22.39ff, Jn:18.1ff). Finally, Mark and Matthew report Jesus as quoting Psalm 22 with virtually his last breath (cf Mk:15.34 and Mt:27.46).

Now, the everyday language of Jesus was Aramaic. So, we need to be aware that the word Jesus would have used for prayer, "shela"[12], would have had different nuances to our word in English which is probably most often interpreted in terms of vocal prayer, or, at least, conceptual prayer. By way of contrast, the Aramaic word communicates a sense of opening oneself to God and listening to God's presence. A quiet attentiveness rather than an active dialogue is the focus. In encouraging his disciples to pray, therefore, Jesus would have been encouraging them to be more aware of God's presence in their lives and to be sensitive to the voice, as it were, of that presence. Interestingly, where the giving of the Lord's Prayer is concerned, in Luke it is given only in response to a request from the disciples and in Matthew after an instruction not to use many words, along with a reminder that the Father, in any event, knows what we need even before we ask (cf Lk:11.1-4 and Mt:6.7-15). Prayer it seems, does not necessitate an abundance of words.

In fact, if we look at another of the sayings of Jesus on prayer, we find that what he recommends provides a foundation for what has been described above as Centering Prayer:

"But whenever you pray, go into your room and shut the door and pray to your Father who is in secret; and your Father who sees in secret will reward you." (Mt:6.6)

The first thing to notice here is the use of the familiar term, Father, or "Abba" [13]. This was a child's term of endearment and would have startled an audience that held the names for God in such reverence that they never pronounced them aloud. Their God was a transcendent God, a God of majesty, power and glory, a Divine King and Judge, far removed from their impoverished lives. And here was Jesus asserting that God was not distant but close, very close, at least as close as their own fathers. This was the God they were to be open to. This was the God they were to embrace and listen to whenever they prayed.

To pray to the Father, they were to go into their rooms. People of the time, of course, would be lucky, we can imagine, to have any kind of four walls. So, we can take it that Jesus is saying here that we should turn within and access our most private selves in silence. When he adds that we should close the door, he is recommending that we close the door on distraction, everyday preoccupation and our unending internal chatter, if we are to be able to listen to God's presence. We also close the door on the unhelpful assumptions that we routinely make about God and on our expectation that our prayer, our listening in silence, will have particular outcomes.

Thomas Keating says that two things go on when we are in the inner room. Our basic goodness is affirmed and the healing of a lifetime's unconscious repressed emotional material is taking place. The affirmation of our basic goodness is not an exercise in building up self-esteem. It is a gradual dawning of the profound realisation that we are rooted in God, find our meaning in God and can only be happy in God. With that realisation comes the ability to begin disengaging from the emotional programmes for happiness which, as we have seen, look for happiness in ever increasing levels of power and control, safety and security and the unquestioning love, affection and esteem of those around us. The healing of emotional scars and accumulated life trauma in the unconscious is also a gradual process. It may, at times involve the surfacing of wounds some of which we mistakenly believe we have dealt with and left behind. This can result in a significant freeing up of previously mis-directed emotional energy.

Finally, Jesus twice uses the phrase, "in secret" in this wisdom saying. We are to pray in secret and the Father sees in secret. The secret place within us is our deepest being, the innermost recesses of our soul. It is a place accessible only by silence. It is our place of intimacy with the Divine, where God is so close to us that miracles, signs, wonders and intellectual argument are of no relevance. We are, in fact, incapable of interpreting this presence. It is mystery and our prayer in secret is the acceptance, in silence, of this mystery. This is why, ultimately, Centering Prayer is a deepening of our faith and our trust in God. Our prayer in secret is a "triumph of faith" that allows us to, "....find God in the only place where he exists, totally beyond our comprehension..." (14)

Transformation and Self-Emptying

As we come to accept our basic goodness and allow the emotional wounds and baggage of the past to be addressed by the Spirit, we create psychological space within us. This is space that can be filled by God. So, to admit the fullness of God's reality into our lives, we have to be prepared to be emptied as Jesus was and as described in the famous hymn in the letter to the Philippians.

"Let the same mind be in you that was in Christ Jesus,
who, though he was in the form
of God,
did not regard equality with God
as something to be exploited,
but emptied himself,
taking the form of a slave,
being born in human likeness.
And being found in human form,
he humbled himself
and became obedient to the point
of death -
even death on a cross.
Therefore God also highly
exalted him
and gave him the name
that is above every other name,

so that at the name of Jesus
every knee should bend,
in heaven and on earth and under
the earth,
and every tongue should confess
that Jesus Christ is Lord,
to the glory of God the Father."
(Phil. 2: 5-11)

Now, for most of us this sounds more than a little threatening, so, what does it actually mean to allow onself to be emptied as Jesus was? A retreat reflection more than thirty years ago offered me such an invitation but, at the time, I lacked the spiritual maturity even to recognise it as an invitation. Making a private ten day silent directed retreat, my spiritual director, kindly advised me to take things easy for the first day and simply take a favourite passage of scripture to ponder over. Fresh from scriptural studies but knowing no better, I chose the above passage from Philippians.

What happened then was unexpected and frightening. As I sat with the passage, I was overcome by a dark foreboding and a feeling of dread that increased as the light of the day faded. The prospect of self-emptying was just too much, I think, for a young man still in the business of proving himself. I cannot remember what I brought to my director the next morning, but the experience coloured the rest of the retreat and I failed to identify it as the natural but high anxiety that accompanies any suggestion that we let go of the ego and create a greater space for God in our lives. Sadly, it was for me an opportunity missed. However, God is more than generous in according us invitations to grow and each day brings possibilities for expanding our awarness of God and our consciousness of God's unconditional, loving presence in our lives. What I also failed to realise, at this particular time, was that I already possessed a means of collaborating in self-emptying. I already had a practice, albeit a faltering and irregular practice, of

Centering Prayer and, of course, where God was concerned, I was loved and I had absolutely nothing to prove.

Self-emptying is about giving up on the misguided programmes for happiness, described earlier, and declining further investment of energy in the false self. It is about naming and curtailing the subtle, and sometimes not so subtle, tyranny of the ego in our lives and opening ourselves to surrender to God. It is acceptance of the kingdom and acceptance of God as the meaning of my existence. Centering Prayer is a spiritual tool for going about all of this, or, more correctly, for consenting to God undertaking this task within us. Self-emptying provides a theological foundation for Centering Prayer[15] and along with the wisdom saying of Jesus in Matthew 6:6, a further scriptural foundation.

Many other methods of meditation are concentrative [16] and seek to attain ever greater levels of consciousness or clarity of mind. They, therefore, necessarily involve a certain participation of the ego. [17] By way of contrast, Centering Prayer engages with the depths of the unconscious. It is a receptive method, seeking only as Thomas Keating has told us, "to evacuate unconscious obstacles to the permanent abiding state of union with God." [18]

As these unconscious obstacles are emptied out, space is created that can be filled with God's transforming love. As the ego loosens its grip and begins to let go, we allow ourselves to be held more intimately in God's embrace. This is what Jesus means when he says to his disciples:

" 'If any want to become my followers, let them deny themselves and take up their cross and follow me. For those who want to save their life will lose it, and those who lose their life for my sake will find it.' " (Mt. 16:24-25)

To lose one's life is to come to a point where we look to God for our identity rather than to the ego. [19] Our frenetic inner dialogue, and usually self-righteous commentary, slows to an insignificant background murmur. Our preoccupation with fears, dramas, ambitions and hurts begins to still. The false self is allowed to die and the true self rises within us offering an entirely new perspective on life, a perspective previously beyond our imagining. This process, which we invoke each time we do our Centering Prayer, is a sharing in the Paschal Mystery of Christ, that self-emptying that was the "core gesture" [20] of his life. After Jesus calls us, as he did Lazarus, out of entombment, it is a removal of the bonds that bind us, until one day we are free and have become more the human being we were created to be. We are a new creation which Bourgeault describes as, "the integral wholeness of Love manifested in the particularity of a human heart." [21]

It is important to note that the manifestation of Love within humanity comes about not through a process of rejection but through a process of evolution. Our human condition, with the development of the ego and the false self system, is the very stuff of the evolutionary journey and of transformation.[22] It is, in a sense, primal matter, the chaos over which the creative Spirit broods.

The evolutionary template can be discerned from the beginning in the Old Testament. God calls Abraham, Isaac and Jacob not just to relationship but to intimacy. Their descendants, enslaved in Egypt are summoned out of bondage to journey to freedom. Shaped into nationhood in the wilderness, they travel to their new home, a land of milk and honey. Though repeatedly called to justice and compassion, they prove to be weak or incapable and Yahweh has to promise them new hearts so that they can truly become his people.

Today, Jesus calls us to relationship and to intimacy with the Father when he asks us to enter the inner room. Consenting to God's presence and action within us, we are summoned out of bondage to journey to freedom. Shaped by silence, we seek to embrace our own darkness and to come home to our true self. Incapable, of ourselves, of dealing with the wounds of the past or with the unconscious, God will eventually heal our hearts and transform us with Divine Love.

Incapable we may be, but, we are not helpless. We are called to action and we are called to discipline. After all, if we do not actually present ourselves and take the time to sit down and be quiet there will be no meditation, no Centering Prayer and no silence within which God can heal us. Bourgeault makes the important point that Centering Prayer is not just a passive type of therapy. It is also prayer and makes available to us Divine assistance, strength and encouragement. [23] Whatever gifts are given to us, either by way of Centering Prayer or in any other way, they are always given for service. We are transformed in love not for ourselves only. We are transformed so that Love can be experienced also in the lives of others.

Summary

Centering Prayer is a non-verbal, non-conceptual method of praying in silence. Free of our images of God, we allow God to communicate with us on God's terms as our interior dialogue is stilled. Standing in the rich tradition of Christian contemplation, Centering predisposes us for contemplation and allows the Holy Spirit to advance the process of our interior transformation and the raising of our awareness of the divine presence all around us.

Repeating the sacred word used in Centering signals both our intent to be in God's presence and our willingness to be transformed. It aids the letting go of thoughts, providing the mind with just enough to engage it. In Centering, we have no goals, no expectations. We do not analyse our prayer afterwards. If we do momentarily lose our awareness of self and time, that is the gift of Centering. There is no such thing as a good or a bad period of this prayer.

It is our preoccupation with life, our assumptions about life and our culturally conditioned attitudes that separate us from God.

Acceptance of ourselves and of God, as God is, are necessary steps on our spiritual journey. Centering Prayer helps us to do both. It is a great adventure that facilitates change in us and through us in the world around us. It allows us to embrace the reality of life that can only be fully lived in God.

Jesus prayed in the temple, in the synagogue and on the hillside. He prayed with his disciples and he prayed alone. When he spoke of prayer, he spoke in the context of opening oneself to God and listening to God's presence. He indicated that prayer did not require a lot of words. He encouraged his disciples to pray in secret, in their innermost selves, to a God they could intimately call "Abba". There our basic goodness is affirmed, the healing that needs to take place can take place and our trust, our faith, in God deepens.

Centering Prayer is a receptive method of prayer and a facilitated self-emptying so we can be filled with God's transforming love. It curtails the tryanny of the ego. We lose our life only to find it and, as the emotional bonds that bind us are removed, we are at last freed to truly serve.

Quotation for Discussion

"It is important to note that the manifestation of Love within humanity comes about not through a process of rejection but through a process of evolution. Our human condition, with the development of the ego and the false self system, is the very stuff of the evolutionary journey and of transformation.[22] *It is, in a sense, primal matter, the chaos over which the creative Spirit broods."*

Questions for Discussion

- What are the usual ways in which you choose to acknowledge and communicate with God's presence and how comfortable are you with silence and with solitude?

- How do you find yourself responding to the hymn from Philippians and its call to "empty" yourself as Jesus did?

1. "Open Mind, Open Heart" by Thomas Keating in "Foundations for Centering Prayer and the Contemplative Life" by Continuum Publishing 2002. Cf p46.
2. Ibid cf. p7.
3. Ibid p8.
4. Ibid p41.
5. Cf "The Theological Principles" in Contemplative Outreach's training materials for presenters of Centering Prayer.
6. "Open Mind, Open Heart" op. cit. cf p36.
7. Ibid p40-41.
8. Ibid p64.
9. Cf Training materials for introducing Centering Prayer and the DVD set of "Six Continuing Sessions."
10. "Open Mind, Open Heart" op. cit. cf p15
11. Ibid p86.
12. "An Introduction to Centering Prayer" Contemplative Outreach training materials for presenters cf. Conference 1, p1 and p6 and note referencing "The Hidden Gospel"; Decoding the Spiritual Message of Aramaic Jesus; Healing Breath by Neil Douglas-Klotz.
13. For the commentary on Mt:6.6 on which this section is based cf. "The Spiritual Journey" DVD series with Thomas Keating, part 5, DVD 26.
14. Ibid 52 minutes following.
15. "Centering Prayer and Inner Awakening" by Cynthia Bourgeault. Cowley Publications 2004, cf p161.
16. Ibid cf p87.
17. Ibid cf p92.
18. "Open Mind, Open Heart" op. cit. cf p86.
19. "Centering Prayer and Inner Awakening" op. cit. cf p81.
20. Ibid p83.
21. Ibid p87.
22. Ibid cf p106.
23. Ibid cf p109.

12. Trying to Live a Life Worthy of the Gospel

What choices do I consistently make around my personal actions and lifestyle? How do I make these choices? Where is our solid moral ground today? What are the factors involved in responsible decision making? What is conscience and how does it operate? What moral guidance do the scriptures offer?

We communicate God's love to other people not just through the kind of people we are in our personal encounters but also through the choices we make in respect of others, including people we have never even met. Our chosen behaviours, our moral choices, personal and communal, impact upon the lives of those around us and, increasingly, upon the lives of those on the other side of the globe. Because of the consequences of our actions and lifestyle, a warm, welcoming and positive personality needs to be complemented by relationships, decisions and choices that are compassionate, just, forgiving, reconciliatory, respectful and supportive.

Likewise, this must be the case with institutions. In the context of Christianity, it has not always proved to be so within my own Church, the Roman Catholic Church, and within other Christian Churches. Many Christians, in fact, have been wounded by moral condemnation within their Churches that fashioned affective and psychological bonds that led to a slow spiritual strangulation. This, in part, has been due to moral teaching and moral requirement that emphasised and had most impact upon personal morality rather than communal and social morality. There was, for example, a strong focus upon approaches to sexual and reproductive morality in particular. In application this tended to restrict rather than to free, despite consistent confirmation of the right to exercise individual conscience.

Now, having made these remarks, it is not my intention, nor would it be within my competence to review the scope, or content, or major effects, of Catholic or Christian teaching. What I do hope to do, is to offer some comments on a Christian approach to morality in general and identify some issues that must now surely become Christian moral preoccupations into the future.

Navigating a Modern Moral Morass

The need to leave behind the certainities of the worldview of classical physics and allow for a worldview that accommodates unpredictability and randomness has already been noted. Of course, this also presents its problems. Veronica Littleton writes that, "... in the combined wake of 18th century philosophy and 20th century science, the modern mind was left free of absolutes, but also disconcertingly free of any solid ground." [1] As elsewhere, the ramifications of this in the moral arena are frightening.

It is, therefore, fair to say that responsible moral decision making is more difficult today than ever it was. Ironically, mass, instant and relentless communication has, arguably, served more to confuse us rather than enlighten us. A constant flood of differing viewpoints compete without moral weighting, relativise everything and reduce the most complex questions to a matter of either personal preference or unexamined cultural approval.

Robin Gill, for example, quotes Alasdair MacIntyre writing some thirty years ago that: "There seems to be no rational way of securing moral agreement in our culture." [2] Gill offers the debate around abortion as an instance of intractable and interminable moral argument which proceeds, decade after decade, without apparent hope of societal resolution. This is so even given that abortion is undeniably, as I see it, an act of violence perpetrated upon the most defenceless human life form.

Social argument is often emotionally charged, and on the basis of feelings alone, at times, little is left unclaimed as an individual's right. So, for example, are our feelings about heart rending cases, the sole factors to be taken into consideration in determining whether a society should make provision for the

Unbinding Christian Faith: Free to Be   Denis Gleeson

legalisation of euthanasia? Is the right of the individual to make personal choices, irrespective of their level of maturity, the only thing to be weighed in the scales when a society addresses a major question such as the use of recreational drugs or something as simple as the wearing of seat belts in cars? Is it a person's own business whether they smoke cigarettes or not, when we now know about the effects of passive smoking and smoking related diseases exert further, and almost intolerable, pressure on already overstretched health systems?

Doubtless, the considerations to be taken into account in all of these issues can be highly complex. But, however complex a situation, we are not excused from making honest and responsible decisions and adopting Christian moral stances that we can defend with integrity. So, how do we do this? What are the factors we need to take into account to be morally responsible? Well, most are fairly obvious. Not only have we the power of reason to bring to bear on our moral dilemmas, we have the considerations of human compassion; the lessons gleaned from practical pastoral experience; the wisdom of Christian tradition and existing Christian teaching; the content of sacred scripture; the delicacy of the balance between the needs and rights of the individual and those of the community; and the promptings of conscience. Keeping all of these in balance is the problem. An over-emphasis on one may distort the picture.

Particular balances have to be maintained and challenging, creative tensions have to be held by Christians. The Church, for example, holds in sacred trust scripture and tradition, interpreting both as best it can, and yet it must also respond to people with the compassion that Jesus showed. The question of divorce is a case in point. Gospel passages dealing with divorce (cf. Mt. 5: 31-32, 19: 3-9; Mk. 10: 2-12; Lk. 16:18) can be debated but there is hardly need to debate the suffering and trauma caused within families when marriages break down. When such breakdown then becomes irretrievable can the Church model the compassion of Jesus and reach out with a healing and sacramental touch to those who are broken-hearted and wounded? Unfortunately, it has not always done so and does not even now, always do so.

Similarly, with those born with homosexual orientation and who want to live lives of committed, responsible relationship. It is inconceivable that the compassionate gaze of the Jesus of the Gospels would not also have rested on them as invariably it rested on all people of integrity and good will who crossed his path. Can the Church, and by this I mean here, the hierarchy of the Church, do otherwise than respond with similar compassion?

Then, take the question of lay and female participation in Church life and how best to balance traditional structure with the needs of those committed to Jesus today. Within the Roman Catholic Church, it is time to examine the traditional, male, clerical, hierarchical structures. We should examine them not just in terms of how to proclaim the Gospel and make available the liturgy and sacraments, but in terms of responsibility and justice? Rather than structure having the major role in determing relationship within the Church, should not relationship play the major part in shaping our structures?

In this regard, Rowan Williams makes some interesting observations when he suggests that Christians make moral decisions in much the same way as other people and that, in the abstract, "they do not automatically have more information"[3] than people who are not Christian. What Christians do have, he says, is a different perspective on relationship with God, others and creation. This is what shapes their response to situations. Williams points out that before Israel was given the Law, God had already entered into relationship with them and they were already being molded into a community. How people behaved and the choices they made then became expressions of their relationship with God, illustrating, or betraying, both God's character and that of the community. As God's character is defined by self-giving and in the person of Jesus, by self-emptying, so too must we seek to give of ourselves, empty ourselves and selflessly engage with the interest of the other.

The relationship perspective, however, is no guarantee that complexity will be simplified, nor does it necessarily dampen disagreement. What it does do is situate morality within community with its wisdom, traditions and pastoral experience, as well as within the context of relationship. It also calls for responses inclusive of compassionate action. Morality, as a result, becomes more than simple assertion of personal opinions, needs and rights, and more than a consideration solely for individual conscience, be it a conscience carefully formed or carelessly uninformed.

Conscience and Culture

Conscience is the profound, personal, inner integrity that we bring to bear on our moral decision making. The free exercise of conscience touches upon the innate dignity of the human person and the depths of the human heart. Conscience calls us to choose love. It calls us to choose good over evil. The integrity of conscience must always be respected, though that integrity is not a guarantee of the correctness of a decision made. [4]

An individual's conscience can be finely tuned, or, dulled by lack of use. It can be over-sensitive or not sensitive enough. It can be well-informed, or, mis-informed. We have, for example, already discussed our instinctive need for safety and security, power and control and love, affection and esteem. We have seen how insatiable these can be, how they can present themselves as programmes for happiness and can feed the false self. When such unconscious, pre-rational factors are at play in our exercise of our conscience, we can see how our ability to distinguish between good and evil stands every chance of being compromised.

Kess Frey distinguishes between our innate spiritual conscience and our outer human conscience[5] and it is good to try and keep his distinction to the forefront as we progress tentatively here. The spiritual conscience, he says, is integral to and situated in our very being. It is the conscience referred to above in terms of a profound, inner, personal integrity. The human conscience is an acquired conscience and is the product of family, upbringing and education, along with the influence of culture and society. Our spiritual conscience and our acquired conscience, continues Frey, "... do not always agree and, at times, are liable to oppose each other in deadly conflict." [6]

Acquired conscience is deeply ingrained. It is most often unconscious and consequently unchallenged and may be inclusive of an unhealthy, cultural over-identification that is acceptable in society but reflects little of Gospel values. Social practice and accommodation may even directly contradict Gospel values. So, for example, a society may find itself able, "in conscience," to ignore, condone or actively support, the waging of war, the destruction of the environment and the neglect of the homeless, the vulnerable and the underprivileged. Now, few of us actively and coldly choose to do evil. So, when we do perpetrate evil, it is usually only after we have convinced ourselves that we are actually in the right, or, that we are justified in doing what we are about to do. Alternatively, we may rationalise that what we are about to do is not that bad after all and as lots of people around us are doing it as well, it must therefore be okay.

To the degree that we accept the values in our society and those values are not true spiritual values, then we can expect that our acquired conscience will be at odds with our spiritual conscience. [7] Happily, of course, this will not always be the case and Gospel values and the values of society can also be in harmony. This is so when there is an overwhelmingly generous response to appeals for aid in the wake of some appalling disaster, be it near to home or in some far flung corner of the world. What follows from all of this is that for a true exercise of conscience, particularly acquired conscience, there is a clear need for us to educate ourselves around moral issues and around our own unconscious motivations and our false self. Such education we will have to seek out ourselves because Western society which celebrates fame, wealth and power, will not offer it to us. It will instead affirm our false self and feed the insatiability of our instinctive needs around security, esteem and control. The wise and healthy alternative according to Frey is harmonious living with the true self. As well as a consciously nurtured spiritual life, this requires deep self-knowledge, insightful comprehension of our real needs and shrewd understanding of options, consequences and the workings of our world. [8] This is what Jesus means when exaggerating for effect he says:

> "Whoever comes to me and does not hate father and mother, wife and children, brothers and sisters, yes, and even life itself, cannot be my disciple." (Lk.14:26)

He is certainly not preaching hatred. That would be totally out of keeping with everything else he said. He is warning against unexamined, naive loyalties, social assumptions, acceptance of stereotypes and overidentification with the cultural mindset around us. Jesus is calling us instead to the exercise of spiritual conscience, personal sacrifice in search of the true self and growth in consciousness.[9] His challenge to us is to stand with integrity on our own two feet. If this means being counter-cultural even to the point of mature, moral, or religious disagreement with family or close friends, then, so be it. Thomas Keating writes that:

> "Such maturity is vigorously opposed by the downward pull of regressive tendencies and overidentification with national, ethnic, tribal, and religious groups from which we draw our sense of belonging and self-worth. These regressive tendencies hinder us from taking responsibility for the injustices that are pepertrated in the name of our particular community."[10]

All of us are culturally conditioned and much of that conditioning is good. We remain grateful for the positive things we have received, but "loyalty is not an absolute." [11] Therefore, just as each individual has a dark dimension and a capacity for evil, so too does each society and this is what we have to engage with and bring to consciousness. We can do so on the individual level by reflection, education and consent, in silent prayer, to healing and transformation by God. [12] It is the absence of this consent to healing and transformation by the Divine that explains why human beings change so little from one generation to the next. Of ourselves, we are simply not capable of real change. Even the Gospel injunction to love each other is, of itself, not enough to transform us, which raises the further question of the part scripture can play in our moral deliberations today.

Morality and the Old Testament

The early Christian communities had their problems relating to the societies in which they were formed but they also had their internal problems. One major debate (cf Acts.15:1-29) concerned whether or not converts who were not Jews should be required to be circumcised and to obey the law of Moses. The outcome of that debate is interesting because the decision was that non-Jewish converts would not be asked to observe all the rules and regulations we find in the Old Testament. Instead, they would only be asked not to eat meat that had been sacrificed to idols, or meat that was not "kosher" and to refrain from unchastity. [13] According to John Rogerson, a "minimalist" view was adopted, a fact that surely holds relevance for us today.

At the very least, the debate recorded in The Acts of the Apostles should encourage us to be aware that we have to struggle with contemporary circumstances and it should caution us against unrestrained use of Old Testmanet texts in our moral debate. The New Testament, Rogerson maintains, makes remarkably little appeal to the Old Testament in matters of conduct and morality.[14] Jesus, for example, adopts a liberal approach to the laws concerning sabbath observance (cf Mk.2:23-28, Lk.13:10-17 and14:1-6) and Paul, when writing at length to the Romans on Christian conduct, unity in Christ and love, offers just a brief summary of the Ten Commandments (cf Romans, chapters 12, 13 and 14, especially 13:8-10).

Many of the laws in the Old Testament, of course, are ceremonial and civil laws that do not have relevance in a Christian context today. [15] In addition, some laws are just time bound. For example, whereas the death penalty is prescribed throughout the Old Testament for a broad range of misdemeanours, many Christians today completely reject the death penalty regardless of the offence. So, we have to use careful, scholarly discrimination and prayerful discernment when appealing to the Old Testament on matters of morals. The way the Old Testament was used in the nineteenth century to justify slavery and racism provides evidence enough of that. [16]

Are we to conclude, then, at this stage, that even the moral content of the Old Testament offers us little in the twenty-first century? The answer must be that this is certainly not the case. Reynolds Price poses question and answer in his own vivid style:

"Who, except Orthodox Jews and certain Fundamentalist Christians, now regards the Law of Moses with any degree of strictness? A partial answer is that all of us in the West, except malign psychopaths and willful villains, make most of our serious choices with the internal navigational aid of the Hebrew Law – the Ten Commandments and a few other broad-gauged injunctions from Leviticus and Deuteronomy, with added shadings from the prophets. However frequently we choose to ignore that guidance, it's nonetheless the base of our moral and civil law; and no broadly acceptable replacement has been found except for the ethic of Jesus– *God loves us; we must love one another."* [17]

What of the New Testament, then, and this "ethic of Jesus". What guidance does it offer us? How does it help us set our moral compass, because Jesus had no illusions about the milieu his disciples would have to deal with:

"See, I am sending you out like sheep into the midst of wolves; so be wise as serpents and innocent as doves." (Mt.10:16)

Morality and the New Testament

The first thing to recognise is that there are distinct nuances that we have to allow for in the portrayal of Jesus' moral attitudes in the Gospels. Allen Verhey draws attention to the different characterisations of Jesus by the evangelists. All four of them had very specific communities in mind in presenting Jesus as a model and calling people to discipleship. [18]

Mark, he says, portrays Jesus as the Jewish Messiah who, though liberal about the law, is faithful to God's will even in the face of terrible suffering. Matthew also presents Jesus as the Jewish Messiah. Jesus is the one who calls his hearers to a righteous observance of the law (cf Mt.5:17-20) but with a discerning interpretation that goes well beyond that of the Pharisees (cf Mt.12:1-8). Luke, writing for Jews and Gentiles, and with the assumption that the former should observe the law and the latter need not, presents Jesus as the champion of the poor and the marginalised. John, of course, presents Jesus as the one who calls his disciples to love one another and to live in unity. He sees the law as giving witness to Jesus as the Christ.

Verhey concludes that the fact that four gospels were accepted as canonical by the early Christians illustrates that they were tolerant of, "a limited but real theological and moral pluralism." [19] Driving the point home, he says that four accounts of the one gospel of Jesus were accepted, four differing portrayals of Jesus were accepted and four ways, "to envison a life that is worthy of one gospel" were accepted. Subsequent generations, then, in applying the gospel to their own social and historical circumstances would have to be similarily tolerant and creative if they are to live "a life that is worthy of one gospel." [20] And again, as has already been noted, the compassion of Jesus affirms such tolerance and creativity for us in the present day.

The incident where a woman, allegedly caught in the act of adultery (cf Jn.8:1-11), is brought before Jesus, is often quoted as an example of his compassion. As well as that, it illustrates his invention when faced with the cynicism and disingenuousness of the scribes and the Pharisees. In the story, Jesus intriguingly writes on the ground before challenging anyone in the crowd, considering themselves without sin, to throw the first stone. After the crowd gradually dissolves around them, Jesus does not condemn the woman but tells her not to sin again and sends her on her way. Though Jesus says nothing about the brutality of the interpretation of the law by his contemporaries, his actions speak eloquently enough. He has no time for harsh punishment. In addition, he is saying to us that, as none of us are blameless, we should not rush to pass judgment on one another even when circumstances appear to be clearcut.

Now, as we scan the gospels for what else Jesus may have to say on moral issues, we might be forgiven if that query is sometimes phrased in terms of what Jesus would have done if faced with particular, modern situations. At first glance this seems a reasonable enough thing to do, but, is it? [21] We have already seen how difficult it is to identify with any certainty the voice of Jesus in the gospels, as distinct from that of the evangelists or the early Christian communities. We have seen how difficult it is to distinguish memory and metaphor and the importance of sensitivity to historical context has been emphasised. None of these issues can be readily dismissed, nor, can we play down the extraordinarily improbable task of situating the first century middle-eastern Jesus in a twenty-first century setting. Gleaning guidance from what Jesus reportedly said and did in the gospels is, I think, challenge enough to both intellect and imagination. So, the question: "What would Jesus do?", though innocently inviting, is not really that helpful. Where does this leave us? Well, as with the Old Testament, we simply have to tread very carefully when interpreting the New Testament in a modern context.

When Jesus himself was pressed as to what in the law was the greatest commandment (cf. Mt.22:35-40; Mk.12:28-34 and Lk.10:25-280), he paired [22] two passages from the Old Testament (cf Deut.6:4-5 and Lev.19:18) to tell us to love God with all our might and to love our neighbour as we love ourselves. On another occasion, he cites the Golden Rule (cf. Mt.7.12 and Lk.6:31) asking us to treat others as we would wish to be treated. These powerful moral guidelines were briefly discussed at the end of chapter 5. Looking at how Augustine placed the love of God and the love of neighbour at the centre of the message of Jesus, the point was made that any interpretation of scripture that ran counter to this double message of love has to be suspect.

Though at the time of Jesus, the Golden Rule is already found within Judaism and is echoed, at least, within other major religions, [23] Bourgeault says that Jesus takes it to its, "outer limits, pushing beyond all traces of enlightened self-interest into a no-holds barred exhortation to love without counting the cost..." [24] She quotes the following passage from the gospel of Luke:

"But I say to you that listen, Love your enemies, do good to those who hate you ... Do to others as you would have them do to you. If you love those who love you, what credit is that to you? For even sinners love those who love them. If you do good to those who do good to you, what credit is that to you? For even sinners do the same. If you lend to those from whom you hope to receive, what credit is that to you? Even sinners lend to sinners, to receive as much again. But love your enemies, do good and lend, expecting nothing in return... Be merciful, just as yout Father is merciful." (Lk.6:27-28, 31-36)

The Christian's love for others and the Christian's treatment of others is to be totally wholehearted and is to be characterised by instinctive selflessness and even reckless generosity. The Christian is one who does not need to ask who his, or her, neighbour is.

So, interweaving the greatest commandment, the Golden Rule, selflessness, generosity, compassion, justice and a reluctance to judge, we have a description of love and a template that Jesus offers us for a life worthy of the gospel. This is a life lived in the spirit of the beatitudes. It is a life grounded in God. It is a life that originates in, is nurtured by, and "consists of a radical centering in God." [25] It is the way that Jesus himself lived his life and he calls us to love God and to love one another in the same way that he loved (cf Jn.13:34).

Finally, we cannot complete a review of morality and scripture without asking what we are to make of the endless moral advice and instruction given by Paul in the thirteen New Testament letters attributed to him? [26] Well, consistency demands that we apply the same principles that we have been applying all along. We look at the historical context in which the letters were written. We look at the specific circumstances of the writer and the recipients. We look at the moral norms of the time surrounding the issue being addressed. Then, we look in detail at our modern setting and determine the helpfulness, or otherwise, of the Pauline passage in question. [27] Given that, as Barton says, "the task of historical reconstruction is ongoing and never complete,"[28] we can see how painstaking, exhaustive and, at times, a little questionable this entire process is always likely to be. Yet, the New Testament and Pauline letters will always have moral relevance. The life of the

Christian community today is not simply a personal challenge, but a communal challenge, to respond to God's presence in our world. At the personal and communal level, then, we remember that our present is informed by how God's invitation to life was understood and communicated in the past and we are open to a future, "which is in God's hands and which has been revealed in the resurrection." [29] Two short Pauline passages from Galatians illustrate this, just as they underline the continuity with the teaching of Jesus in the gospel. The first is as follows:

> "As many of you as were baptized into Christ have clothed yourselves with Christ. There is no longer Jew or Greek, there is no longer slave or free, there is no longer male or female, for all of you are one in Christ Jesus. And if you belong to Christ, then you are Abraham's offspring, heirs according to the promise." (Gal.3:27-29)

For Paul, baptism is baptism into the passion, death and resurrection of Christ. This paschal mystery of Christ is at once the good news of God's presence in the world and evidence of God's transformational power. [30] Not only may things be different, they are already different. Old dualistic categories may still punctuate our vocabulary but they no longer apply. They have been transcended by a new and unitive reality.

People, therefore, may still talk about Jew and Greek, black African and white European, but in Christ such distinctions are meaningless. People may still talk of slave and free, ordinary person in the street or celebrity, but in Christ such distinctions are meaningless. People may still talk of male and female, adult and child, but in Christ even these distinctions are meaningless. In Christ, all are equal, all have the same dignity, all are deserving of the same respect. The paschal mystery changed all human relationships and, "forced the early church to re-examine fundamental questions of personal identity, social obligation, and power and authority." [31] It demands no less of Christians today, albeit in very different social and cultural contexts. Have we the appetite for it? Can we model a way to relate that would change the world? The place to begin is with relationships within the Christian community itself and the way to begin is by being inclusive where we are now exclusive.

The second Pauline passage from Galatians is:

"For you were called to freedom, brothers and sisters; only do not use your freedom as an opportunity for self-indulgence, but through love become slaves to one another. For the whole law is summed up in a single commandment, 'You shall love your neighbour as yourself." (Gal.5:13-14)

Here Paul continues with his theme of radicalised relationship and picks up, as Jesus did, on the Golden Rule from Leviticus (19.18). This rule, McKenzie points out, was originally articulated in a situation where your neighbour was another Israelite. However, he adds that this did not stop either Jesus, Paul, or after them, Augustine, from appropriating, "a commandment that was initially situational" [32] into a universal principle. The template offered by Jesus of a love that is selfless, generous, compassionate, just and non-judgmental is Paul's "more excellent way" described in poetic prose in his first letter to the Corinthians (cf.1 Cor.12:31-14.1) [33] Without love, who we are as persons and how we are as Church counts as nothing. Brueggeman writes:

"The Bible is not concerned with right morality, right piety, or right doctrine. Rather it is concerned with faithful relationships between God and the people, between all the brothers and sisters in God's community, and between God's community and the world God has made. Faithful relationships of course can never be reduced to formulae but live always in the the free, risking exchange that belongs to covenanting.

It is this kind of exchange rather than fixed absolutes that is the stuff of biblical faith." [34]

So, using the scriptures in approaching moral siutations today is by no means straight-forward, but neglecting the scholarship, reflection and prayer needed to do so can never be an option. To navigate our modern moral morass, we have to exercise spiritual conscience. In addition, we have to be sensitive to scripture and tradition and, when necessary, counter popular culture. Most importantly, however, we have to place relationship at the heart of our concerns and engage with contemplative silence. Perhaps these two dimensions are what was missing in the past when, failing to balance our understanding, such as it was, with our compassion, heavy burdens were sometimes placed on people's shoulders (cf Mt.23:4). Let us learn from our past mistakes and bring them to that silence that can become occasion for our transformation.

Summary

Today we seem to lack solid moral ground and a means of arriving at moral agreement. Social debate is often emotionally charged and about an individual's "rights". But, in making responsible decisions, reason, compassion, experience and conscience, along with Christian tradition and sacred scripture can all play their part, if held in balance. Christianity also has to hold a creative tension between the interpretation of scripture and the compassion that Jesus showed. Furthermore, it needs to allow relationship play its part in shaping structure. Situated within the context of relationships, morality draws on the wisdom, experience and traditions of the community.

Conscience is the profound, personal, inner integrity we bring to bear on our moral decision making. It can be well-informed or ill-informed. Its exercise is no guarantee of a right decision and our culturally acquired conscience and our deeper spiritual conscience can be at odds with one another. We need too to explore unconscious motivations and our false self. To follow Jesus, we are called to examine all the assumptions and loyalties of our upbringing. Aware too of our individual and communal capacity for evil, we must open ourselves to transformation by God because we are not able to transform ourselves.

Western society, by and large, operates with a moral compass based upon the Ten Commandments. However, scholarship and discernment are needed in any appeal to the Old Testament on matters of morals. In the New Testament, Mark is more liberal than the stricter Matthew, Luke puts the focus on the poor and marginalised and John calls us to love. Overall though, to live a life worthy of the gospel is to observe the Golden Rule and to be selfless, tolerant, compassionate, just, generous in our giving and slow to judge. For Paul, this is the "excellent way" and he sees all of us as equal in Christ, regardless of social status. Relationship is always the key.

Quotation for Discussion

"....for a true exercise of conscience, particularly acquired conscience, there is a clear need for us to educate ourselves around moral issues and around our own unconscious motivations and our false self. Such education we will have to seek out ourselves because Western society which celebrates fame, wealth and power, will not offer it to us. It will instead affirm our false self and the absolute insatiability of our instinctive needs around security, esteem and control. The wise and healthy alternative according to Frey is harmonious living with the true self. As well as a consciously nurtured spiritual life, this requires deep self-knowledge, insightful comprehension of our real needs and shrewd understanding of options, consequences and the workings of our world. [8] "

Questions for Discussion

- What do you see as the greatest challenge Christians face as they try to live a life worthy of the gospel?
- Have you ever experienced a conflict betweem culturally acquired conscience and spiritual conscience and what were the things that helped you resolve that conflict?

1. "Eternal Music" by Veronica Littleton, publised by the author (2009) p33.
2. "The Cambridge Companion to Christian Ethics" Second Edition, edited by Robin Gill. Cambridge University Press 2012. Cf "Sexuality and religious ethics" by Robin Gill p271.
3. Ibid cf "Making Moral Decisions" by Rowan Williams p6ff.
4. "Vatican Council II" General editor, Austin Flannery O.P, Costello Publishing 1975. Cf "The Pastoral Constitution on the Church in the Modern World" par. 16, p916.
5. "Human Ground Spiritual Ground" by Kess Frey, Portal Books (2012) cf. p135.
6. Ibid p.135.
7. Ibid cf. p.136.
8. Ibid cf. p.138.
9. "Invitation to Love" by Thomas Keating in "Foundations for Centering Prayer and the Contemplative Life" by Continuum Publishing 2002. Cf p157. Also, "The Human Condition" by Thomas Keating. Paulist Press 1999. Cf p33.
10. Ibid p.231.
11. Ibid p.217.
12. Op. cit, "The Human Condition", cf p35.
13. "The Cambridge Companion to Christian Ethics" Second Edition, edited by Robin Gill. Cambridge University Press 2012. Cf "The Old Testament and Christian ethics" by John Rogerson. Cf p29.
14. Ibid cf. p31.
15. Ibid cf. p32-33.

16. See, for example, "Bible Babel" by Kristin Swenson. Harper Perennial (2011) cf p.75-77. Also "The Bible: The Biography" by Karen Armstrong, Atlantic Books (2007) cf p.179-181 and "The Rise and Fall of the Bible" by Timothy Beal, Mariner Books (2012) cf p.155-156.

17. "A Serious Way of Wondering" by Reynolds Price. Scribner (2003) p.125.

18. "The Cambridge Companion to Christian Ethics" Second Edition, edited by Robin Gill.
    Cambridge University Press 2012. Cf "The Gospels and Christian ethics" by Allen Verhey, cf p.42ff.

19. Ibid p.44.

20. Ibid p.45.

21. Reynolds Price, op. cit. cf p.48ff, for an extended reflection on the origins and applicability of the question, "What Would Jesus Do?"

22. Ibid cf. p.57 and "Bible Babel" by Kristin Swenson. Harper Perennial (2011) cf p.103-104.

23. "The Cambridge Companion to Christian Ethics" Second Edition, edited by Robin Gill.
    Cambridge University Press 2012. Cf "Sexuality and Religious ethics" by Robin Gill, cf p.283f. Also, Kristin Swenson op. cit. p115 quoting Stephen Prothero's "Religious Literacy: What Every American Needs to Know – and Doesn't", Harper (2007) p.182.

24. "The Wisdom Jesus" by Cynthia Bourgeault, p27. Shambhala (2008).

25. "Jesus" by Marcus Borg, HarperCollins (2008), p.218.

26. "How to Read the Bible" by Steven L. McKenzie. Oxford University Press (2009). Cf p.151 & p.154.

27. Ibid. cf p.148 & p.173.

28. "The Cambridge Companion to Christian Ethics" Second Edition, edited by Robin Gill.
    Cambridge University Press 2012. Cf "The Epistles and Christian Ethics" by Stephen C. Barton. P58.

29. Ibid p.59.

30. Ibid cf. p.56ff..

31. Ibid. p.62.

32. Steven L. McKenzie, op. cit. cf p.176.

33. Stephen C. Barton, op. cit. cf. p.57.

34. "The Bible Makes Sense" by Walter Brueggemann, published by St. Anthony Messenger Press (2003) p121.

13. The Issues of Our Times

Why is morality a religious concern? Why is so much suffering caused globally by humanity itself? Has the rejection of traditional family values caused suffering? Has extreme individualism weakened our sense of community? Is there any solution to poverty and hunger in our world? Does Christianity speak loudly enough on environmental and ecological issues? What could be possible if the major world religions were to find a common voice?

It is suffering which makes moral concern integral to religious belief. [1] So much of the suffering around us derives from human action or inaction and is, in theory therefore, avoidable. These are the sufferings that have their origins in such things as deceit, ignorance, cruelty, violence, selfishness, irresponsibility, injustice, prejudice, negative projection, lack of forgiveness, negligence, hatred and malice and they directly oppose and challenge the selfless, generous, compassionate, just and non-judgmental love discussed in the last chapter.

One of the realities of human existence that the garden story touches upon, as we saw, is the inevitability of the choices we have to make in life between good and evil. Each one of us has a capacity for evil and each one of us has the potential to consciously inflict gratuitous suffering on others. These are facts that we do not like to admit to. When we are faced with them our response is often one of vehement denial, or, if necessary, self-righteous justification.

Peter Abbott[2] quotes Alexander Solzhenitsyn to the effect that, "the line dividing good and evil cuts through the heart of every human being." Abbott then adds an assertion by Raymond Williams that, "evil as it is now widely used, is a deeply complacent idea. When we abstract and generalize it, we remove ourselves from any continuing action and deliberately break both response and connection." Abbott picks up on the word 'connection' here, reading it as that manifestation of evil resulting

Unbinding Christian Faith: Free to Be   Denis Gleeson

from the inability, or the failure, to exercise empathy towards others. This inability or failure is the consequence of our complacency around the presence of evil within us. It is the consequence of our denial of the darker depths of our own unconscious shadow material.

If, however, we were to loose the bonds that restrict the full expression of our religion and our trust in God and, at the same time, set aside our complacency and lack of empathy and acknowledge our own shadow, what are some of the issues that we could apply ourselves to? Where could we focus redirected energy? Well, this chapter offers a few suggestions. None of these suggestions is an attempt to pass judgment. They are simply some of the areas I believe Christianity should seek to be identified with over coming decades if we are to take the gospel seriously.

Supporting Family as a Value

Sexual morality has long been a contentious, controversial and multi-dimensional area of concern for Christianity in the Western World. To be a community worthy of the gospel, all of the issues involved need to be approached with the generosity, love and compassion just discussed in the last chapter. Abortion, understandably, but also contraception and homosexuality have tended to dominate the agenda. Here, however, I will not attempt to add to the literature on those topics. I will just touch briefly on one issue that I believe is neglected. It is marriage and the family. The Churches have supported the traditional family structure as the expression of healthy heterosexual relationship and the preferred environment for raising children. Yet, the Churches need to do even more because over the last five decades, or so, the traditional family has been progressively undermined with divorce, including 'no-fault' and unilateral divorce,[3] becoming ever more widespread, many couples choosing to cohabitate and children often being raised by a single parent.

These developments are generally supported by a current affairs and entertainment media that "probably constitutes the greatest single challenge parents face..." and is, "...diametrically opposed to traditional family values of stability, interdependence and fidelity." [4] These are the words of Gerard Hartmann, who is an Irish, internationally renowned, sports injury physical therapist based in Ireland. They echo those of Jim Wallis, a well-known American writer, broadcaster, theologian, lecturer and preacher. Wallis has observed that his audiences nod in agreement when he comments that, "parenting is a countercultural activity." [5] Two very different people, with contrasting professional backgrounds from opposite sides of the Atlantic, both of the opinion that in order to raise children today parents have to be prepared to resist the predominant social culture. Hartmann, in fact, adds that traditional family values as such are countercultural and that fits with my own experience having spent a lifetime in education.

Now, let me be clear, the traditional family structure will not always be without exceptions and relationship cannot always withstand the pressures that are exerted upon it by human shortcomings and modern society. However, the alternatives explored in the last few decades have caused harm and can be seen to have failed. Dan Browning says that although initially family changes were not seen to have negative consequences, that view began to change worldwide by the end of the 1980's. Now, academics in the fields of sociology, psychology and economics are, "much more willing to acknowledge that they have been damaging to large numbers of people."[6] Young women especially have suffered, often struggling alone to sustain a family in the absence of the father. And single motherhood has proven to be linked with poverty. Browning quotes research by Sara McLanahan and Gary Sandefur:

"Using sophisticated statistical tools to analyse the data of four national longitudinal studies in the USA, these authors have concluded that children raised outside

Unbinding Christian Faith: Free to Be   Denis Gleeson

biological two-parent families were twice as likely to do poorly in school, twice as likely to be single parents themselves, and one-and-a-half times more likely to have difficulties becoming permanently attached to the labour market. This was true when the data was controlled for race, education, age and place of residence of parents. Income reduced these disadvantages, but only by one-half. Stepfamilies had no advantage over single parents; both were less successful than intact biologically related families. This is so even though average income of stepfamilies is higher than for intact families, thereby challenging the idea that income rather than family structure is the chief predictor of child well-being" [7]

The conclusion Browning draws from this and from other research he examines is that, within society and within Christianity, there should be *"a presumption toward encouraging the formation and maintenance of intact families."* [8] He acknowledges exceptions but still advances his presumption as a guideline.

The enormous challenge for the Christian Churches, therefore, is to work for communal support of all families, irrespective of structure and without any hint of judgment whilst, at the same time, somehow finding its voice in unequivocal support of traditional family structure. This will call us to keep personal and communal relationship, rather than absolutes, at the heart of our concern for family and to try always to respond, with generosity and a creative compassion, to families finding themselves in vulnerable circumstances. In the absence of marital structure, it is not enough to rely on a simple promise of committed relationship. In the absence of personal and community support it is not enough to have social acceptance and state welfare. [9] Into the future, Christian communities must have family structure, especially traditional family structure, at their heart without any hint of judgement or exclusion. In these times of "exaggerated individualism," [10] it may seem strange to make an appeal to communities, Christian or otherwise. But that is exactly what I believe needs to be done and, if it is to be done effectively, Christian communities need to achieve levels of collaboration far beyond what now exists.

Individualism and Community

It is, perhaps, ironic that respect for the dignity, uniqueness and autonomy of the individual is grounded in Christianity, given the well-deserved ecclesial reputation for authoritarianism. Yet, despite occasional and appalling aberrations and departures [11] by Churches themselves, respect for individuals is one of the most important contributions of Christianity to Western society. Such has been its impact, however, that the balancing concept of community has been seriously undermined and eroded. This has certainly been the case in industrialised and urbanized countries. In fact, in the face of an individualism that is increasingly intolerant of any limits, parish structures and other Church communities have not been strong enough to resist and to retain perspective.

Individualism has almost become an absolute, and a moral absolute at that. Extreme individualism and a denial of interdependence and interconnectedness are at the root of arguments for abortion on demand, for example. Likewise, an appeal to the rights of the individual - which is often an emotional appeal and is sometimes supported by the ready assertion that no harm will be visited on anyone else - is sufficient for an argument to be put forward supporting voluntary euthanasia. Effects upon other people, attitudes towards life in society at large and the possibility of precedent are held as secondary, if not irrelevant, considerations. Life can be terminated because the fact that an individual desires it to be terminated is held to be the proper concern only of the person making the decision. Morality is precariously reduced to a matter of personal preference and one has to wonder how long the fabric of any society can withstand such exclusive self-interest. [12]

The reality is that every day of our lives, we are undeniably dependent upon others and are indebted to countless people whose names we will never know. We are dependent upon others for our food, our clothing, our electricity, our transport and everything else. Our society is premised upon an ever more complicated network of services which are made available to us by other people and to which we ourselves contribute. Who we are as individuals and the decisions we make as individuals matter to all those around us and has an impact upon their quality of life. My decisions about drink, drugs, sex, money and relationships do make a difference. Community does matter and shared values also matter. Community, in fact, validates the idea of individuality itself. Vardy and Grosch write:

> "… communitarian theory assumes that society is rather more than merely the sum of its parts. Moreover, it takes as its starting point the view that being an individual is only made possible if society recognizes the concept of individuality in the first place." [13]

The task of Christianity, then, is to continue to honour the uniqueness of the individual who is made in God's image, while at the same time providing experience of community and working models of community. Unless a creative tension can be held between individual freedoms, commitment to community and collective responsibility, self-interest dominates and the gross inequalities characterizing our world today will continue to develop unchallenged. [14] As before, selflessness, generosity and compassion are the gospel qualities that can nurture such creative tension for us. They call for Christian love. They require "agape" which is love without self-interest, a love which "calls individuals to a high level of personal responsibility." [15]

Even though our love is without self-interest, it profoundly forms and shapes us. Writing in the context of a feminist approach to medical ethics, Margaret Farley posits two elements integral to personhood. [16] They are autonomy and relationality. We become who we are not just because we are free to do so, she writes, but also because we can transcend ourselves by knowing and loving others, including God, and being known and loved in return. The centre of our being is found not just within us, it is also beyond us. To put it another way, we need others to become ourselves. To attain truly human individuality, we actually need community.

When pain and suffering are shared and love manifests as compassion, our response to the other person, or persons, "constitutes a bridge between ourselves and others." Love, as compassion, spans individuality and community. [17] Farley proposes a framework for medical ethics consisting of responsible and "structured discernment" [18] incorporating the concepts of compassionate respect and compassionate justice. This approach twinned with due accommodation of individuality and autonomy also offers us a model for building Christian communities.

Take the hospice movement as a case in point. [19] It has been exceptionally successful in helping people in great pain die with dignity. Then, there is L'Arche, the inspirational, international federation that provides homes, programmes and networks to help people with intellectual disability to live with dignity. Imagine a Christian Church with such sensitivity to the individual and such a highly developed sense of community that it could offer unlimited, non-judgmental support to all those struggling with issues such as abortion and voluntary euthanasia. The impact would be enormous and many proven precedents are already there. As a Christian response, debate is never enough. We must act and we must act by building upon what we already have. We have a long way to go.

Poverty and Hunger

Towards the end of chapter fourteen in the gospel of Luke, we come across some uncompromising words uttered by Jesus:

".... none of you can become my disciple if you do not give up all your possessions." (Lk. 14:33)

Now it is difficult to take anything from these words other than what they plainly say. We must give up all our possessions or, even allowing for some poetic emphasis, as good as all our possessions, if we are to follow Jesus. Peter McVerry offers some equally uncompromising words by way of commentary on this saying and those preceding it in Luke. He writes:

"The criteria for entering the community that Jesus established was: can you live in radical solidarity with others, in a relationship of equality, respect and dignity with everyone else in this community, including the poor, and thereby ensure that the needs of everyone, including the poor are met? If so, then you are welcome; if not, you may be a wonderful, hard-working, upright, morally just person – and God will love you for it – but a place in this community is not for you." [20]

Plain words again, and this time, I would suggest, no room for poetic emphasis. So, is the case being overstated? I do not think so. Jesus often made those who heard him feel uncomfortable and it should come as no surprise that as we listen to his words today, we too feel more than a measure of discomfort. We live in a world of dire poverty and obscene opulence. Children die of starvation every day whilst others waste food and struggle with obesity. Some are without the most rudimentary medical services when elsewhere fortunes are spent and made on cosmetic surgery. Millions live without adequate shelter and basic amenities when governments around them spend without hesitation on armaments and national security. We live in cities where the homeless lie on the streets at night outside bright, expensively lit financial offices. We endlessly repeat economic policies that are proven only to make rich people richer and those who are already poor even poorer.

The system, however, does not change, nor is it even consistently challenged, and all kinds of arguments are advanced to justify continuing with the status quo. It is the system that is the problem because, paradoxically, ordinary people repeatedly demonstrate the most extraordinary generosity in giving to charitable organizations. Collectively, however, the picture is different. The United Nations pledge by rich countries to dedicate 0.7% of gross national product to international aid has rarely been honoured by governments [21] complacently secure in the knowledge that the pledge will never become an election issue.

The truth is that those who endure poverty and hunger are simply not our collective priority, locally or globally. We have learned to shield ourselves from our discomfort. We do so, in part, by giving paltry percentages from national budgets but we do not persist with questions about the system. Alternatively, we succumb to collective paralysis and convince ourselves that the issues are just too complex and are on a scale that puts them beyond the tools of analysis we have available to us. Thomas Keating puts it forcefully:

"One cannot be a Christian without social concern. There is no reason why anyone should go hungry even for a day. Since the resources are there, why do millions continue to starve? The answer must be greed. It is, for most people, an unconscious greed stemming from a mindset that does not ask the right questions and a worldview that is out of date." [22]

As Keating says, we do have the resources. That is not in dispute. What has to be disputed is an economy of greed and a worldview that limits both our obligation to share and our responsibility for others. Consumerism encourages us to buy, throw away and buy again. When we purchase beyond our means, the economy goes into recession and then to take us out of recession, the drive begins to get us to resume spending again. We are asked to believe that the very policies and mind-sets that led us into crisis will lead us out of crisis. [23] This is "market fundamentalism," [24] says Wallis. And, the "obvious untruth" and the "unspoken message" [25] we are given by governments and the culture, adds McVerry, is that all this consumption will make us happy, will make us feel better about ourselves, will put us in control and will make us feel secure. But, our perceived needs are insatiable and in a culture of greed, enough is never going to be enough. [26] But, how can we set about changing such a culture?

The first step is to name what is happening around us and to question it openly. If we begin to do this individually we will soon find that others share our disquiet and our questions. It is hard to believe that we would not reach a tipping point, and change would not be inevitable, if every Christian and every Christian community on the planet began to question our collective response to poverty and hunger. It is hard to believe that change would not edge closer if every homily in every Christian service encouraged us to persist with our questioning. If is hard to believe that momentum for change would not build up if every advertisement appealing for charitable donation did not also appeal for economic justice.

Could the power brokers, the media and the policy makers ignore such a collective outcry? Maybe some of our brilliant economists would break ranks and step forward with new and imaginative economic policies and a vocabulary that included words like, solidarity, sharing, sustainability and redistribution? Maybe some of our political parties would set aside "tired" political ritual and shallow financial debate amounting only to "a little more of this and a little less of that" [27] and really inspire people by offering a vision of change for national and global economics. Small chance of any of this happening, you might be thinking and you are right, unless some of us take that first step and begin talking with disquieting passion. The Christian Churches need to put poverty and hunger on the agenda and make sure that they stay there.

A second step would be to take up Peter McVerry's [28] call to go beyond compassion to solidarity. Solidarity exceeds compassion in two ways, he says. It identifies with all people who are suffering irrespective of identity and all other circumstances and it is, "a radical commitment to do whatever is required to alleviate their suffering, at whatever cost to ourselves." [29] In other words, solidarity demands those gospel qualities of selflessness and non-judgmental generosity already identified and discussed. As Christians we have to be prepared to see our own lives change in recognition of the truth that to neglect others is to be ourselves diminished. [30] Jim Wallis puts this succinctly when he writes:

"Ultimately, the common good is our own good, and the best thing for all of us is the right thing for the least of us." [31]

This means that if to save lives in one part of our planet, economies and standards of living in another part of the planet have to retract then that is the price that Christian people are called to pay. Church leaders must not shrink from speaking this truth internationally and the rest of us must not shrink from speaking this truth to our immediate political representatives, though they will not want to hear it. In the world in which we live today, the politics of popularity and short-term advantage is the politics of irresponsibility.

This line of thinking brings us to our third and final step and it is redistribution. For individuals and nations who are super rich, of course, redistribution is a word that engenders fear. Yet, we have conveniently short memories. There was no problem with redistribution when it meant gold laden galleons sailing back to

Unbinding Christian Faith: Free to Be   Denis Gleeson

Europe, or the world's art and antiquities somehow ending up museums in London and Paris, or industrial empires being built with cheap labour, or cheap oil and minerals finding their way to the West. Clearly, precedence for redistribution does not have to be established. It can happen. However, instead of being the product of grasping greed, it must be planned, phased and compassionate redistribution aimed at meeting the needs of the poorest. This is actively encouraged in the scriptures.

In the Old Testament, in the Book of Leviticus, there was allowance for a year of jubilee every fifty years (cf. Lev.25:10). It was a year when debt was forgiven, people were released from slavery, property was returned to its original owners and families were reunited. [32] The magnanimity of jubilee finds resonance [33] in the life and teaching of Jesus. We see it when he reads from the scroll in his home town of Nazareth (cf Lk.4:18-19 and Is.61:1-2, 58:6). The passage he reads from Isaiah amounts to his mission statement and speaks of proclaiming, "the year of the Lord's favour."

We see it also in Jesus' constant theme of forgiveness. One example is his exchange of words with Simon the Pharisee over the anointing by the sinful woman. Jesus says that the woman has been forgiven much because she has loved much. It is during this incident that he tells the parable of the two debtors (cf. Lk.7:36-50). Both of them had their debt cancelled, with the one with the bigger debt having greater cause to love in response. It was no mere accident that the first Christian community adopted the lifestyle that is described in Acts and chose to hold things in common and give to everyone as they had need (cf. Acts 2:44-47). Can these passages of scripture inspire us today?

There was a brief but bright ray of hope for the world with the Jubilee 2000 movement that led to international agreement on the forgiveness of international debt. Promises made were not followed through in full, by any means, but as an initiative that some believe was largely driven by public opinion, it was an imaginative and heartening step in the direction of redistribution. Who knows what would result if Christian leaders and Christians en masse were to take up the call to revisit the issue of international debt forgiveness and persist with it?

To deal with the obscenities of hunger and poverty in our world, we do need, as Aidan Donaldson suggests, "a revolution of heart and mind that only the people of God can bring about by recalling the dangerous message of Jesus." [34] Let us not wait for someone else to take the lead. Let us open ourselves to this gospel inspired revolution of heart and mind straight away. We are the people of God, so let us name the need and deprivation that we see around us, challenge our economic culture, make the move from compassion to solidarity and take the first step towards redistribution by speaking loudly for international debt forgiveness.

The Environment

Another big issue for our day and another big topic for the exercise of various forms of denial is the environment. Though we have left it late, attitudes here are slowly beginning to change with scientists proclaiming the interconnectedness of things and acknowledging the reality of climate change. Ordinary people too, are much more prepared to accept as fact the negative effects of our human footprint.

Yet, we still resolutely believe we are really in charge of this world of ours and its future is ours to determine. Is this belief founded on anything more than our destructiveness? We cannot still a raging storm. We cannot change night into day. We cannot splash the red and orange glow of sunset across the sky. We cannot quiet the howl of the wind, or stop the rain or the snow from falling. Do we see ourselves in control because we can clear the rainforest, exhaust the fish stocks, or hunt lion and tiger to extinction? Are we not at our greatest when we seek collaboration with nature rather than control over it, when our relationship with nature is positive rather than negative? Rather than seeking to destroy, do we not excel when we ride the airstream in flight, harness the wind and the waterfall for electricity, farm organically, explore nature's own healing properties in medicine and copy nature's ingenious design in our engineering and architecture?

As we saw in the first chapter, part of the problem is that having removed the earth as centre of the universe, we filled the vacuum by effectively making ourselves not just the centre of the universe but, as Michael S. Northcott puts it, "the principal *locus* of consciousness and moral purposiveness in the cosmos." [35] Planet earth had been removed from centre stage and so too had God. Creation came to be seen as our possession, to do with as we wished, and God was positioned somewhere outside of creation looking on as an observer. This allowed us, and still allows, us to abuse creation with impunity and, freed of consequences, apply human ingenuity to the mindless, commercially motivated exploitation of our planet.

Northcott, however, explains that the Jewish and Christian traditions saw creation as gift for humanity and not in terms of an absolute possession devoid of responsibility. So, he writes:

> "The duty of respect for natural order arises, then, from original recognition that the world is not ours but God's and that in its design and order it displays not an independent order of being from human being, available for human remaking at will, but a shared realm of *created* being." [36]

For the Christian, the good news of Jesus is that both the meaning of life and of creation is situated in God. Both are embraced by God's love in the mystery of the incarnation and the kingdom, the new creation, as has been said, is both existing reality and developmental possibility. As Littleton expresses it, the love that Jesus reveals is, "the love that pervades the cosmos" and it is also the love that is yet to come to completion in humanity. [37]

Jesus is the Christ and the Christ is a cosmic Christ. Creation was fashioned in love and it was fashioned for love and it is through love that creation will move towards its fullness.

Just as humanity experiences aloneness and incompleteness without God, so, creation in its entirety is incomplete without God, as it were. Both humanity and creation, therefore, are embraced in the incarnation. The whole of creation evolves towards completion by means of its relationship with God. The proof that this completion is not an empty promise is found in the resurrection of Christ, and it is constantly being brought to reality by the power of the Spirit. Northcott adds: "There can be no more solemn and morally weighty conception of the moral value of created order than this incarnational tradition." [38]

Is it not extraordinary then, that the Christian Churches have been so relatively silent on environmental issues and climate change? How can it be that our understanding of the mystery of the incarnation itself is so greatly impoverished when that mystery is at the very heart of Christianity? How is it possible for a Christian not to see the sacredness of all that surrounds us? How can we not champion protection of the environment, ecological responsibility and positive action in response to environmental degradation, ecological interference and climate change?

Where this latter is concerned, it is becoming increasingly clear that it is inextricably tied to matters concerning global peace and justice. If climate change continues to evolve into climate crisis, no one can doubt that it will be poor people and poor countries that will suffer most and that it will be rich people and rich countries that will be best insulated. Now is the time for Christians to speak and to take action. With lives at stake, wealthy people, governments, industries and corporations have to be asked to respond with courage and new heights of generosity rather than pursue self-interested, short-term, protectionist policies. Christian leaders are well placed to offer this challenge and are obliged by the gospel to do so in unambiguous terms. What a contribution to humanity this creative challenge can be and now is the time to make it - while levels of climate change still allow us to speak to each other with a measure of calm and some objectivity. It will be too late when, as is most likely, further disasters occur, levels of tension arise over precious resources of food, water and fuel and the finger of angry accusation is raised.

The encyclical letter of Pope Francis, "Laudato Si' " is a timely and magnificent articulation of the challenge Christians can offer the global community on all aspects of the ecological crisis. It calls for an international, interdisciplinary dialogue and advances an approach that integrates social, political, economical and technological strategies. In doing this, the Pope appeals to our integrity and generosity, arguing that ecological questions are also social questions and questions of justice and, therefore, we must position ourselves, "...so as to hear both the cry of the earth and the cry of the poor." [(39)]

Finally, the combined reports of the Intergovernmental Panel on Climate Change (IPCC) provide us with a good map of the way forward and it is on these reports and the human cost of further hesitancy that Christians must focus. The values of the gospel may be our motivation but the IPCC provides us with a language and a scientific fact-file that should get the ear of those of us not moved either by the words of Jesus or, the seriousness of the situation in which we find ourselves.

Inter-Religious Dialogue

At this moment in time, it may seem somewhat fanciful to suggest that the great religions of the world could speak with one voice on any of the issues discussed in this chapter, or, on any issue at all. As is the case with inter-denominational relationships within Christianity, inter-religious relationships have a sad and shameful history even in our own times, so much so that dialogue between the major religions, and with the major religions, is one of the great contemporary moral demands. We have seen the dark and ugly face of the alternative to this, even to the extent of the most obscene violence, shockingly justified by fundamentalist religious stances. But, of course, religion itself is not the problem. We are the problem. It is time, therefore, for the great faiths to exercise leadership and exploit the benefit of inter-religious dialogue on our most serious issues. Acknowledgment of Ultimate Reality[40], in whatever form it takes, lays down a foundation for mutual respect and is a source of inestimable creativity and goodness for humanity.

In what was to prove to be a tragically fateful journey, Thomas Merton, with the permission of his Abbot, set out in October 1968 to attend a conference of Asian monastic orders. On his journey, he had the following to say during a brief informal address at another conference he attended in Calcutta. This particular conference was to promote understanding among the world's religions. Merton said:

> "...the deepest level of communication is not communication, but communion. It is wordless. It is beyond words, and it is beyond speech, and it is beyond concept. Not that we discover a new unity. We discover an older unity. My dear brothers, we are already one. But we imagine that we are not. And what we have to recover is our original unity. What we have to be is what we are." [41]

Specifically, Merton was speaking of monastic life but his words beg application not just to monks, but to all spiritual searchers and to all human beings. We are one in our humanity and we are one in our spiritual depths. At our most profound level of existence we share a unity that needs to be proclaimed only because of our willingness to allow diversity and difference obscure it. It is so obvious that our common humanity is its own moral imperative, but as we look around us we can see that that frequently fails to register with us. Our world order is almost universally premised upon injustice, inequality and failure in relationship.

Why is it that good religious people so often fail to communicate at all with each other, never mind carry their communication to communion? Are we so insecure in our own religious identity that we have to assert it aggressively against all others? Are our concepts of the divine and of mystery so impoverished that they can bear only familiar, traditional and sometimes tired interpretations? Have we so neglected our psychologically rich heritage of spiritualities that we are oblivious to the unconscious sources of our motivation and blind to the sharp perspective offered by humility?

Merton maintained that he would be a better Catholic if he could affirm the truth in other denominations and religions and take it further. However, he rejects a carelessly accepting, freely accorded, unthinking tolerance of everything. There are, indeed, many things, he says, that cannot be mutually affirmed and accepted. He cautions that the first step, though, is always to find the things that can be accepted. Otherwise, we are much the poorer.

> "If I affirm myself as a Catholic merely by denying all
> that is Muslim, Jewish, Protestant, Hindu, Buddhist,
> etc., in the end I will find that there is not much left for
> me to affirm as a Catholic: and certainly not much
> breath of the Spirit with which to affirm it."[42]

Quoting from "The Asian Journal of Thomas Merton", King [43] notes that Merton calls for "scrupulous respect for important differences". Therefore, to avoid pointless and damaging debate, there must be clarity around those areas about which there is no understanding or agreement. We must respectfully agree to disagree.

Drawing on Richard Niebuhr's ideas on dialogue, King does not hesitate to add to what Merton has to say. He points out that,

"True dialogue involves self-disclosure, openness, vulnerability, risk and willingness to change." [44] So, as with contemplative practice and social action, true inter-religious dialogue results in the transformation of those who are engaged in the dialogue. Inter-religious dialogue is by no means just a matter of an abstract sharing of theological and religious concepts. It is, in fact, based on a common set of social values. King [45] sees this cross-cultural and inter-religious dynamic as a "movement towards a universal community of responsibility". This movement finds expression as the major religions take up involvement with contemporary global issues.

Just imagine what an influence for good such a universal community of responsibility could be! Free, hopefully, of all political wrangling, transparent in its procedures, calm and prayerful in its deliberations and intent only on contributing to the common good, it could speak with authority on a wide range of global issues. In unparalleled fashion, it could be a balanced voice on the environment and a calmly credible voice on international economic injustice. It could challenge governments with integrity when basic human rights were denied. On behalf of the weak, it could speak the truth to the powerful. It could be an advocate for the poor, the hungry and the excluded. Where there was conflict, it could appeal for peace and sanity. When natural disaster struck, it could be a conduit for reliable local information and help to focus aid effectively and without agenda. Its very existence could model dialogue, empathy, compassion and celebration of diversity. It could witness powerfully to an alternative to political posturing and aggression. Finally, as a community enabled by prayer to rise above conceptual differences, it could evoke the depth dimension of the human person. In response to Ultimate Reality, it could call all of us to become more than we are and more than we allow ourselves to be.

The world's major religions could speak together because together it is they who witness to the existence and experience of

Ultimate Reality. [46] However this Ultimate Reality may be named, faith and religious practice are a response to it, though it is also experienced through nature, the arts, other human beings, self-transcendence and the selflessness of service. Actual denial of Ultimate Reality is, in fact, the embrace of illusion and a further cause of human suffering. This is because a sure foundation for all human growth, development, potential and transcendence is to be discovered only in Ultimate Reality. But, we do not always acknowledge this. Instead, we consistently rely on our own limited abilities and feeble efforts.

This chapter began with the issue of religion and suffering and I want to return to that issue as I bring the chapter to a close. Margaret A. Farley says that:

> "All major world religions have endured as world religions, at least in part, because they have had something to say in response to the large questions in people's lives, including the question of suffering." [47]

In the face of so much global suffering, it is time now for some of these world religions to respond to large questions together. Such response is urgently required and needs to be international, local and individual. It is the responsibility not just of those in religious leadership. It is the responsibility of each and every person who professes religious belief and so is the responsibility of all Christians.

Summary

It is suffering which makes morality a religious concern because so much suffering is generated by humanity itself. This, in part, is because in choosing between good and evil, we can deny our own capacity for evil. If, however, we were to honestly accept our capacity for evil and at the same time entrust our lives totally to God, what contemporary moral issues would merit priority?

Supporting Family as a Value: The traditional family has been under pressure in recent decades, with modern culture advancing different kinds of family variation and experiencing rises in divorce and separation. In all families parenting has also become, in many respects, a struggle against culture. Academics now acknowledge this and the harm that has been caused. The challenge for Christianity is to unequivocally support every type of family while finding proactive ways to promote, non-judgmentally, the traditional family.

Individualism and Community: Christianity always fostered the value and uniqueness of the individual. Today, however, an extreme, absolute individualism tends to undermine the concept of community with moral decisions, that affect everyone, being reduced to personal preference and an individual's assumed rights. It is the community, however, which recognises individuality in the first place. Christianity must honour both the individual and the community with a love that respects autonomy and is grounded in the relational. Add compassionate respect and compassionate justice and we have a model for building up Christian communities that will be relevant and will make a difference.

Poverty and Hunger: The uncompromising call of the gospel to treat all others with respect and to meet the needs of the poor makes for uncomfortable reading. This is all the more so as we live in a world where gross inequality and injustice, along with appalling excess are, in effect, supported by the global economic system. Christianity must consistently question rampant consumerism and an economy based upon greed. The *first step* is to articulate our questions very clearly and put poverty and hunger on the agenda. The *second step* is to combine solidarity with compassion and speak our readiness to accept change in our own lives and in our standards of living. The *third step* is to face the issue of redistribution. The generosity and magnanimity we hear Jesus talking of in the gospel could begin to find contemporary expression in following through on the Jubilee 2000 movement that led to international agreement on the forgiveness of international debt.

The Environment: Attitudes are slowly beginning to alter and there is greater acceptance of the human contribution to climate change. We have had a very negative effect on our planet. We have also shown that we can learn from nature and sometimes harness natural forces creatively. Yet, we are still capable of unthinking abuse, disastrous short-sightedness and commercial exploitation. Respect for creation, however, is strongly present in Judaism and also in a very particular way in the Christian mysteries of the incarnation and the resurrection. It is strange, so, that the Christian Churches have been so relatively silent on climate change and even more so when we consider the link with matters concerning global peace and justice. We must find our voice on these issues. "Laudato Si' " is a magnificent beginning.

Inter-Religious Dialogue: Acknowledgment of Ultimate Reality is a source of inestimable creativity and goodness for human kind. We are one in our humanity and one in our spiritual depths. The great religions need to be confident in their own identity, secure in the knowledge that in exploring truth we draw closer to each other. Bound by contemplation and united in social action, imagine what a voice for good the major religions could be? There is so much suffering in the world and it is now the responsibility of all who hold religious belief to join together to try to address that suffering.

Quotation for Discussion

"We live in a world of dire poverty and obscene opulence. Children die of starvation every day whilst others waste food and

struggle with obesity. Some are without the most rudimentary medical services when elsewhere fortunes are spent and made on cosmetic surgery. Millions live without adequate shelter and basic amenities when governments around them spend without hesitation on armaments and national security. We live in cities where the homeless lie on the streets at night outside bright and expensively lit financial offices. We endlessly repeat economic policies that are proven only to make rich people richer and those who are already poor even poorer. The system, however, does not change, nor is it even consistently challenged, and all kinds of arguments are advanced to justify continuing with the status quo."

Questions for Discussion

- What are the social issues that you are passionate about and what is it that feeds your passion?
- What priorities do you think Christians should have in a world where traditional family values are threatened, the demands of individualism abound, the gap between rich and poor grows daily, our planet is abused and religion is often fundamentalist and a source of division?

1. "Compassionate Respect" by Margaret A. Farley, Paulist Press (2002). Cf p.45.
2. "Values & Ethics" edited by Harry Bohan and Gerard Kennedy. Céifin Conference Papers published by Veritas (2003). Cf "A Framework for a New Reality: 2" by Peter Abbott, p109.
3. "The Cambridge Companion to Christian Ethics" Second Edition, edited by Robin Gill. Cambridge University Press 2012. Cf "World Family Trends" by Dan Browning, cf p.260.
4. "Values & Ethics" edited by Harry Bohan and Gerard Kennedy. Céifin Conference Papers published by Veritas (2003). Cf "Why Do We Need Champions?" by Gerard Hartmann, p19.

5. "Rediscovering Values" by Jim Wallis, Howard Books (2011) p.164.
6. Op. cit. Dan Browning p.257.
7. Ibid. p.258.
8. Ibid. p.260.
9. Ibid. cf p.261.
10. "Compassionate Respect" by Margaret A. Farley, Paulist Press (2002) p.26.
11. Ibid. cf. p.50-p.51.
12. "The Puzzle of Ethics" by Peter Vardy and Paul Grosch cf. comment on Alasdair MacIntyre and emotivism and contemporary culture, p.92.
13. Ibid. p.135.
14. Ibid. cf p.203.
15. Ibid. p.128.
16. "Compassionate Respect" by Margaret A. Farley, Paulist Press (2002). Cf p.37.
17. Ibid. p.65 and p.61. Cf Farley's reference to Nussbaum's metaphor of the bridge.
18. Ibid. cf. p.42-p.43.
19. Vardy and Grosch op. cit. cf p.162.
20. "Jesus social revolutionary" by Peter McVerry. Veritas (2008) p.79.
21. Cf http://www.unmillenniumproject.org/press/07.htm
22. "Invitation to Love" by Thomas Keating in "Foundations for Centering Prayer and the Contemplative Life" by Continuum Publishing 2002. p231-232.
23. Jim Wallis op. cit. cf. p.4
24. Ibid. p.3.
25. Peter McVerry, op. cit. p133.
26. Jim Wallis op. cit. cf p.42.
27. "The Cambridge Companion to Christian Ethics" Second Edition, edited by Robin Gill.
    Cambridge University Press 2012. Cf "Business, economics and Christian ethics", by Max L. Stackhouse with David W. Miller. p.240.
28. Peter McVerry, op. cit. p.82ff.
29. Ibid p.83.
30. Ibid. cf. p.83.
31. Jim Wallis op. cit. p.91-92.
32. Ibid p.93ff.
33. "Simply Jesus" by Tom Wright. SPCK (2011) cf. p.76-82 and "Jesus" by Marcus Borg, HarperCollins (2008), cf. p.202.
34. "Come Follow Me: Recalling the Dangerous Memory of Jesus and the Church Today" by Aidan Donaldson. Columba Press (2012) p.138.

35. "The Cambridge Companion to Christian Ethics" Second Edition, edited by Robin Gill. Cambridge University Press 2012. Cf "Ecology and Christian ethics" by Michael S. Northcott, p.234.
36. Ibid p.234.
37. "Eternal Music" by Veronica Littleton, publised by the author (2009) p73.
38. Northcott, Op. cit. p.235.
39. "Laudato Si' " encyclical letter of Pope Francis. Veritas Publications 2015, par 49.
40. Cf. "Points of Agreement" concerning spirituality among the world religious traditions: Snowmass Interreligious Conference (1984) http://api.ning.com/files/daDseKHUDJFV8XU05gXXxaA426F8QUBCJ SYS3c7NdMdyQTDliRI-kxHX8SLW7UJsxK2-ocCO9M5plksuu
41. Cf. "Thomas Merton and Thich Nhat Hanh" by Robert H. King. Continuum (2003) cf. p. 114. The quote is from "The Asian Journal of Thomas Merton," edited by Naomi Burton, Brother Patrick Hart and James Laughlin. New Directions (1975) cf. p.308.
42. "Conjectures of a Guilty Bystander" by Thomas Merton. Image Books (1989) p.144.
43. Robert H. King. Op. cit. p117. The quote is from "The Asian Journal of Thomas Merton" p.316.
44. Ibid. p.37.
45. Ibid. cf. p.37-38.
46. Cf. for this section, "Points of Agreement" op. cit.
47. "Compassionate Respect" by Margaret A. Farley, Paulist Press (2002). p.45.

14. The Church of the Future

What kind of Church do we need for the future? What are the gospel fundamentals we must build upon? Why will relationships be a defining characteristic? Why will our personal experience be so central? What offers us hope? Can the Church really be political? How can we be transformed?

It is no surprise that in trying to conjure up an image of the ideal Church or ideal Christian community, we invariably go back to this familiar passage from the Acts of the Apostles:

> "They devoted themselves to the apostles' teaching and fellowship, to the breaking of bread and the prayers. Awe came upon everyone, because many wonders and signs were being done by the apostles. All who believed were together and had all things in common; they would sell their possessions and goods and distribute the proceeds to all, as any had need. Day by day, as they spent much time together in the temple, they broke bread at home and ate their food with glad and generous hearts, praising God and having the goodwill of all the people. And day by day the Lord added to their number those who were being saved." (Acts 2:42-47)

Driven by the Spirit, still in the grip of first fervour and buoyed by the experience and excitement of a new togetherness, the first Christians did indeed enjoy a honeymoon period. Soon enough though, as the Acts of the Apostles tells us, they faced the strain of tension and disagreement from within the community itself and the threat of persecution from without. Similarly today, we may think that we know what we need to do to accompany one another on the journey but being open and responsive to the promptings of the Spirit always remains a challenge. Too easily, we become embroiled in pointless squabbles and distract ourselves from dealing with our own failings by projecting anger onto those who are critical of Christianity from the outside. We are also more than accomplished, as we have seen in these pages, at wrapping ourselves up in all kinds of theological, scriptural, spiritual, moral and psychological bonds. We are our own worst enemies.

The contemporary Church is in crisis and Pope Francis is in no doubt as to the sources and effects of this crisis. [1] Among the sources he mentions there are many that have already been alluded to: the lack of dialogue within the family; negative media influences; moral relativism; consumerism; the neglect of the poor; unwelcoming Church institutions and disregard for the mystical and the contemplative. Among the effects he mentions are disillusionment and, most worryingly, a breakdown in passing on the faith to children and young people. If then, we are to begin to address all of this, what kind of Church do we need? What might the Church of the future look like?

A Gospel Church

The Church has always been a gospel Church but it has not always been overtly so and it certainly has not always been emphatically so. There were times when dogma, doctrine and liturgy seemed to take precedence. Pope Francis comments:

> "In some people we see an ostentatious preoccupation for the liturgy, for doctrine and for the Church's prestige, but without any concern that the Gospel have a real impact on God's faithful people and the concrete needs of the present time. In this way, the life of the Church turns into a museum piece or something which is the property of a select few." [2]

In the Church of the future, therefore, and in all Christian communities of the future, we must look first to the gospel in all that we do. The gospel must be our constant concern. In our relationship with Jesus and our experience of him, prayerful reflection on the gospel must be our primary point of reference. Contemplation of the words and actions of Jesus are an invitation to the Spirit and a response to the Father because the meaning of the gospel message of Jesus is that God is to be found in all of life and the fullness of life is to be found in God.

A focus on the gospel actively nurtures our relationship with Jesus, the incarnation of the Divine. It reminds us that God loves us unconditionally and totally beyond our imagining and that although nothing we can do, or fail to do, will change that love, God does implore us to respond to Divine love by loving each other and treating each other justly. These are the Christian fundamentals, but they remain fundamentals that we struggle with and somehow fail to comprehend. The task of the Christian community, is to keep affirming them and reminding us of them and encouraging us in our response. What we do not need is a Christian community that judges, or condemns, or excludes. That was not the way of Jesus in the gospel, which is not to say that Jesus was at all afraid to speak the truth, and speak it plainly, when there was need to do so.

Jesus consistently and courageously challenged the religious authorities of his day when they allowed the rules and ritual of the temple to exclude and obscure the reality of God's love for his people. The High Priests had made access to God conditional and placed it only within reach of the rich and the privileged. The poor were effectively excluded. Citing the account of the cleansing of the temple in Matthew, Aidan Donaldson[3] notes that in the verse immediately after the incident the blind and the lame come to Jesus for healing in the now cleansed temple (cf. Mt:21.14) and Jesus cures them. The function of the temple has been restored. It is once again a place for God's people, especially the poorest of the poor, to be welcomed by God's mercy and healing power.

Two thousand years later, can we say unequivocally that our places of worship are welcoming of the poorest of the poor? Have we not recreated something akin to the temple worship that so angered Jesus, as a means of keeping his radical gospel message at a safe distance? [4] Having posed this question, Donaldson answers with a quote from Peter McVerry:

"Today, as in the time of Jesus, sacred space is safely separated from those who makes us uncomfortable, the poor, the unwanted, the despised. Today, as in the time of Jesus, we access God through the priests, not the poor. We have removed God from our streets, our prisons, from our hostels and our drug clinics, from trailers at the side of the road – and we have locked God safely up in our tabernacles." [5]

For the Church to truly be a gospel Church, we cannot forget the poor and they are all around us. We do not have to look very far. Remembering the poor is, "the key criterion of authenticity" says Pope Francis [6] noting that this is the sole instruction the apostles give to Paul and Barnabas as they send them to preach the gospel to the Gentiles (cf. Gal.2:10). The good news comes in tandem with a concern for the poor and can only be embraced along with a concern for the poor. It was, in fact, this very concern that inspired the newly elected Pope to choose the name Francis and signal his desire for, "a Church which is poor and for the poor." [7] A gospel Church can be nothing other than this.

A Relational Church

In the last supper narrative in John's gospel, Jesus says:

"I give you a new commandment, that you love one another. Just as I have loved you, you should also love one another. By this everyone will know that you are my disciples, if you have love for one another." (Jn.13:35)

The manner in which we treat each other is, as we have seen, a key theme in both the Old Testament and the New Testament. So, what is new about this commandment of Jesus? Surely it is that Jesus himself has underlined for us how we are to love. We are to love as he loved. We are to love unconditionally, generously, totally. We are to love with a love that radiates from the Father who seeks us out to breathe vitality and warmth into all of life. Just as the love of Jesus did, this love will coax us, and everyone we encounter, into growth and into the fullness of humanity. It is the love that will be the defining stamp of Christian community and the characteristic by which Christians are known.

Christian community is about relationships, as difficult and perplexing as they always are. Relationships are the stuff of community, the very means by which community forms and they are also the measure of that formation. This "complex interweaving of personal relationships" [8] describing human interaction is the way that God attracts us. It is the reason that the good news is for all people and the reason that Church has to be a place "where everyone can feel welcomed, loved, forgiven and encouraged to live the life of the Gospel." [9]

There is no room for exclusion within Christian community, and dare I say it, there is no room for hierarchy that is self-important. Christian leadership is about service (cf. Mt.20:24-28), washing the feet of others (cf. Jn.13:12-15) and being prepared even to lay down one's life for those who are served (cf. Jn.10:11-18). Just as all Christians are called to serve, therefore, all Christians are called to leadership. Unfortunately, in the Roman Catholic Church, we have tended to confuse and associate leadership, with authority and power, and with an exclusively male clergy. This has been the case despite countless, outstanding examples of non-clerical, lay, male and female leadership down through the centuries.

If this kind of exclusion continues, relationships within the Church of the future will not be well served. The laity, and particularly women, must be afforded full participation in the life and activities of the Church. This means they must be given real responsibility and genuinely involved in decision making at local, national and international levels. As this happens, it might allow, for example, a different kind of discussion around the issue of the ordination of women. That discussion could then more credibly take place on the role and nature of priesthood itself rather than on that of the much wider matter of access to full participation in the life of the Church. If women are to be admitted to ordination, it has to be on the basis of an evolution and transformation in our understanding of the purpose and expression of the sacrament, rather than as an admission to power and an extension of clericalism.

To use Mark Patrick Hederman's memorable image, [10] we must learn to dance with the dinosaur - that incredibly successful institution which is the Church - for this kind of change to come about. This dance is the dance of relationship. It is the dance of love and love is dynamic, it is never static. It constantly calls us to respond, to grow, to be more than we presently are. The dance of loving relationship and the dialogue of love, are what the Church is always about. Hederman writes: "The only thing that endures is love. Love began the Church and love is her only end." [11] A Christian community, which is robustly relational, with open communication and commitment to dialogue and which, of course, relates to God in sacrament and prayer, has the means to resolve any difficulty and is assured of a future.

An Experiential Church

A relational Church is also an experiential Church, a Church where there is genuine experience of community. It is experienced in the warmth of welcome received, the instant sense of inclusion, the patience and understanding shown, the respect that is given. Many local parishes are a focus for all kinds of community activity and community support, with facilities for young people, attention to the needs of the elderly and referral provided for an array of social,

Unbinding Christian Faith: Free to Be   Denis Gleeson

spiritual and professional services available in the parish and in the larger locality. All of this builds a sense of community. However, community building is hard work and has to be consciously undertaken and adequately resourced. In addition, it is always necessary to be aware that there will be those will feel isolated and reaching out to them sometimes presents a challenge. When Zacchaeus, a despised tax collector, looked on from the branches of the sycamore tree, he needed an invitation. The encounter he was to experience with Jesus changed his life (cf. Lk: 19.1-10)

So, in the local and the wider Christian community, concern is about people and not about procedure, or liturgy, or dogma, or anything else. This is precisely because Christianity itself is essentially about experiencing and relating to a person, the person of Jesus Christ. Pope Francis says that he never tires of repeating these words of his predecessor, Benedict XVI:

> "Being a Christian is not the result of an ethical choice or a lofty idea, but the encounter with an event, a person, which gives life a new horizon and a decisive direction." [12]

Asked what he, or she, believes in, a Christian's reply has to be that they believe in, they trust in, the person of Jesus. Belief in creed and Church only follow. As Mark Patrick Hederman[13] puts it, written words and dogmatic formulae are "secondary theology." That "inexpressible mystery" which is the person of Jesus, experienced in silence within oneself but also with and through other persons in the Christian community, is "primary theology." Hederman quotes the great Karl Rahner:

> "In the Spirit of God all of us 'know' something more simple, more true and more real than we can know or express at the level of our theological concepts."

Good liturgy facilitates this knowing. It accommodates a conscious encounter with Jesus that is pure gift and has the potential to change one's experience of life. This is why the better celebration of Eucharist always presents a challenge and never succumbs to dull routine. It offers the experience of recognizing Jesus, having our eyes opened and having our hearts burn within us (cf Lk: 24.13-35). So, we break open the word and we break the bread. There is song as well as silence. There are moments of solitary reflection, there is solemnity and there is joy and there is inclusive fellowship. Pope Francis says that what we have to experience in the Eucharist, "is not a prize for the perfect but a powerful medicine and nourishment for the weak." [14]

Perhaps, what the world needs more than anything else at the moment is hope and hope is precisely what the eucharist offers us. Our memory in breaking the bread is the memory of a community participating in a cosmic event, an event without boundaries of time or place, the paschal mystery of Christ. This is the event in which the hope of humanity lies. Our participation, therefore, is an experience of hope not just for the Christian community. It is hope for humankind and for all of creation.

Our hope cannot be a vague, ill-defined hope. We cannot sit back and wait for divine intervention. God takes action in the world through us and, as ever, the first to whom we offer hope have to be the poor. The poor remain the yardstick of our authenticity and integrity. In offering them hope by standing with them, by listening to them, by hearing of their suffering and learning from their wisdom, we "find Christ in them." [15] Then, we are ourselves evangelized by the poor and our own experience becomes an experience of hope. Lifeless, spectator liturgies do not change lives. That is why so many people find attendance at Church on Sunday difficult. But, lives are changed and enriched when liturgy is an experience of the person of Jesus Christ, the experience of genuine Christian community, and the joyous experience of hope.

A Vocal Church

The Church of the future has to be a vocal Church. Unfortunately, at present, the voice of the Church seems to be associated more with matters of sexual morality rather than with the advance of social justice, global economic equality, peace, environmental sustainability, or even authentic contemporary spirituality. Some of the reasons for this are outside of the control of Church. For example, the communications media can at times be selective in what is covered and can be disinterested in, or dismissive of, religious views that are expressed and the Church leaders who express them. However, sometimes the clarity of the Church's expression of the Gospel message itself and the commitment to have it heard are also open to question.

Furthermore, there is a cultural perception in Western societies that it is fine for the Church to be seen but its voice should not be heard, as that could be construed as trespassing on political ground. There is a degree of hypocrisy in this view, because the voice of the Church and the Christian community is lauded in so far as it is viewed as contributing to social stability, the rule of law and the maintenance of the status quo. But when the Church is perceived to step outside these parameters there is strong, negative reaction. Yet, to preach the Gospel, the Church must be prophetic, so must it not also be, to some degree, political? Democracy and freedom of speech are for everyone.

The word "prophetic" is, I think, a key word here, for most of us today, would probably support the appropriate separation of Church and State on the basis of difference of function. The function of the Church is to proclaim the Good News, celebrate in the sacraments the gift of Christ's healing and transformational presence and attempt to model Christian community and the new creation. The function of the State is to provide for and protect all of its people, irrespective of race, colour, class or creed and to pursue internal and international relations that will achieve this.

Where the Church and individual Christians are entitled to be properly prophetic is where policies pursued or systems created are unjust, foster inequality, are abusive of the dignity and basic rights of people or are destructive of the environment and the planet on which we live. But, as we know very well from the scriptures, the prophetic voice is rarely accorded a positive reception.

I have already quoted, in chapter nine, Peter McVerry's [16] insistence that we actually require a "revolution" in our global social, economic and political structures, if the Christian vision for a new world order is to unfold. We may recall that this insistence was accompanied by an unambiguous warning. It was a warning that any initiatives, or words of Christians, that are designed to bring about such a revolution would attract very strong reaction. Around the world, in fact, we have seen, and continue to see, violent and even murderous opposition.

A vocal Church, as a consequence, needs to be a Church that has its eyes wide open and cannot be naïve about the way the world operates. Jesus was certainly not naïve and warns us in the Beatitudes that if we are genuinely witnessing to the Gospel by the way we live, then we can expect extreme treatment.

> "Blessed are you when people revile you and persecute you and utter all kinds of evil against you falsely on my account. Rejoice and be glad, for your reward is great in heaven, for in the same way they persecuted the prophets who were before you." (Mt: 5.11-12)

Strong criticism of the Church is sometimes deserved, but it is a different matter when that criticism results from an entirely appropriate assertion of gospel values. This latter criticism, no matter how sustained and strong it may be, is actually affirmation that the uncomfortable truth of the gospel, especially in relation to the poor and marginalized, is being proclaimed. If Christians are to be deemed political for holding to their values and voting with integrity and according to spiritual conscience, then "political" they must be.

Commenting on what constitutes a "healthy pluralism", Pope Francis says that it "does not entail privatising religions in an attempt to reduce them to the quiet obscurity of the individual's conscience or to relegate them to the enclosed precincts of churches, synagogues or mosques." [17] That would be tantamount to discrimination against religion he maintains, and he adds that the respect due to those who do not believe should not be used to impose silence on those who do. We see examples of this kind of discrimination when an employee is prevented from wearing a small cross around her neck at work or objection is raised to having a crib in a public space at Christmas. If simple things like these provoke hostile reaction then we can be sure that when the Church is vocal on social issues there will be hostile reaction also. For that, the Church of the future must be prepared.

A Transformational Church

The unconditional love of God demands a response from each one of us daily. It also demands a response from the Christian community. As we saw in the chapter on centering prayer, to respond to God's love is to open ourselves to change and, ultimately, to personal transformation, in silence, by God. There are institutional changes that we need to address also and it is not difficult to identify some of the areas within the Church that are in need of transformation.

The safeguarding of children is one area where a painful transformation has already taken place and is continuing. Sexual abuse and other forms of abuse occur when a lack of respect for the person is combined with an inappropriate use of power. As we now know, the results can be catastrophic, especially when visited upon those who are young and very vulnerable. In the recent past, many shocking incidents of abuse within the Church have come to light around the world and the question remains as to how profoundly lessons have been learned.

Initial Church reaction to incidents of abuse was not good, to put it mildly. The survival instincts of the institution came to the fore and it took too long for Church officials to make the survivors of abuse their primary concern. Since then, progress has certainly been made and new procedures for safeguarding children are in place and appear to be working as they should. Wider issues around treating people with respect and exercising power appropriately have to remain an everyday concern as well, however, for they are at the root of all abuse within the Church and within society at large. The language we use to each other and the sensitivity and consideration we show to each other and our willingness always to be of service are indicators as to whether or not we are going in the right direction.

Here, recent liturgical changes for English speaking nations are a case in point. Based on bemusing concern for accurate reflection of texts in Latin, the liturgical clock was turned back at least fifty years. Little was done to make the English text more inclusive and nothing was done to make the supporting theology more contemporary. The opportunity to increase participation by congregations was missed. The changes made only underscored the need for a truly profound liturgical transformation that would allow sacramental celebration flexible enough to meet the real needs of people and engaging enough to offer genuine spiritual experience.

This brings us back again to changes that need to take place in the roles of clergy and laity. We have witnessed, for many years now, a steady decline in vocations to the priesthood and shrinking Church attendance. There are a number of reasons for both, but we cannot blithely assume that all of these relate to external factors. Could it not also be that the Holy Spirit is trying to tell us something about priesthood itself and about the experience people are having when they do attend Church? Only arrogance, I think, could suggest otherwise. At every level of the life of the Christian community, there is a need to accept the necessity for ongoing transformation and there is no guarantee that it will be achieved quickly or easily.

Religious Life in the Catholic Church has been in the throes of renewal and transformation ever since the Second Vatican Council. It has been a long journey that has dramatically changed the face of Religious Life but, interestingly, has not arrested the decline in membership. Many Orders and Congregations have questioned an over-involvement with ministry and apostolic work that often came at the expense of commitment to growth in prayer and the difficult task of building healthy community relationships. Therefore, I believe that the lessons that have been learnt are that the contribution of Religious Life to the Church of the future will revolve around the building of Christian community, the nurturing of prayer and the sharing of the spiritual search. Religious, of course, will continue to serve and accompany the poor.

In learning these lessons, Religious had to invest heavily of their time and resources. Local parishes and dioceses must begin to do the same. And if we care to look, there are encouraging signs of transformation that illustrate where money might be spent. Even without Church assistance, lay people are pursuing programmes in theology, spirituality and scripture studies. There is consistent interest in contemplative prayer and the great spiritual classics. There is no shortage of volunteers for work with the homeless, the elderly, refugees and immigrants. And many lay people have had immersion experiences in developing countries.

To transform the Church, we must start spending less money on buildings and more money on educating the laity, training lay catechists, liturgists and spiritual directors. We must seek to support single parents and marriages that are under pressure and to further assist the homeless, the financially disadvantaged and the marginalized. Where we spend the money we have, will indicate where our priorities really lie in the Church of the future.

Summary

The contemporary Church is in crisis. Many social factors, a lack of welcome within the Church itself and the neglect of the contemplative, contribute to this. Serious disillusionment and difficulty in passing on the faith are the results.

The Church of the future must keep its gaze fixed on the gospel and its message that God is to be found in all of life and the fullness of life is to be found in God. The gospel reminds us that God's love for us is beyond imagining. It implores us to love each other and to treat each other justly. The poor always have a special place in the Church and our concern for them is the measure of our integrity and gospel authenticity.

The way we love each other is the mark of the Christian community, so relationships within the Church are pivotal. All men and women must have access to decision making and to full participation in Church life. Clericalism needs to diminish and the priesthood needs to evolve. Healthy relationships, good communication and dialogue, the sacraments and prayer will guide us in this kind of evolution.

An experience of the Church of the future, will be an experience of the person of Jesus and an experience of community. People will be the primary concern, rather than dogma, liturgy, procedure, or anything else. Encountering the person of Jesus is what changes lives. Jesus will be experienced in the poor, in the Christian community, in the breaking of the bread and in contemplation. The experience will be an experience of hope.

The Church of the future will be a vocal Church. It will fearlessly challenge economic, social and political inequality and injustice. Most likely, it will be unpopular for doing so. Working for transformation within society, it will also humbly embrace transformation within itself at every level. The desire for internal transformation will be evidenced by the way financial resources are invested in people, in their education and in their training and in the supports provided for those who are most vulnerable.

Quotation for Discussion

"A focus on the gospel actively nurtures our relationship with Jesus, the incarnation of the Divine. It reminds us that God loves us unconditionally and totally beyond our imagining and that although nothing we can do, or fail to do, will change that love, God does implore us to respond to Divine love by loving each other and treating each other justly. These are the Christian fundamentals, but they remain fundamentals that we struggle with and somehow fail to comprehend."

Questions for Discussion

* What areas of Church life do you see as most in need of transformation and how would you envisage this transformation unfolding?
* How do you see your own role in the Church of the future and what steps do you need to take to claim that role?

1. "Evangelii Gaudium: The Joy of the Gospel" Apostolic Exhortation by Pope Francis. Veritas (2013). Cf par. 70.
2. Ibid par. 95.
3. "Come Follow Me: Recalling the Dangerous Memory of Jesus and the Church Today" by Aidan Donaldson. Columba Press (2012) p.95.
4. Ibid cf. p.111.
5. Ibid p.111 quotation from "Jesus social revolutionary" by Peter McVerry. Veritas (2008) p.55.
6. Pope Francis, op. cit. cf par.195.

7. "I Ask You to Pray for Me: Opening a Horizon of Hope" Speeches and homilies of Pope Francis. Libreria Editrice Vaticana and Paulist Press (2013). P18.
8. Pope Francis, "Evangelii Gaudium: The Joy of the Gospel" par.113
9. Ibid par.114.
10. "Dancing with Dinosaurs" by Mark Patrick Hederman, The Columba Press (2011) cf. p.26.
11. Ibid. p.74.
12. Pope Francis "Evangelii Gaudium: The Joy of the Gospel" par 7. The quotation is from the Encyclical Letter of Benedict XVI, "Deus Caritas Est" (25 December 2005), 1: AAS 98 (2006), 217.
13. Hederman op. cit. p59. The quotation from Karl Rahner is from "Theological Investigations 14" p.251.
14. Pope Francis "Evangelii Gaudium: The Joy of the Gospel" par 47.
15. Ibid cf. par. 198.
16. Cf p.128-129 and "Jesus social revolutionary" by Peter McVerry. Veritas (2008) p.119.
17. Pope Francis "Evangelii Gaudium: The Joy of the Gospel" par 255.

15. Free to Be

Handing on the faith, teaching the faith and accompanying people on their faith journey are not the easiest of tasks in themselves and some of the values that are prevalent in Western society certainly do not help. It is the duty, therefore, of anyone charged with these tasks to see that those for whom they have a responsibility are not unnecessarily hampered, restricted or bound as they pursue their spiritual search. The journey is difficult enough without any self-imposed, culturally imposed, or Church imposed additional difficulties, be they conscious or unconscious. Identifying and trying to address such needless difficulties has been the theme of this book.

Instruction in the faith is not primarily about acceptance of a creed. It is about asking questions with honesty and freely exploring inner experience and mystery. At every opportunity, then, the Christian is to be encouraged to aspire towards and cultivate an inner freedom that is based upon a personal relationship with Jesus, a mature, in-depth understanding of the good news, an informed conscience attuned to the complexities of contemporary reality and a basic insight, at the very least, into one's own compulsions, motivations and psychology.

We are made in the image of God and our humanity, freedom and destiny are to be found in God and in God's love which is unconditional. The unconditional nature of God's love means, as I have repeatedly said, that nothing that I can do will increase God's love for me and nothing that I can do will decrease God's love for me. Coming to some realisation and acceptance of all of this, along with an acceptance of ourselves and honest acknowledgement of our circumstances, is the spiritual journey and constitutes, in fact, our life's journey. Thomas Merton writes:

"To say that I am made in the image of God is to say
that love is the reason for my existence, for God is love.
Love is my true identity. Selflessness is my true self.

Love is my true character. Love is my name. If, therefore, I do anything or think anything or say anything or know anything that is not purely for the love of God, it cannot give me peace, or rest, or fulfillment, or joy." [1]

Ultimately, our happiness lies in the exercise of our free will to choose God in love and to choose to love others. No other choices will make me happy and no choice of God other than out of a genuine love will make me happy. Too often, in the past, unhealthy guilt and fear have featured in Christian spirituality and been actively promoted by Christian theology. But, all Church teaching and authority are, "subordinate to the Holy Spirit and to the law of love." [2] Love must always be freely given, so, this makes the Church itself a guarantor and protector of spiritual freedom and the exercise of spiritual freedom. This is so despite perceptions and, it has to be said, more than occasional evidence, to the contrary.

Created in the image of God, we are called to grow in love. Our freedom is freedom to be, freedom to become fully human, freedom to realise our potential in God by surrendering to transformation by God. It is God who does all the work and this realisation takes a great weight from our shoulders. All that we have to do is to be open to God's presence and consent to God's creative action is our lives.

More usually, of course, we follow all kinds of diversions and distractions, surrendering not to transformation but to what amount to addictions in one form or another. Doing so, we reject not just God, we unconsciously reject our own being, our own selves. [3] We condemn ourselves to frustration, disorientation and misery. Sometimes, though, it is actually fear for our very being that holds us back. We fear that if we allow ourselves be drawn towards God, we are risking being overwhelmed by the mystery that is God. We fear being swallowed up, or devoured, by the Divine. Such an interpretation of the nature of God's love, however, is a projection because God's love is not at all like our love. God's love needs nothing. The Divine love is the purest of loves, it does not seek to possess, as human love does. [4] It seeks only to give of itself and to give in abundance, offering us the fullness of our humanity, the fulfillment of our being. In the incarnation, as we have discussed, Jesus emptied himself of his divinity to show us what it is to be human. (cf Phil. 2:5-11) Paul exhorts us to be of the same mind as Jesus. In freely giving of ourselves, we will become ourselves. Jesus wants us to have all that the Father wishes for us in life. He wants this for each human being and for humanity. This is creation ongoing, this is a new creation. This is the kingdom at the heart of the message of Jesus. God's intention was clear from the beginning: "God saw everything that he had made, and indeed, it was very good." (Gen.1:31)

The Spirit of the risen Jesus, therefore, appeals to us:

"The time is now! The place is here!
You are the people!
This is my invitation to you.

Come follow me to the edge, into the deeper and wider dimensions of Living
that you may discover the God who awaits you.
It is at the very heart of existence that you will find life at its fulness.

I came to bring Life and I wish you to live it to the full,
and to carry it to the very edge of the Universe.

Enter into the core of your being, into your stories.
You know me in your stories, in your living traditions and in your deepest moments of joy and pain.

Have courage.
Let go the chains with which you would bind me.

I am awaiting for you beyond the boundaries,
your concepts, your understandings.
I walk with you in the places of the heart beyond your
wildest imaginings.
I am the source, your energy, your passion.

Fly free as the courageous did before you to new
horizons, to the unknown, the not-yet-imagined.

Throw open your windows and let the fresh air in...
Open wide your shutters and allow me to inflame you.

Dare to enter my Mystery and become hope for all
children and the people you encounter on your journey.

Risk being different!
Risk leaping and falling!

Remember, falling is the privilege of the living and
even as you encounter loss, fear, despair and death,
know that I have been there before you and will be with
you always.

Trust me.
Dare to be my disciples.
In you I am doing something new." [5]

1. "New Seeds of Contemplation" by Thomas Merton, Shambhala Publications (2003) p.63.
2. "Conjectures of a Guilty Bystander" by Thomas Merton, Image Books (1989) p.89.
3. "Heartfulness: Transformation in Christ" DVD series with Thomas Keating and Betty Sue Flowers. Cf DVD 3.
4. "The Sign of Jonas" by Thomas Merton, Harvest/Harcourt (1981) cf. p.346.
5. Apapted from the Munnar 2008 Document of the Congregation of Christian Brothers.

Bibliography

"ARCS", "Parabola" Volume 24 Number 4 November 1999.

Abbott, Peter. Cf. "A Framework for a New Reality" in "Values & Ethics" edited by Harry Bohan and Gerard Kennedy. Céifin Conference Papers published by Veritas (2003).

Armstrong, Karen. "The Bible: The Biography", Atlantic Books (2007).

Barton, Stephen C. Cf "The Epistles and Christian Ethics" in "The Cambridge Companion to Christian Ethics" Second Edition, edited by Robin Gill.

Beal, Timothy. "The Rise and Fall of the Bible" published by Mariner Books (2012).

Borg, Marcus J. "Jesus". HarperOne Publications (2006).

Borg, Marcus J. "The Heart of Christianity", Harper (2003).

Bourgeault, Cynthia. "Centering Prayer and Inner Awakening", Cowley Publications (2004).

Bourgeault, Cynthia. "The Wisdom Jesus", Shambhala (2008).

Browning, Dan. Cf "World Family Trends" in "The Cambridge Companion to Christian Ethics" Second Edition, edited by Robin Gill. Cambridge University Press (2012).

Brueggemann, Walter. "The Bible Makes Sense", published by St. Anthony Messenger Press (2003).

Chown, Marcus. "Quantum Theory Cannot Hurt You." Faber and Faber (2007).

Congregation of Christian Brothers. Adapted from the Munnar 2008 Document.

Conn, Marie A. "C. S. Lewis and Human Suffering", Hidden Spring Books, (2008).

Contemplative Outreach, "An Introduction to Centering Prayer", Training materials for presenters. Contemplative Outreach: Vision Statement and Its Foundations, "The Theological Principles".

Coomaraswamy, Rama P. "On the Morals of the Manichaeans" Augustine, quoted in "Fruits of Knowledge", "Parabola" Volume 24 Number 4 November 1999.

Deignan, Kathleen. "Thomas Merton: A Book of Hours", Sorin Books (2007).

Donaldson, Aidan. "Come Follow Me: Recalling the Dangerous Memory of Jesus and the Church Today", Columba Press (2012).

Farley, Margaret A. "Compassionate Respect" published by Paulist Press (2002).

Fiand, Barbara. "Awe-Filled Wonder", Paulist Press (2008).

Finley, James. "Merton's Palace of Nowhere", Ave Maria Press, (2003).

Flannery, Austin O.P. "Vatican Council II" General editor, Costello Publishing 1975. Cf "The Pastoral Constitution on the Church in the Modern World".

Francis, Pope. "Evangelii Gaudium: The Joy of the Gospel" Apostolic Exhortation, Veritas (2013).

Francis, Pope. "I Ask You to Pray for Me: Opening a Horizon of Hope", Libreria Editrice Vaticana and Paulist Press (2013).

Francis, Pope. "Laudato Si': on care for our common home" encyclical letter, Veritas Publications (2015).

Frey, Kess. "Human Ground Spiritual Ground", Portal Books (2012).

Gill, Robin. Cf "Sexuality and religious ethics" in "The Cambridge Companion to Christian Ethics" Second Edition, edited by Robin Gill. Cambridge University Press (2012).

Hart, Patrick and Montaldo, Jonathan. "The Intimate Merton: His Life from His Journals", Lion Publishing (1999).

Hartmann, Gerard. Cf "Why Do We Need Champions?" in "Values & Ethics" edited by Harry Bohan and Gerard Kennedy. Céifin Conference Papers published by Veritas (2003).

Hederman, Mark Patrick. "Dancing with Dinosaurs", The Columba Press (2011).

Huesman, John E., S.J. "The Jerome Biblical Commentary" (3:36), op. cit. Commentary on Exodus 15:1-21.
Jung, Carl G. "An Answer to Job", Routledge Classics (2002)
Keating, Thomas. "The Human Condition", Paulist Press (1999).
Keating, Thomas. "Divine Therapy and Addiction" Lantern Books (2009).
Keating, Thomas. "Foundations for Centering Prayer and the Christian Contemplative Life" (Invitation to Love) Continuum (2002).
Keating, Thomas. "Open Mind, Open Heart", Continuum (2006).
Keating, Thomas. DVD set of "Six Continuing Sessions."
Keating, Thomas. DVD set on, "The Spiritual Journey".
Keating, Thomas with Betty Sue Flowers. "Heartfulness: Transformation in Christ" DVD series. Cf DVD 3.
King, Robert H. "Thomas Merton and Thich Nhat Hanh", Continuum (2003).
Kushner, Harold S. "When Bad Things Happen to Good People", Pan Books, (2002).
Lewis, C.S. "A Grief Observed", Faber and Faber (1966).
Littleton, Veronica. "Eternal Music" published by the author (2009).
Marsh, John. "St. John", Penguin (1976).
McKenzie, John L. "The Jerome Biblical Commentary", op. cit. Commentary on Mt. 7:12 in "The Gospel According to Matthew" (Article 43.51).
McKenzie, Steven L. "How to Read the Bible", Oxford University Press (2005).
McVerry, Peter. "Jesus: Social Revolutionary?", (Veritas 2007).
Merton, Thomas. "Conjectures of a Guilty Bystander", Image Books (1989).
Merton, Thomas. "New Seeds of Contemplation", Shambhala (2003).
Merton, Thomas. "No Man is an Island", Shambhala (2005).
Merton, Thomas. "The Seven Storey Mountain", SPCK (1990).

Merton, Thomas. "The Sign of Jonas", Harvest/Harcourt (1981).
Northcott, Michael S. Cf "Ecology and Christian Ethics" in "The Cambridge Companion to Christian Ethics" Second Edition, edited by Robin Gill. Cambridge University Press (2012).
Peck, M. Scott, "The People of the Lie", Arrow Books (1998).
Polkinghorne, John. "Quantum Theory: A Very Short Introduction", Oxford (2002).
Price, Reynolds. "A Serious Way of Wondering", Scribner (2003).
Rogerson, John. Cf "Sexuality and religious ethics" in"The Cambridge Companion to Christian Ethics" Second Edition, edited by Robin Gill. Cambridge University Press (2012).
Rohr, Richard. "The Naked Now", Crossroad Publishing (2009).
Sandford, John A. "The Man Who Wrestled With God", Paulist (1981).
Schwartz, Jeffrey M.D., and Begley, Sharon. "The Mind and the Brain" Regan Books (2002).
Shaw, Miranda. "The Transcendent Fury of Palden Lhamo", "Parabola" Volume 24, Number 4, November 1999.
Smith, Richard F. "Inspiration and Inerrancy", Article in "The Jerome Biblical Commentary" (1968) Published by Geoffrey Chapman.
Stackhouse, Max L. with Miller, David W. Cf "Business, Economics and Christian Ethics" in "The Cambridge Companion to Christian Ethics" Second Edition, edited by Robin Gill. Cambridge University Press (2012).
Suelzer, Alexa. "Modern Old Testament Criticism" article in "The Jerome Biblical Commentary" (1968) Published by Geoffry Chapman.
Swenson, Kristin. "Bible Babel", Harper Perennial (2011).
The Pontifical Biblical Commission "The Interpretation of the Bible in the Church". Published by the United States Catholic Conference (1996).
Ulanov, Ann Belford and Dueck, Alvin. "The Living God and Our Living Psyche", Eerdmans Publishing (2008).

Vardy, Peter and Grosch, Paul. "The Puzzle of Ethics", Fount (1999).

Verhey, Allen. Cf "The Gospels and Christian Ethics" in "The Cambridge Companion to Christian Ethics" Second Edition, edited by Robin Gill. Cambridge University Press (2012).

Wallis, Jim. "Rediscovering Values", Howard Books (2011).

Wheatley, Margaret. Source as yet not known.

Williams, Rowan. Cf "Sexuality and religious ethics" in "The Cambridge Companion to Christian Ethics" Second Edition, edited by Robin Gill. Cambridge University Press (2012).

Wright, Tom. "Simply Jesus", SPCK (2011).

Index

I

image of God, 24, 25, 33, 36, 39, 43, 125, 150, 226, 227
imagination, 4, 13, 17, 35, 37, 72, 81, 85, 91, 129, 155, 177
individualism, 17, 185, 189, 205, 207
instinctive needs, 143, 144, 147, 148, 172, 182
IPCC, 200
Isaac, 7, 14, 29, 36, 162
Israel, 28, 30, 32, 65, 72, 73, 74, 76, 77, 80, 85, 86, 113, 115, 116, 117, 169

J

Jacob, 30, 36, 72, 162
Jerome, 64, 69, 86, 87, 232, 233
Jesus, viii, 2, 16, 19, 20, 22, 28, 33, 35, 36, 38, 40, 51, 54, 55, 58, 62, 63, 65, 67, 69, 71, 73, 78, 81, 83, 84, 85, 88, 89, 94, 95, 96, 99, 100, 102, 103, 104, 105, 106, 107, 108, 109, 110, 113, 114, 116, 117, 118, 119, 120, 121, 122, 123, 126, 127, 128, 129, 131, 132, 133, 134, 136, 138, 147, 150, 155, 156, 159, 160, 162, 164, 165, 168, 172, 174, 175, 178, 179, 180, 181, 184, 192, 196, 198, 206, 208, 212, 213, 214, 216, 219, 223, 224, 225, 226, 228, 230, 231, 232, 234
Job, 40, 47, 49, 50, 51, 54, 55, 56, 79, 232
John, i, 7, 26, 30, 37, 56, 66, 67, 70, 73, 86, 91, 94, 95, 96, 99, 100, 104, 106, 108, 111, 113, 114, 122, 173, 175, 182, 183, 213, 232, 233
Jonah, 73, 74, 75, 85
Joseph, 30, 61, 72
jubilee, 128, 196
Jung, Carl, 46, 47, 56, 133, 232

justice, 4, 20, 36, 101, 116, 118, 129, 132, 154, 162, 169, 178, 191, 194, 199, 205, 218

K

Keating, Thomas, 21, 23, 35, 37, 141, 143, 145, 146, 148, 149, 150, 151, 152, 154, 155, 158, 161, 165, 172, 183, 193, 208, 229, 232, 233
King, Robert H, 209, 232
Kingdom, ix, 2, 19, 34, 53, 88, 94, 98, 99, 100, 101, 103, 104, 105, 106, 107, 109, 110, 113, 114, 116, 117, 118, 120, 121, 123, 127, 129, 130, 131, 132, 133, 135, 136, 144, 155, 156, 161, 198, 228
Kushner, Harold S., 41, 42, 43, 48, 54, 56, 232

L

Lazarus, v, vii, viii, 35, 88, 93, 101, 162
leadership, 100, 129, 201, 204, 214
Lewis, 43, 56, 230, 232
Littleton, Veronica, 131, 133, 134, 137, 148, 167, 183, 198, 209, 232
love, 2, 8, 24, 25, 30, 33, 36, 39, 49, 51, 53, 55, 56, 82, 83, 84, 85, 101, 107, 108, 111, 113, 119, 120, 124, 126, 127, 130, 132, 135, 136, 138, 141, 143, 144, 145, 146, 147, 148, 151, 152, 158, 161, 163, 164, 166, 170, 173, 174, 175, 177, 178, 180, 182, 185, 186, 190, 192, 196, 198, 205, 212, 213, 214, 220, 223, 224, 226, 227
Luke, 61, 66, 83, 92, 95, 98, 101, 115, 157, 175, 182, 192

M

Mark, 66, 67, 91, 95, 115, 156, 175, 182, 215, 216, 225, 231
Marsh, John, 56, 66, 70, 122, 232
Mary, 19, 22, 54, 61, 98, 108, 113, 115, 117
Matthew, 59, 66, 84, 87, 92, 95, 99, 101, 115, 156, 161, 175, 182, 212, 232
Maxwell, James Clerk, 10
McKenzie, John L., 87
McKenzie, Steven L., 70, 72, 74, 86, 184
McLanahan, Sarah, 187
McVerry, Peter, 101, 106, 128, 129, 134, 192, 195, 208, 213, 219, 224, 225, 232
Mechanical Universe, 7
media, 1, 4, 18, 187, 194, 211, 218
memory, i, 50, 76, 77, 86, 88, 89, 94, 104, 105, 176, 217
mercy, 34, 74, 103, 110, 144, 212
Merton, Thomas, 1, 2, 3, 13, 15, 26, 33, 37, 52, 56, 130, 134, 136, 140, 144, 146, 148, 149, 201, 202, 209, 226, 229, 231, 232
metaphor, 26, 36, 81, 85, 88, 90, 100, 104, 105, 118, 176, 208
Meyers, Robin R., 97
mindset, 9, 10, 13, 16, 18, 20, 21, 22, 34, 39, 65, 99, 112, 115, 128, 172, 193
ministry, v, 78, 92, 112, 156, 222
morality, 166, 170, 174, 178, 180, 181, 185, 186, 204, 218
Moses, 28, 30, 36, 60, 65, 72, 78, 81, 84, 173, 174

N

new creation, 116, 117, 119, 121, 123, 128, 131, 132, 162, 198, 218, 228
Newton, Isaac, 7, 14

Niebuhr, Richard, 202
Northcott, Michael, 198, 199, 209, 233

O

ordination, 215

P

Palden, Lhamo, 45, 56, 233
parable, 83, 93, 104, 114, 196
Paradise, 115, 123, 124
Passover, 109, 111, 120, 156
Paul, 59, 77, 79, 112, 119, 142, 174, 178, 179, 180, 182, 208, 213, 228, 234
peace, 28, 101, 106, 109, 116, 120, 130, 146, 155, 156, 199, 203, 206, 218, 227
Pentateuch, 65, 68
Pentecost, 90, 117
Peter, 81, 93, 94, 101, 105, 106, 113, 117, 128, 134, 185, 192, 195, 207, 208, 213, 219, 224, 225, 230, 232, 234
Pilate, 40, 81, 109, 113, 114
Planck, Max, 9, 10, 11
pluralism, 176, 220
Polkinghorne, John, 7, 15, 233
Pope Francis, 211, 213, 216, 217, 220, 224, 225
post-Easter Jesus, 90, 97
poverty, 2, 21, 22, 38, 110, 128, 185, 187, 192, 194, 205, 206
prayer, viii, 19, 22, 34, 35, 37, 81, 113, 123, 126, 133, 142, 147, 150, 151, 152, 154, 155, 156, 158, 163, 164, 173, 181, 203, 215, 220, 223
pre-Easter Jesus, 97
presence, 24, 29, 30, 33, 35, 36, 37, 46, 67, 73, 78, 80, 84, 85, 86, 109, 110, 116, 117, 121, 126, 136, 141,

147, 148, 151, 152, 157, 158, 160, 162, 163, 164, 179, 186, 218, 227
primal narratives, 76, 77, 85
psychology, vi, 5, 47, 143, 187

Q

quantum physics, 9, 12, 14
quelle, 66
Qumran, 63

R

Rahner, Karl, 216, 225
randomness, 12, 14, 15, 50, 55, 167
reconciliation, 53, 60, 101, 116
redistribution, 194, 205
relationship, 1, 3, 9, 13, 21, 24, 25, 30, 31, 32, 33, 35, 36, 37, 39, 49, 52, 55, 72, 73, 80, 85, 97, 99, 103, 105, 116, 126, 127, 131, 132, 133, 138, 142, 150, 151, 154, 155, 156, 162, 169, 180, 181, 186, 188, 192, 197, 199, 202, 212, 215, 224, 226
resurrection, 28, 52, 55, 78, 88, 94, 96, 104, 106, 107, 116, 117, 118, 119, 121, 179, 199, 206
Rohr, Richard, 16, 17, 21, 23, 28, 37, 233

S

sacrament, 9, 215
sacred word, 150, 152, 153, 163
sacrifice, 29, 51, 103, 104, 107, 110, 120, 172
Sandefur, Gary, 187
Sarah, 29
Satan, 47, 59
Schrodinger, Erwin, 11
science, 1, 3, 7, 8, 11, 12, 13, 15, 22, 167
Scotus, Duns, 26
serpent, 59, 147

silence, viii, 1, 35, 53, 55, 82, 150, 152, 153, 154, 155, 156, 158, 162, 163, 164, 181, 216, 217, 220
Simon, 7, 64, 114, 196
sin, 2, 41, 108, 132, 135, 141, 144, 176
Smith, Richard F., 62, 69, 233
solidarity, 108, 192, 194, 205
Soloveitchik, Rabbi Joseph, 42
Solzhenitsyn, Alexander, 185
Song of Miriam, 71, 84
Spirit, 28, 33, 84, 85, 96, 117, 151, 154, 156, 159, 162, 163, 164, 199, 202, 210, 212, 216, 221, 227
spiritual conscience, 170, 181, 183
spirituality, i, 81, 118, 126, 209, 218, 222, 227
suffering, 24, 38, 39, 40, 42, 43, 45, 48, 49, 51, 53, 54, 55, 56, 100, 107, 113, 119, 120, 128, 141, 168, 175, 185, 191, 195, 204, 217
Swift, Jonathan, 58
symbolism, 81, 85, 91, 109, 111, 120
synoptic gospels, 67, 92, 94, 111

T

temple, 103, 107, 109, 110, 120, 156, 164, 210, 212
Tolkien, J.R., 58
Torah, 82, 84
tragic interpretations, 125
transformation, vi, 73, 78, 82, 101, 102, 103, 112, 131, 132, 135, 151, 152, 153, 162, 163, 164, 173, 181, 182, 203, 215, 220, 223, 224, 227

U

Ulanov, Ann, 46, 47, 53, 56, 234
Ultimate Reality, 201, 203, 206
unconditional love, 126, 146, 147, 152, 160, 220, 226

V

Vardy and Grosch, 190, 208
Vulgate, 64

W

Wallis, Jim, 187, 195, 207, 208, 234
Watson, John, 8
Wellhausen, Julius, 66, 69

Wheatley, Margaret, 19, 20, 23, 234
Wigner, Eugene, 12
Williams, Raymond, 169, 183, 185, 234
Wright, Tom, 106, 113, 116, 122, 127, 128, 134, 208, 234

Y

Young, Thomas, 10

Unbinding Christian Faith: Free to Be   Denis Gleeson